CECILY MACKWORTH

was born in Wales but has made her home for most of her adult life in France. She is married to the Marquis de Chabannes la Palice. Her other books are *I came out of France* recounting three months wandering in Petain's France before she escaped to Britain: *The Month of the Sword*, a book of the Middle East: a novel *Spring's Green Shadow*: *A Mirror of French Poetry: François Villon* and *The Destiny of Isabelle Eberhardt*.

*Guillaume Apollinaire
and the Cubist Life*

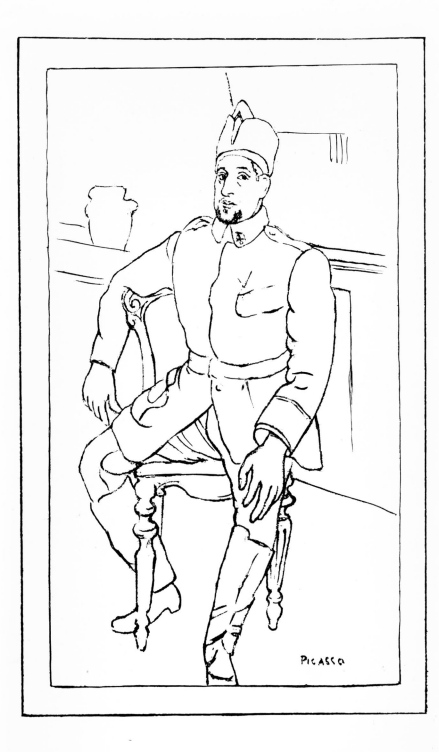

Guillaume Apollinaire and the Cubist Life

CECILY MACKWORTH

Horizon Press

NEW YORK

1963

First American edition 1963
Horizon Press

Library of Congress Catalog Card Number: 63-11181

© *Cecily Mackworth 1961*

Printed in Great Britain

Contents

Illustrations

Acknowledgements

I am grateful for the generous help of many people in Paris and elsewhere, who knew Apollinaire and have helped me to form in my own mind a picture of his personality. Two of them—Serge Jastrebzoff (Férat) and Louis de Gonzague Frick—died shortly after my conversations with them. Among others, I should like specially to mention Madame Louise Faure-Favier and Madame Sonia Delaunay, André Salmon, André Breton (who kindly lent me an unpublished manuscript containing an account of his relationship with Apollinaire), Ossip Zadkine, Tristan Tzara, Pierre Albert-Birot, and Paul Fort, 'the Prince of Poets', who, at the age of eighty-nine, could recall the début of young Guillaume Apollinaire in the *Closerie des Lilas* in 1902.

I should also like to record my gratitude to M. Marcel Adéma, whose researches have done so much to shed light on the mystery of Apollinaire's birth and whose vast collection of Apollinairiana has been of such value to me; to M. Michel Decaudin, who introduced me to the hitherto unknown rough draft of *Zone*; to M. Chapon and his assistants at the Bibliothèque Doucet, who have given me such patient and precious help. –

Prologue

Every epoch has its representative figure, someone who incarnates the subtle and intricate elements in which a new spirit can be recognised. There is never a total, immediate break with old and new, but rather a re-arrangement, a new perspective, a new light on permanent problems, a throwing into relief of hitherto unsuspected aspects. An aesthetic attitude that has been valid for a certain time becomes, for no immediately apparent reason, untenable. Times are changing and the world is not what it was ... and it is surely the business of the artist to feel and translate change almost before it occurs, to be sensitive to the future rather than to the past and to crystallise in himself and his work the stirring of time.

The man who became Guillaume Apollinaire was the personification of Cubism, at the moment when Cubism had become a necessity. Placed, as Georges Ribemont-Dessaignes has said: 'in the centre of his times, like a spider in the centre of its web, computing the value of the passing flies; or like a lonely man who cannot resign himself to his solitude', he spoke with the voice of the twentieth century, and it was perhaps through him that that voice was heard for the first time.

Photographs taken of him at various periods of his life suggest matter rather than spirit and the portrait that probably most resembles him is the 'decomposed' picture painted by Metzinger. It was the first time the Cubist technique had been used in portraiture and it provoked considerable mockery because it distorted the subject out of immediate recognition; yet it was really the only way in which he could reasonably have been painted. No character could be more diverse and multiple, or show more contradictory aspects. There was the mystic and the mystificator, the bohemian and the good soldier, the cynic and the sentimentalist, the scholar and the iconoclast—and many more. When the old people who were the friends of his youth talk of him to-day, it is as if each were speaking of a different man. Even the essential facts vary, and it soon becomes evident that Apollinaire, when he talked about himself, invented stories which would amuse or intrigue his listeners. Perhaps he believed in them himself, in all of them, successively. Or perhaps he simply allowed his friends to build up whatever legends they liked about him. Or perhaps he was not sure of his own origins, or preferred to forget them. In any case, until the time when he appears in Paris, as a disciple of Moréas, the great Master, and of the terrible 'Super-male' Alfred Jarry, he has left us only the hints and allusions in his poems, and a few confidences to an almost unknown and soon abandoned fiancée, to go on. It is perhaps symbolic that this man of the twentieth century should have effaced his own traces, or drawn red herrings over his tracks, until the opening of that century. He can only be discovered as a child and youth by an indiscreet breaking down of doors that he himself had been careful to lock and bar against the curious.

I

'Who is he?'

Le Soleil d'Or, Au Père Jean, Le Caveau du Rocher, Balzar . . . one
might choose any one of these cafés to give a glimpse of the young
Guillaume Apollinaire in the winter 1902–03. Perhaps it was the
Closerie des Lilas that played the most important role, during these
months when he first stormed a section of Paris's literary life that
was not always welcoming to newcomers. It was a place of great
literary traditions and we shall see that Apollinaire, in spite of his
later passion for innovation and the most mobile aspects of art,
was and remained a man of tradition.

The café still exists. It is situated at the angle of the Boulevard
Montparnasse and the Boulevard Saint-Michel. There is still the
same wide, raised terrace where Verlaine once set up his headquarters, where his friends—among them the young Rimbaud—
met to drink absinthe, recite poetry and watch the spectacle in the
street below. To-day, white-jacketed waiters serve expensive
meals there, but at the beginning of the century it was an un-
pretentious place, hidden by trees so immense that they were soon
felled by order of the municipality, as a public danger. The famous
Bal Bullier was then at the height of its reputation. In the evening,
the gay music of polkas and waltzes drifted across the street and a
noisy crowd of pleasure-seekers wove in and out of soft pools of
light shed by the gas lamps. There would be groups of midinettes,
giggling, arm-in-arm, trying to attract the attention of lonely
young men on the look-out for partners; young workmen, and
men of fashion come up from the Champs-Elysées or the *Grands
Boulevards* for the thrill of mixing with low life, and bringing with
them the 'lionesses' of the day—women celebrated for their wit,
beauty and lack of virtue, the possession of whom was one of the
attributes of social success. All this must have made a charming
picture for the poets and artists who crowded the terrace, and it
was probably one of the reasons for the café's long popularity.

Though the aspect of the place was as gay as ever, many things had changed by the turn of the century. Verlaine was dead, killed by drink and debauch, and with him had disappeared the last of the *poètes maudits*, the decadents of the Romantic Agony. The *Closerie* was still the poets' café, but the mood was more robust. Three men dominated the discussions, imposing themselves, either by their achievements or by the force of their personality, as leaders. First of all, indisputably, there was Jean Papadiamantopoulous, the Greek aristocrat who, under the name of Jean Moréas, wrote the purest French of any man of his time and could never forgive his colleagues, who had the luck to be born Frenchmen, for their ignorance of their own language. Even to-day the old men who were young when they knew him thrill to his name. He was the great teacher, listened to with love and respect by writers of every tendency, because of his intransigent devotion to poetry and the elegant, stoic pessimism of his attitude to life. Although he spent the greater part of his days and nights in one or other of the bohemian cafés he had adopted in various parts of the city, and drank beyond reason, he was always impeccably dressed and immensely dignified. Some of his friends could remember his arrival in Paris, the 'charming arrogance of his youth, his showy clothes, the fresh flower in his button-hole; a very courtly young foreigner, a bit of a swashbuckler, wearing a monocle, constantly caressing his blue-black moustaches and judging our great men in a few curt words that rang out like insults'.[1] Now the flat, almost violet-hued curls and the famous moustaches were streaked with grey and the gestures were less lively, but the man was ageless, living out of time, entirely consecrated to his 'divine mania' for poetry. Moréas had not only studied the classics, he had penetrated them to such an extent that he lived and thought like a man of antiquity. It was not really surprising that he should soon have deserted Symbolism, to the shocked horror of his friends, and founded the 'Roman' school of poetry with Maurras, Barrès and Ernest Raynaud. Superficial acquaintances who saw him drinking and playing dice in the cafés were often astonished to hear him compared to the austere Stoics of ancient Greece; only his intimate friends guessed something of the sadness and

[1] For this, and all numbered references to sources, see pp. 238-239.

solitude of his life and the immense renunciations that had made possible the composition of *Les Stances*.

Moréas' judgements were peremptory and his harsh Greek accent seemed to lend them added weight: 'Flaubert? He is perfect, of course, but it is the perfection of sterilised water.' . . . 'Chateaubriand? A baroque writer!' (And the term baroque, on the lips of this pure classicist, was the most terrible of insults.) When the conversation turned on free verse, as it often did, the ageing master, who could bear nothing less than perfection, would cut into the debate: 'Free verse is the least free of all; it is the slave of its theme.' He had tried it himself and renounced it, but the young men to whom it meant liberation, would be up in arms at once, defending Gustave Kahn, Marie Kryzinska, Vielé-Griffin and the other free-versifiers. The subject was a favourite one and generally ended in terrible vociferations and broken glasses.

Moréas was the king of this society of poets, but the prince was undoubtedly young Paul Fort. He was still under thirty at this time but already, to even younger men, he seemed to be pointing a way down a new road. His simplicity disquieted the men of the old school, as did his refusal to adhere to any established rules. For many of the habitués of the *Closerie* he represented the Future, but he was passionately, generously devoted to Moréas and always ready to proclaim he had learned everything from this master who was at the same time the companion of wild nocturnal expeditions and homeric drinking bouts. 'Yes, everything!' he would cry, his soft, dark eyes flashing with enthusiasm, 'the value of words, the art of choosing them and of linking them together . . .' He was always a great reciter of his own poems, and towards midnight, when the saucers were piled up on the tables to help the waiters tot up a complicated and still distant total of drinks, he would improvise astonishing ballads, in a high, squeaky voice, renewing an ancient form that had been long forgotten and to which he brought a new grace and ardour.

The third of this brilliant and disparate trio was utterly unlike either Moréas or Paul Fort. Both were essentially gentlemen, and even dandies, in spite of their wild life and extravagant behaviour. Alfred Jarry, with his long black hair separated by a parting in the middle and falling almost to his shoulders, his face already heavy with unhealthy fat, his thick body supported by extremely short legs, was uncouth, violent and could even be dangerous. He spoke with an accent of extraordinary vulgarity that seemed to the uninitiated to be of peasant origin but which they could never identify with any special region. It was, in fact, the accent of 'Ubu', invented by Jarry himself for the use of that unique character— symbol of the triumph of human stupidity, cruelty and wickedness in the world—who had earned a sudden blaze of celebrity for his author, a few years earlier. When Lugné-Poe had had the temerity to produce the play at the *Théatre de l'Œuvre*, it had divided Paris into Ubuists and anti-Ubuists, with, it must be admitted, a vast majority of anti-Ubuists. At the opening night the critics had joined the audience in booing the play; some of them had left the theatre in protest and the sole critic who published a favourable account lost his job next day. But Ubu had entered French literature and was becoming, slowly but surely, almost a classic figure.

Unfortunately, Jarry could not content himself with creating Ubu; he had set himself to *become* Ubu, and that monstrous buffoon was not a comfortable companion. He had replaced food by drink and balanced his diet according to a logic of his own: two absinthes equal one beefsteak; one absinthe equals a pound of bread, and so on. 'Ubu' had been King of Poland and Jarry invariably used the royal We in speaking of himself. In his lucid moments he contributed to the famous *Mercure de France*, where the editors were doing their best to save him from himself. His friends were gradually deserting him, fearing the scandals he created in his drunken frenzies. Moréas tolerated him, as he would tolerate anyone who was amusing and free of prejudice, but allowed neither him nor anyone else to penetrate the closely guarded sanctuary of his inner life. As for the younger men—for there was always a group of them surrounding these three dominating figures during the evenings at the *Closerie*—perhaps they understood the tormented 'Super-male'* better than their elders could. 'Revolt' during the nineteenth century had been synonymous

---

* Jarry liked to refer to himself by this promising title, which was that of a play—his last—which he produced in 1902. It was all the more unsuitable since he had never been known to love a woman.

with 'Romanticism', but they—the rising generation—were sure of one thing about themselves: they were not Romantics and had no time for the bric-à-brac of Romanticism. Jarry, who was himself only twenty-nine, would sometimes murmur a phrase that opened a new perspective, shed a ray of light on a singularly uncertain future. Before the young André Salmon, for instance, he had let fall the mask of Ubu at least once, to pronounce words that corresponded to the instinctive urge he and some of his companions were already feeling: 'You are right to dedicate yourself totally to poetry as you do . . . go ahead. . . . It's your job to create a fairyland out of the things of daily life . . . ah! the things of daily life. . . . Life, life waiting there, ready to be moulded by you. . . . ' Perhaps the tragedy of his own unhappy existence arose from his own incapacity to seize hold of reality, or, simply, to live.

Beside the slender, fair-haired boy, Salmon, with his exquisite imagination and cruel tongue, with the slightly exotic charm that came from early years spent in Russia, there was Marinetti, a boisterous Italian who was soon to found the Futurist Movement in Italy and stupefy the relatively reasonable circles of the French avant-garde. Then there was Jean Royère, who was immensely argumentative and enjoyed nothing better than a terrible verbal battle with Moréas on the eternal subject of free verse, of which he was a fanatic champion; and the Spanish sculptor and apprentice-poet, Manoli, who idolised Moréas and whose incomprehensible accent and semi-ignorance of the French language never discouraged him from composing poems which he believed to be in the purest classic vein. Among the minority of non-poets there was Augustus John, with his fine beard and always with a woman—never the same woman twice running—hanging on his arm. Rumour accredited him with four separate *ménages*, one at each of the cardinal points of Paris.

And sometimes there was a good-humoured little Russian, a great chess-player and always trying to find a partner, who took tremendous interest in art and poetry but admitted that he was incapable of drawing a line or rhyming a verse. His name was Vladimir Ilitch Lenin and he spent what were probably some of the pleasantest evenings of his exile in this unlikely company.

A newcomer had lately joined this bohemian band and had almost immediately begun to play a leading role. He called himself Apollinaire, but this was known to be a pseudonym for a more unpronounceable name. He was younger even than his friend Salmon. In appearance, he was sandy-haired, with a long, fleshy-chinned face, rather like that of a Roman emperor, a long, very delicately-modelled nose and a small mouth with rather thick, sensual lips. He was long-bodied and short-legged, with an air of solid health and good humour. He was a foreigner, like Moréas and Marinetti, but spoke French without a trace of accent, and greatly resented—with sudden rages that had an irresistibly comic effect on his friends—any allusion to his supposedly Slav origin. Sometimes he affected a slight stiffness, a cold glare from the light-coloured eyes that drooped at the corners, a ceremoniously frigid manner. It was his Prussian ego, soon recognised as such by his friends, and probably invented in order to recall to himself or to others that he had recently returned from an inexplicable and perhaps mythical *wanderjahr* in Germany. Luckily, the Prussian mood never lasted long and he would turn within a few minutes from a haughty Junker into one or other of the rapidly inter-changeable personalities that kept his friends amused and in-trigued. Nearly all these personalities were unconsciously comic, and all the more so for the seriousness and concentration with which he threw himself into them. Apollinaire the chess player, especially, was a continual source of gaiety and Lenin would play game after game, doing everything possible to lose, but always winning in spite of himself even though he was generally helpless with laughter.

Yet nobody, in spite of the successive metamorphoses, the too-noisy, childlike bursts of laughter which he usually stifled behind his hand, the transparent lies, and the funny little bowler-hat, several sizes too small, with which he crowned an impressively Roman head—could consider Apollinaire as a clown. Even for those who had not read the curiously baroque short stories that had been appearing for nearly a year in *La Revue Blanche*, it was impossible not to recognise that this young man was a force to be reckoned with. His conversation was outstandingly brilliant, even in this company where only brilliant conversationalists were admitted, and it revealed an amazing erudition. Perhaps not all the curious and fantastic facts which enlivened his talk were exact, but all were amusing. He had a warmth of manner, an almost feminine charm, an evident joy in life that radiated from him in what sometimes seemed an almost tangible way so that he was already, in spite of his youth, the 'magician of pleasure' he was to become for his friends. This habitual gaiety sometimes gave way to sudden, but always brief, fits of melancholy that added to the enigma of his character; just as the bohemianism to which he gave himself up with such gusto in the evenings contrasted strangely with a taste for order and economy that came into its own each morning, when he took his place behind the counter in a bank in the rue d'Antin.

As to his origins, he was evasive and secretive. He was known to live with his mother, whom he obviously admired and of whom he was as obviously terrified. Occasionally, he had introduced one or other of his friends to his home and they brought back stories of a handsome virago who welcomed her son at the threshold with screams of: 'What have you done now? What have you been up to again?' and, as often as not, slammed the door in their faces. Others, for no apparent reason, had been received with an almost royal welcome, stuffed with wonderful meals and sent away loaded with good things. The lodgings changed frequently, were sometimes handsomely furnished, sometimes hardly furnished at all. Altogether, this mother was as unpredictable and incomprehensible as her son, and much more alarming. As for his father, Apollinaire occasionally hinted that he was the son of a great Prelate, intimately connected with the Vatican. Something unctuous in his manner and priestly in the gestures of the beautifully shaped, rather fleshy hands, with their finely pointed fingers, seemed to give credence to this supposition. Perhaps he enjoyed the slight air of mystery that surrounded him; certainly he cultivated it to some extent. At any rate, it is almost certain that he could not, at that time, have answered with any precision the question his friends often discussed among themselves: Who is he?

*   *   *

For the answer to that question, we must go back to Rome

during the papacy of Pius IX.* It was then a gay, frivolous, superstitious city, whose brilliant social life was enhanced by the arrival of numerous noble refugees from the storms that had struck Europe in the middle of the century. Among them had come a certain Michael Apollinaris Kostrowitsky, a Pole who had lost his fortune during the anti-Russian insurrection in his country and escaped just in time to avoid being exiled to Siberia with his brothers. As Madame Kostrowitsky was of Italian origin, it had been natural for them to come to Rome and apply for help, like so many other Catholic refugees, to the Vatican. Kostrowitsky had been lucky enough to be nominated Papal Chamberlain and they had settled down, like so many others, to keep up an appearance of prosperity on a narrow income and hope for a miraculous restitution of former glories.

The couple had brought with them their little daughter, Angelica Alexandrine, born in Helsinki and obviously destined to be a beauty. She was a difficult child, even at that early age, and her parents must have been relieved to hear that the Pope himself had intervened to procure a place for her in the French convent of the Sacred Heart. At that time most of the daughters of the Roman aristocracy were educated in this exclusive and expensive establishment and they must have hoped that the perfect finish provided by the nuns would compensate for an insufficient dowry when the time came to arrange a marriage.

It had soon become evident, however, that Signorina Kostrowitsky would be too much for them. Even her piety had been too ardent, too excessive, and her indomitable will, violent temper and precocious sensuality had made her an undesirable companion for rich little Romans. By the time she was sixteen, not even the Papal patronage could persuade the Mother Superior to keep her. She had been removed discreetly and her parents had launched her, a little earlier than they had wished, into the social life they still hoped might lead to a reasonably good marriage.

---

* A French scholar, M. Marcel Adéma, has patiently and pertinaciously unearthed the facts about this nearly eighty-year-old mystery. The proofs he brought back from a recent journey to Rome (birth certificates, legal documents, even verbal recognition of the facts by a member of the Flugi d'Aspermont family) must be considered as finally establishing the truth on the subject of Apollinaire's parentage.

They had soon been disillusioned. In the salon of some society hostess, Angelica Alexandrine had made the acquaintance of a handsome ex-officer of the Royal Army of the Two Sicilies. Francesco Flugi d'Aspermont was at that time already over forty but he retained a charm that had always got him what he wanted. He was the youngest son of the Italian branch of an aristocratic Swiss family with a long military tradition, alleviated now and again by the spasmodic appearance of a poet. He was a traveller, a wanderer with a mysterious past and a somewhat tarnished reputation, but apparently reconciled with his family. At first sight there had been nothing unsuitable, in spite of the difference in age, about his courtship of Mademoiselle Kostrowitsky. The two families moved in Vatican circles and shared solid Legitimist principles; one of Francesco's brothers was a high dignitary of the Benedictine Order; the pomp and ceremonies of the Church were as familiar to the couple as the gay social life outside the Vatican walls. It had seemed, on the whole, a suitable union and normally they would have been married with the approbation of cardinals and a papal blessing.

Perhaps Francesco had picked up a wife in the course of his travels; perhaps he was simply not a marrying man. In any case, instead of a marriage, there had been an elopement. The couple had disappeared, leaving their two families to conceal the scandal as best they could. After a time news had begun to arrive from various fashionable resorts where there were casinos and opportunities for gambling, but it had generally taken the form of claims for debts. The young people had been living on a grand scale, on credit all too easily forthcoming with the guarantee of the Flugi name.

They had returned to Rome in 1880. Alexandrine was pregnant and they had had to decide on the child's future identity. He was born on August 26th and they had solved the problem in a muddled, incoherent way that was to be typical of his mother for the rest of her life. The baby had first been registered under the fictitious name of Dulcigni, and baptised a month later with the Christian names of Wilhelm Alberto Appollinario. Then, after six months had elapsed, she had changed her mind and signed a declaration recognising him as her illegitimate son and conferring on him her own name of Kostrowitsky. Two years later, a second boy had been born and christened Alberto. He was a fair, cuddly child, not in the least like his brother, and Alexandrine had preferred him from the beginning. As for her middle-aged lover, his absences had been growing more and more frequent and lasting for longer and longer intervals, till at last he had disappeared from her life.

II

In the Chrysalis

Je suis Guillaume Apollinaire
Dit d'un nom slave pour vrai nom
Ma vie est triste toute entière
Un écho répond toujours non
Lorsque je dis une prière.*

Although Wilhelm Kostrowitsky was only five years old when he arrived in Monaco, his whole childhood was passed in the shadow of the Vatican. Back and forth from Rome came Dom Romarino—otherwise Nicholas Flugi, elder brother of Francesco and now Abbot-General of the Benedictine Order—devoted and anxious, determined to repair as far as possible the harm done by his irresponsible brother. Alexandrine and her children were placed under the personal protection of Mgr Theuret, Bishop of Monaco; the two little boys were accepted at the Collège Saint-Charles, where the Marist brothers educated the children of the best families of the Principality, and funds were provided for their upkeep. Perhaps this excellent uncle served as a model for Father Benedetto Orfei—'theologian and expert in gastronomy, pious and greedy', and deaf into the bargain—whom the disrespectful nephew imagined, in *L'Hérésiarque*, as the inventor of a strange new heresy. At any rate, he was ill-rewarded for his kindness. The mysterious origin of the two children and his persistent interest in them soon gave rise to the rumour that he was their father and Guillaume himself, as he grew up, was inclined to encourage this idea, though he later improved on it by hinting that a cardinal had been responsible for his birth.

So the children were safely installed in the kindergarten of the college, high on the rock above the sea, where their names were gallicised into Guillaume and Albert and Sister Odile and Sister Henri taught them to speak French. Alexandrine—who now called herself Countess de Kostrowitsky—swooped down on them

* Apollinaire: *Le Guetteur mélancolique.*

11

for visits that were dreaded by the good Marists, because she found fault, vociferously, with everything. As for the pupils, the poet Louis de Gonzague Frick recalls the excitement the appearance of this beautiful and elegant woman, with her vividly painted face, jewels and plumed hats, caused among the older boys, who used to hang about the passages to watch her pass. The children adored their glamorous and seldom-seen mother. For Guillaume, she was still connected with strange and rather disturbing memories of visits to miracle-working hermits or to sorcerers and fortune-tellers in terrifying yet fascinating slums; but also with the wonderful Roman sweetmeats that were to reappear so often in his stories: nuts candied in honey, fondants flavoured with rose-petals, dried figs stuffed with nuts and aniseed, *cotanniata* and *cuccuzata*, with their delicate flavouring of quince and peach. It was she who had taken him to see the Carnivals (the chariots decorated with flowers and bells, the masked figures in the streets, the confetti, the rubber balls full of scented water that slapped and splashed against the faces of the onlookers, became confused in later life with memories of the carnivals of Nice and Monaco) and to the marionette shows, with the great, life-size figures that acted oriental dramas to the gaping Roman crowds. And always in the background of these Roman memories, there was the mysterious, yet strangely familiar, figure of the Pope, that dominated the life of the city. The idea of the papacy was to haunt him throughout his life, as something at once majestic and absurd. It was one of the many problems he would never be able to solve to his own satisfaction, and like so many of those problems, it was intimately, though unobviously, connected with his mother.

Meanwhile, he was shedding the skin of a Polish-Roman child and learning to be a Frenchman. The long poem *Zone*, in which he reveals himself more directly than anywhere else, gives a glimpse of the child who was no longer Wilhelm, but Guillaume:

> Tu es très pieux et avec le plus ancien de tes camarades René Dalize
> Vous n'aimez rien tant que les pompes de l'Eglise
> Il est neuf heures le gaz est baissé tout bleu vous
>   sortez du dortoir en cachette
> Vous priez toute la nuit dans la chapelle du collège
> Tandis qu'éternelle et adorable profondeur améthyste
> Tourne à jamais la flamboyante gloire du Christ. . . .*

The pupils of the Collège Saint-Charles lived in an enchanting world of symbol and mysticism. Within its bounds, nature was the mirror of eternity. The cry of the cock became: *Christus natus est*; the passing of bread to a neighbour was a religious gesture; and even the fish, swimming among the seaweed, deep in the clear Mediterranean water, became, for Guillaume and his friends, not merely fish, but 'the image of the Saviour'. He was writing poetry already, encouraged by an understanding master, and although none of these early verses survives, they must surely have reflected this ardent and joyful piety. *Comment faire pour être heureux— Comme un petit enfant candide?*,† he wrote twenty years later, when the sad and sordid aspects of life had become all too familiar to him; and all through his work, right to the end, there runs this thread of nostalgia for the days when everything was clear and simple . . . the time of belief.

This period of childhood came abruptly to an end in 1895, when the College was closed. Sister Odile and Sister Henri disappeared into their own convent, and the Brothers from whom he had acquired a solid grounding in classical culture and a vast repertory of antique and biblical legends were dispersed to other establishments. Guillaume was sent to continue his studies at the Collège Stanislas in Cannes and it was there that he made, at the age of fifteen, his first real contact with the outside world. It was certainly an important, and indeed, a decisive period. The young man who left Cannes two years later, to prepare for his *baccalauréat* at the Lycée in Nice, had practically nothing in common with the

* You are very pious like your oldest friend René Dalize
  Loving nothing so much as the Church's mysteries
  It is nine o'clock the gas-jet lowered from the dormitory you steal
  You will pray all night in the college chapel
  While the eternal and adorable depth of amethyst
  Turns for ever the flaming glory of Christ.
  (from a translation by W. S. Strachan).

The punctuation disappeared from Apollinaire's poems at the time of the publication of *Alcools* in 1913 (see p. 150). Quotations follow his own practice in this respect. Many of the poems that refer to his early life were, of course, written much later. Sometimes, as in *Zone*, we know the year and even the month when the poem was composed, but in other cases it is impossible to fix even an approximate date.

† What can I do to be happy like an innocent little child?

child who had arrived from Monaco. He was morally unrecognisable. Something had happened, and although there is no witness to
this period, it is not hard to reconstitute a crisis that was inevitable
in the circumstances.

A minor poet called Ange Toussaint Luca, who later became an
admiring disciple, has left a vivid little portrait of his friend when
he arrived in Nice at the age of seventeen.

'We spent all our recreations discussing the new poets we
were discovering,' he recalls, 'and as Guillaume was already
a great smoker, he used to offer me cigarettes that I smoked
in a distant corner of the classroom where we did our preparation. Literature had drawn us together, and was to make intimate friends of us. . . . What a delightful person he was, and
how marvellously he talked. His curiosity led him to search for
anecdotes, eccentric stories, the funniest and least-known
details. Already he knew all the witty remarks, all the small
adventures that make up the bypaths of history, and also its
pleasures. He could have told you that a certain wizard wore
blue brocade and a pointed hat, that a certain fairy wore a
dress the colour of Time. He knew all about succubus and
incubus. He lived in the midst of legend, anecdote and
minor history . . . '

But Guillaume had another side to him which would have been
far more disquieting to his masters in Monaco. Luca shows him as
a militant atheist and an anarchist . . . or at least a subscriber to
anarchist newspapers; a rebel who lost no time in founding a
review entitled *The Avenger*, described as being 'against our teachers,
our ushers, even against certain of our comrades'; a 'Dreyfusard',
who revered Zola, the anti-clerical, the 'friend of the Jews', the
enemy of established society, yet who was intransigent enough to
despise the gallant, desperate Colonel Picquart, for 'allowing
himself to be tortured'.

Obviously, this rebellious, contemptuous, independent Guillaume had come into being during the two years at the Collège
Stanislas. During that time, the world he had lived in for fifteen
years had been shattered, leaving only a nostalgia that never left
him and that wells up in his poetry, like a spring bursting from a
crack in the rock, at every period of difficulty or unhappiness.

During those two years, we know that he lost his faith in God, and it is almost certain that he lost, at the same time, faith in his mother.

Alexandrine (or Angelica, or Olga—for she changed her Christian name according to successive whims) de Kostrowitsky was a woman of violent and indomitable character. She was determined to live as she pleased and never submitted to the pressure of circumstances. Although she was critical of unconventionality in others, she felt that she herself, as a Polish noblewoman, was exempt from ordinary restrictions, and this conviction was so firm that she often managed to impose it on other people. Thus she had succeeded, in spite of all the prejudices of the day, in forcing her way into the best society in Monaco, openly acknowledging her two children and at the same time continuing the easy-going life to which she was accustomed. For a time at least, the strict principles she preached—and applied to everyone except herself—her piety that was doubtless sincere in a rather spectacular way, the ecclesiastical patronage she owed to Dom Romarino, and her own remarkable beauty, prevented Monégasque society from asking too many questions about her past. As for her children, safely sheltered from reality in the College, it was natural that they should admire her blindly and accept unquestioningly the picture of herself as she intended them to see her.

It was impossible, of course, that these illusions should last for ever. At Cannes, Guillaume was no longer a boarder, but a day-boy, living with his mother. He must soon have understood the real meaning of the succession of 'uncles' who had appeared during his holidays; he must have discovered that the chaotic finances of the family were due to her overwhelming passion for gambling. Perhaps he even discovered that she was listed in the police archives of the Principality as a 'kept woman'. Certainly he must have begun to ask questions about his own birth. Alexandrine's social position was not as secure as it seemed, in spite of her false title, and he must have been a witness to a good many snubs and slights. The world was crumbling around him. He understood that the brilliant, capricious mother he idolised was a sinner in the eyes of the Church and of Society. That Madame de Kostrowitsky herself arrogantly refused to admit the existence of a dilemma, only made the situation more difficult. Guillaume was forced to make a choice and he remained firmly on the side of his mother—as he was to do for the rest of his life and in spite of everything she did to discourage him. The choice for his mother and against the Church and Society was made without any illusions. There can be no doubt that, by the time he arrived in Nice, Guillaume knew exactly what his mother was, and that the knowledge caused him bitter suffering. He had discovered the truth at the moment when he entered into adolescence, thus, at the most impressionable age. And with the discovery, the two stable elements of his life disappeared. Deprived of them, he was forced to define himself anew, and thus discovered himself to be a foreigner and a bastard, uprooted and stateless.

The new Guillaume who arrived at the Lycée in Nice was already a young man, with precociously ripened tastes and talents. He was writing a good deal: ('Prose! How difficult it is! It is much easier to compose good poetry', he was soon exclaiming in a letter to his friend Luca); translating from Mediaeval Italian, considering the possibility of publishing a volume of verse at his own expense. He gained great prestige with Luca and a few other literary-minded boys, when he was found to be familiar with the work of poets like Henri de Régnier, Rémy de Gourmont and Vielé-Griffin, who were then at the avant-garde of the poets in Paris. As for the great Mallarmé, he was the pole, the magnetic centre of the fascinating, esoteric Symbolist School with its exciting doctrine that 'to name an object is to destroy half the pleasure of the poem. Suggestion . . . there lies the ideal!'

Symbolism was at its apotheosis. The May number of *Cosmopolis* (which the two young men had probably read, since their tastes naturally led them to the 'little reviews' of the period) had published what must have been one of the most extraordinary poems ever to have appeared in print. In *Un Coup de Dés jamais n'abolira le Hasard*, the lay-out became, for the first time, an integral part of the poem itself; the blank spaces—silence—assumed an equal importance with the words scattered ('like stars' explained Mallarmé) over the pages. The central idea, although it was difficult and perhaps impossible to seize entirely or to define, represented the logical conclusion to the poet's obsession with annihilation, with nothingness and the preference he shared with his own hero, Igitur, for 'non-being rather than being, for the hymn to life rather than life itself, for divinity rather than God'. It was, in fact, poetry assimilated to music, aiming at the expression of pure thought, pure emotion. 'This manner of using an idea in all its nakedness, with all it comports of reticences, prolongations, flight,' explained Mallarmé in his preface, 'results, if [the poem] is read aloud, in a musical score.'

From the other end of the scale came news of the 'Naturist' movement, that opposed the Symbolist 'decadence' and sought to use reality, in its most simple and easily perceptible forms, as the matter of poetry. 'It is our aim to make of the great laws of Nature the very laws of Art', Saint-Georges de Bouhélier had declared a year earlier at the Naturist Congress in Brussels, and after him a young disciple had suggested in more concrete terms:

'A man appears on the scene—he is a mason, or a warrior, or a fisherman. The aim is to take him by surprise in a moment of eternity; the sublime instant when he leans forward to polish a cuirass or cast his net into the water. We know that his attitude at such a moment is in harmony with God....'

The young men who followed Bouhélier* demanded 'a renewal of the national spirit, the cult of the earth and of heroes, the consecration of civic energy'. In other words, they were in violent reaction against Symbolism. These two apparently isolated events —the publication of *Un Coup de Dés* and the Naturist Congress— appear to-day as a preliminary confrontation of the two main literary tendencies of the twentieth century: abstraction and 'commitment'. From that time on, French literature was to hesitate between these two radically different conceptions of the relationship between life and art. Guillaume himself can hardly have imagined that he was to play in this dual evolution a part as important as it was ambiguous.

Meanwhile, he and Luca were sure that they were Symbolists

---

* It is curious to note that this 'Naturist' movement, which had considerable importance in its day and influenced many talented young men of the next generation (especially the group who called themselves *L'Abbaye*: Romains, Duhamel, Vildrac and others) produced no writers of any importance. Even Saint-Georges de Bouhélier, who had a good deal of prestige at the end of the century, is remembered only by literary historians.

though this did not prevent them from an eclectic admiration for Zola the Naturalist, Barrès, the Neo-Classicist and even Balzac. Naturally, they dreamed of Paris where these fascinating literary clashes were taking place, where Mallarmé freed the imagination of the young poets, weaving around them, during the prestigious Tuesday evenings in the rue de Rome, the magic web of Symbolism. For these Mediterranean schoolboys, it was the centre of the world, although they must have found it hard to imagine a climate and rhythm of life so different from that of the nonchalant South. There, writers and painters were not considered as mere eccentrics; they influenced the course of events and directed the current of ideas. Zola—a man of the South, like themselves—was about to launch the terrible blast of his *J'accuse* and force the nation to examine its own conscience in face of the ugly tissue of lies, forgeries, treachery and high-sounding words, that the Dreyfus affair had become. The manifesto appeared and Guillaume was transported by enthusiasm. The Dreyfus case had affected him, and perhaps in a more personal way than he ever admitted. Surely he must have identified himself to some extent with the exile in Cayenne, with the little captain whom the *bien-pensants*—the Church, the Army, the Nationalists, the men of wealth and position— accused of being no true Frenchman because he was a Jew. Like himself, Dreyfus was beyond the pale through a mere accident of birth.

Although Guillaume already imagined himself launched on the conquest of Paris, there seemed to be little chance of him ever getting there. For some reason this erudite youth, with his stock of extra-scholastic learning, never passed his examination. At eighteen he was still dependent on his mother and probably found it natural to be so. Alexandrine's apron-strings were tough, and her son was securely tied to them. It looked as if he might spend the rest of his life writing rather frigid alexandrines for the delectation of amateur poets on the Côte d'Azur.

It was then that the versatile mother met a temporarily wealthy Jewish financier named Jules Weil. He was her junior by eleven years and was accustomed to live by rather questionable expedients, but he had the advantage of being a gambler as passionate as herself. At any rate the link must have been a strong one, for he remained her faithful and submissive companion for the rest of her life.

The couple moved to Lyons, then to Aix-en-Provence. The two boys accompanied them, for their mother had no intention of abandoning them to the temptations of the worldly Riviera. At each stage poor Jules Weil lost a little more of the fortune that had helped him to woo his Alexandrine. Guillaume and Albert took odd jobs, read in public libraries, packed suitcases and moved on again. And so they arrived, in April of the last year of the century, in Paris.

It was not at all the Paris of which Guillaume had dreamed, and he himself was still a far cry from the brilliant young Apollinaire of the *Closerie des Lilas* and the *Soleil d'Or*. The great Mallarmé had died a few months earlier, worn out by the lonely struggle to express the inexpressible. As for Henri de Régnier, Barrès and Moréas, they might have been dead too, for all the possibility he had of meeting them. The nearest he could approach to these great figures was to imagine them in the form of passers-by, rendered ethereal by dusk or dimmed by mist, encountered during long, solitary walks by the banks of the Seine. He was poor, friendless and, above all, insecure. His mother had taken lodgings in a fashionable quarter and had soon discovered certain private gambling clubs, where she quickly ran through the remains of Weil's small fortune. They were soon deep in debt, but she was well used to that, of course, and considered herself far above such sordid nuisances as bills and bailiffs. When things became too hot for her, she would resort to the simple expedient of changing her address and even, on occasion, her name. When at last her creditors became so pressing that they could no longer be avoided, she merely removed her whole family to Spa, in the hope of winning back her losses at the famous Belgian casino.

Presumably she had some success there, or perhaps she pined for Paris. In any case, she was off again in no time, leaving her sons in a small family pension at Stavelot, in the Ardennes. The bills were to be paid from Paris, but naturally the money never arrived. Instead, after two months had passed and the innkeeper was growing uneasy, there came a letter imperiously commanding the boys to escape by night, not forgetting their belongings. Guillaume and the timid Albert obeyed, as usual, and carried off the affair successfully, though not painlessly. Guillaume described it succinctly in a letter to one of his friends in Monaco: 'Stay in

Belgium, no money. Flitted by night, frost, trunk on back, suit-case in hand, through five miles of forest, smell of mushrooms, from Stavelot to Roanne-loo, luckily met no one. Two hours in the cold in front of the station at Roanne-loo and departure for Paris. . . .' On arrival they found their mother in new lodgings, transformed into 'Madame Olga Karpoff' and, according to her new identity card, aged twenty-six.

This stay in the Ardennes, apparently so brief and unimportant, marked in fact the emergence of a writer from the chrysalis of a mere literary-minded schoolboy. It was long enough for Guil-laume to learn the racy Walloon dialect, to make love to the innkeeper's daughter, and above all, to compose the greater part of a novel in the mediaeval style and owing, it must be admitted, a good deal to Chrétien de Troyes's *La Charrette*. It was to be pub-lished some years later under the title of *L'Enchanteur Pourrissant*— 'The Decaying Magician'.

L'Enchanteur Pourrissant is one of Apollinaire's most neglected works, but he himself set great store by it and referred to it later as 'this testimony to my first aesthetic position'. It is quite obvious-ly, and in spite of all the romantic bric-à-brac, the work of a poet. It reveals the boy of nineteen as already in possession of his essential themes and methods: 'simultaneity', religious satire, the juxtaposition of mythical figures of different origins in order to create a personal myth. In the Forest of the Ardennes ('that immense womb, that gives birth to ceaselessly renewed lives and miracles') the taste for Celtic legends, acquired from the Marist Brothers, revived and became an irresistible impulsion. It was natural that he should transplant into its leafy shadows the figures of Merlin, Morgan la Fay, Vivien, who had haunted the unknown forests of Wales and Brittany. Then gradually, in this northern landscape of rocks and trees, appear figures whose presence is more surprising: Vulcan, Pan; Caspar, Melchior and Balthazar (or deceptive emanations of those three Wise Kings, for every-thing here is deception); Delilah, Simon Stylites, Helen of Troy and the Druids. It is a story of enchantments, of reciprocal spell-bindings, of the falsity of all things. Above all it is a picture of the fundamental chaos of the world, and under the treachery and shifting illusions one can detect a personal chaos and the brutal revelation of the falsity of accepted truths. The Surrealists have adopted Apollinaire, like Rimbaud and Lautréamont, as one of their precursors, and *L'Enchanteur Pourrissant*, if it can be classified at all, seems to deserve the title of a pre-Surrealist work. The return to Paris brought him face to face with hard reality. Alexandrine, impulsive as ever, met him there with an ultimatum that left him disorientated and helpless. A short poem entitled *La Porte*, published many years later, but apparently related to this crisis, suggests how crushingly the mother had invited her elder son to cease living at her expense:

> La porte de l'hôtel sourit terriblement
> Qu'est ce que cela peut me faire ô ma maman
> D'être cet employé pour qui seul rien n'existe
> Pi-mus couples allant dans la profonde eau triste
> Anges frais débarqués de Marseille hier matin
> J'entends mourir et remourir un chant lointain
> Humble comme je suis qui ne suis rien qui vaille
>
> · Enfant je t'ai donné ce que j'avais travaill*

But it was not easy to find work in Paris. For the first time, Guillaume realised the disadvantages of being a foreigner in France. The Civil Service for instance—the refuge of so many poets and novelists—was closed to him. Nor had he any compensatory academic qualifications. There remained only the sort of jobs that are advertised in the vacancy columns of newspapers. . . ill-paid and generally with a catch in them somewhere. Guillaume did his best, tramped the city from one dingy office to another, acted as tutor-nursemaid to backward little boys, even followed a course in shorthand-typing in the hope of improving his prospects.

A letter to an old school-friend, James Onimus, describes this bitter period that left him with a permanent terror of poverty:

'. . . A difficult winter in Paris. We began to think we should have to eat bricks. I even used to write blurbs for an advertising firm at four sous the line, which is the worst thing of all, among

---

*The door of the hotel has a terrible smile—What can it matter to me, O my mother—If I am this employee for whom alone nothing exists—Pihi couples setting out on the deep, sad water—Angel-fish freshly unloaded at Marseilles yesterday morning—I hear a distant song dying and redying—Humble as I am myself, who am worth nothing—Child I have given you what I had. Work.

In the manuscript version Apollinaire wrote: *pour qui seul tout existe*—'for whom alone *everything* exists'.

jail-birds, penniless ex-lawyers, adventurers returned from the gold-mines. I used to meet people trying unsuccessfully to join up for the Transvaal and I mingled with the hungry, plebeian crowds. Then, at the end of the month, I got out, with twenty-three francs fifty centimes handed over by the boss of the firm, who is Galuzot's mistress and pays the down-and-outs herself by burning scented paper to drown their smell. That is the most terrible of my memories. . . .'

These months of misery were reborn many years later when he came to write the long poem *Zone*, that has caused so much controversy and in which he watches the events of his life passing like a film before his eyes. Among the scribbled notes—expurgated from the final version—there is a passage that refers directly to the experience described to Onimus, and suggests that it taught him the immense tolerance he always showed towards the failings of others:

> I have known the misery of all sorts of people,
> Shady bankers, writers, very poor poets,
> (Blank) actors, writers . . .
> Penniless painters with syphilis,
> Pimps, men who hand out prospectuses,
> Sandwichmen, newspaper-sellers,
> We must not blame them if they are sometimes unpleasant.
> Nothing leads to evil like the lack of money . . .

Luckily, he had inexhaustible physical and mental energy. Scenes at home and harassing jobs were powerless against an immense appetite for life. He was beginning to make friends—and for him friends were always to be one of the essentials of his existence. There was René Nicosia, there was Ferdinand Molina da Silva, both of whom he exhausted by dragging them on endless walks through Paris, on a voyage of discovery that never ended and never palled. He must see every play, hear every concert, drink in every bar . . . and somehow earn enough money to do it all. A less expensive joy was to be found in the great libraries. It was in the Bibliothèque Mazarine that he met Léon Cahun, historian, explorer, latinist, hellenist, author of historical novels and adventure stories in the style of Jules Verne, philologist, fluent in such unlikely languages as ancient Turkish. Besides all these seductive talents, Cahun was a Hebrew scholar and Cabbalist, descendant of a long line of rabbis and wonderfully versed in the legends of his people. His nephew, Marcel Schwob, was a semi-invalid, already well-known in the world of letters and attached to Alfred Vallette's famous literary review, *Le Mercure de France*. He had started his career by collaborating with Catulle Mendès, chief of the Parnassian school of poets, and he was a friend of Claudel and the young André Gide. He had a passionate admiration for R. L. Stevenson, with whom he had kept up a long correspondence, and it was he who had introduced Meredith to French readers.

The uncle and nephew fascinated Guillaume. They were his first contact with the literary world and in them he recognised his own taste for the byways of history, for fantastic characters, little-known languages and bizarre facts. Through them he learned a smattering of Hebrew and discovered the ritual of orthodox Jewry. It enthralled him as the rites of Catholicism had once done, while the secrets of the Cabbala haunted his imagination for many years. It was Léon Cahun who introduced him to the *Bibliothèque Nationale* where he was later to obtain the not uncongenial job of cataloguing its famous *Enfer*—the collection of erotic or subversive books that can only be consulted by permission of the Director. As for Marcel Schwob, who had written that 'We must destroy because all creation is based on destruction', his influence was probably as deep and lasting as that of Jarry was to be. Later, he was to play an important part in his friend's life by introducing him to Paul Fort and the society of the *Closerie des Lilas*. Meanwhile he opened the door to what Guillaume called 'alimentary literature', notably by bringing him into contact with a certain Esnard, a novelist whose imagination had never carried him beyond the first two or three chapters of a novel. Guillaume, who had plenty of that quality to spare, entered his service as 'ghost' and thus embarked on an intermittent career that stood him in good stead, over a considerable number of years, whenever funds ran low.

René Nicosia, at the age of nearly eighty, has left a portrait of this exhausting companion of his youth. Like all the portraits traced by his friends, it is at once true and false. For Nicosia, the Parisian, Guillaume appeared almost incredibly naïve and was often embarrassing because of his aggressive vanity and absence of any sense of the ridiculous. 'He was extremely intelligent, rather bohemian, but bourgeois at heart. Something of an opportunist where his own interests were concerned, but incompetent in money matters. Perhaps a bit of a liar, unstable and jealous, but with great charm.' And the old friend sums up: 'I think he was a little unbalanced mentally, or perhaps he was playing a part with himself as audience.'[1]

There were, of course, many things about Guillaume of which his friend knew nothing. Madame de Kostrowitsky approved of him and believed him to have a good influence over her son, but Nicosia never suspected the difficult relationship between the two of them. There can be no doubt that Guillaume suffered deeply on her account and that the bourgeois principles which the astute Nicosia had detected in him were constantly revolted by her conduct. He never ceased to admire her ('She is so tremendously distinguished!' he confided once to a friend, although no one else ever noticed a quality which had, in fact, disappeared with her youth) and to worry over her, even when it became impossible to live with her. 'She begins cursing me as soon as she sees me,' he confided to his friends, and eight years later in a letter to Toussaint Luca he confided something of the difficult, anxious relationship he had with her:

> 'Mother is well but we are not on good terms. Her exclusive character has separated us for the time being and, in fact, we have not seen much of each other for some time. I am very fond of her, but as she cares nothing for my work, or for the art and literature I love, there are more and more subjects of friction between us. I hope it is only temporary. . . .'

In the meantime he was obliged to live with her, to support her scenes and reproaches. To Nicosia she complained that her son only came home when he needed to change his shirt, but she certainly exaggerated. When he was there, under her wing, she treated him like a child, refused furiously to answer questions or even to discuss the question of his birth that obsessed him. 'Why can't you be more like your brother?' she would scream at him, and indeed, the gentle, timid Albert was no trouble to anyone and had already found a steady job as an accountant. Guillaume was deeply attached to him, in spite of this humiliating favouritism, and they corresponded (often, on the elder brother's part, by means of ideograms that must have gravely puzzled the recipient) throughout the whole of their lives.

There were other troubles, too, that darkened this first experience of Paris. The child of those two ardent seekers of pleasure, Francesco Flugi and Alexandrine Kostrowitsky, was unlikely to be indifferent to women, and Guillaume had a singularly explosive temperament. He had already known brief and varied triumphs (though perhaps not quite so many as he liked to boast of), including the mistress of his employer, Esnard, through whom he took a pleasant revenge when he finally realised he would never be paid for his work. Now, for the first time, he was in love. Ferdinand Molina da Silva was a closer and more intuitive friend than Nicosia, and Guillaume was soon adopted by the whole family. The Molinas were Spanish Jews, rich, cultivated and forming the warm, happy family cell he had never known and had probably always longed for. Naturally, he fell in love with Ferdinand's pretty sister, Linda. She responded to his spate of poems with nothing more satisfying than friendly pity and went off for a holiday by the sea. There was a correspondence, 'Don't begin your letters "My poor Kostro". I find it revolting', wrote Guillaume. Linda was kind, and really fond of him and Guillaume exaggerated whatever encouragement he could find in her kindness. Presently he turned up, wearing his most formal clothes, to ask for her hand. Monsieur Molina, who had appreciated him as a friend for his son, would not hear of him as a son-in-law and refused even to discuss the matter. Poor Guillaume, whose vanity hid a self-esteem far more fragile than any of his friends imagined, was terribly hurt. The disappointment was passing, but it seemed like an augury. Guillaume, at twenty, already saw himself as the *mal-aimé*, the 'ill-loved', that he was to remain till the end of his life, without ever suspecting it was his own fault.

In fact, the century could hardly have begun more badly, but Guillaume had a robust, optimistic side to his temperament that protected him from the romantic—and at that time, fashionable—despair of misunderstood youths. Paris had proved a failure for the time being. Now, in August of the year 1901, he received a proposal which had little in common with the literary career he longed for, but at least offered a change of scene. It came from the

Vicomtesse de Milhau, daughter of a rich German businessman and widow of a Frenchman of the minor nobility. She was seeking a cultured young man to accompany her to her estates in the Rhineland and act as tutor to her daughter, Gabrielle. This child —for whose education, decidedly, nothing was being neglected— already had a young English governess and Madame de Milhau was in a hurry to pack the whole household off to Germany.

If Guillaume hesitated at all, the first interview with his future employer soon put an end to his doubts. First of all, he caught a glimpse of the governess, who was very young and remarkably pretty. Then he discovered that Madame de Milhau actually possessed a motor-car and proposed to set out with him and her chauffeur for what must have been the unusual adventure of crossing the whole of France by this means. The idea enchanted the improvised tutor. He was already fascinated, in a poetic and entirely unpractical way, by the new mechanical inventions that were beginning to make their appearance. Perhaps he was already beginning to suspect that they were the real sign under which the twentieth century had been born. At any rate he accepted. Madame de Milhau herself was in too much of a hurry to insist on the question of qualifications, and a few days later the party set out for Neu-Glück.

III

'I, who know songs for sirens'

Moi qui sais des lais pour les reines
Les complaintes de mes années
Des hymnes d'esclave aux murènes
La romance du mal-aimé
*Et des chansons pour les sirènes**

Time passed and from Germany came letters, addressed to Madame de Kostrowitsky and Albert, giving conscientious details of Guillaume's daily existence and of German cities visited in the company of his employer and his pupil. As for René Nicosia, who had worn out so much shoe leather tramping the streets of Paris with his indefatigable friend, he received a single postcard, containing the words: 'I am at my apotheosis.' As Guillaume had never confided in him, he was merely puzzled and put it aside for later explanations.

It was perfectly true, and perhaps more absolutely true than the writer himself understood. This year in Germany was really an apotheosis, as well as a beginning. Apollinaire's poems are always, like those of his spiritual ancestor, Villon, rooted in fact. It was always some immediate event or emotion, something entirely personal, that provided the springboard for each poem. A landscape, a legend, a love affair . . . but always its immediate impact on himself, never idealised, impersonalised in the style of the Parnassians. If one analyses the whole of *Alcools* one soon realises that the 'sources' are restricted and easily discernible: regrets for lost youth, a few violent, involved and unhappy loves, certain aspects of Paris, the terrifying experience of prison, and

* Apollinaire: *La Chanson du Mal-Aimé.*

27

almost all the rest can be traced back to this year of 1901–02, beginning with the exquisite short poems grouped under the title *Rhénanes* and culminating in one of the finest long poems in the French language: *La Chanson du Mal-Aimé*. This year in the North provided not only a store of impressions into which he would dip long afterwards for the subjects of poems and stories but was also a period of extraordinarily concentrated production, which must form almost a record of creative activity. He had arrived in Germany as Guillaume de Kostrowitsky, an assimilative but uncertain youth with a vast store of half-digested learning; he left it as Guillaume Apollinaire, having found his style and discovered a personal medium for the transposition of daily life into poetry, with a baggage of verse and prose that was to place him later in the front rank of contemporary writers.

Yet life in the Milhau household was not apparently stimulating. Madame de Milhau's mother, Frau Holterhoff, who had lived with them since her daughter's widowhood, was sordidly avaricious and immensely impressed by her own indirect affiliation to the French nobility. Her favourite occupation was to supervise the decoration of every available space of the walls and ceilings of the sham-Gothic villa in Neu-Glück with the gilded arms of the Milhau family. Madame de Milhau resembled her and utterly lacked charm. They never received visitors, were interested in nothing and were totally uncultured. The tutor and governess were made to understand that they were merely upper servants. They had very little to do and had probably been engaged to act as the visible signs of their employer's wealth rather than to occupy themselves with the education of the eight-year-old Gabrielle.

For Guillaume, the Southerner accustomed to the brilliant landscapes of the Mediterranean, there was something infinitely melancholy and even sinister in the German countryside. The brief stay in Stavelot had given him a glimpse of a gentle, romantic North, but Neu-Glück was a brutal contrast with everything familiar. The absence of light, the wind in the great fir-trees, then, when winter came, the snow he had probably never seen before— all these impressed him as tragic and indeed uncanny. The poems written in the little, unheated bedroom, where he could watch from the window the ceaseless swaying of three pine trees in the garden, all reflect this mood:

> Oh! les cimes des pins grincent en se heurtant
> Et l'on entend aussi se lamenter l'autan
> Et du fleuve prochain à grand'voix triomphales
> Les elfes rire au vent ou corner aux rafales. . . .*

Or he wanders in the cemetery where the owls hoot and the winds blow out the candles that the children tirelessly relight before the graves; or, haunted by the ubiquitous presence of the great, conical trees that replace the familiar orange groves of the Riviera or the gay chestnut trees of Paris, he imagines their endless cycle of transmutation, their occult force—'indoctrinated in the seven arts'—their successive transformations into astrologers, rabbis, old crones, musicians chanting ancient carols or accompanying the thunder with their great bass voices.[1]

The young tutor soon made friends in the region. He was good-humoured, interested in everything he saw, ready to talk to anyone and drink with anyone. Soon he was a familiar figure at the village inn, where his friend, the farmer Johann Dahs, played the flute and taught him the German of the common people. After a few beers, these Rhinelanders would be in a sentimental mood and ready to sing the local *lieder*. The Lorelei, who had lured so many fishermen to their death from her rocky castle 'high above the Rhine', was naturally a favourite and so were the ballads recounting the exploits of the terrible brigand, Schinderhannes, whom Guillaume, who mistrusted the Teutonic *bonhommie,* shows at dinner with his band, 'grow-ing sentimental in the German style', before he sets out to murder a rich Jew.[2]

Indeed, for Guillaume the theme of such legends was never sufficient in itself, but rather a hint, a signpost pointing to obscure regions in the destiny of mankind. It is typical of him that the Lorelei of *Rhénanes* is not the traditional siren whose misdeeds were so often crooned in the long winter evenings

---

* The pine-tops creak as they shock together—And you hear the Auster wind lamenting—And from the nearby river the triumphant voices of elves —Laughing at the wind or trumpeting with its blasts.

in the inn, but the Loreley of the philosopher-poet Clemens Brentano, a witch victim of her own beauty, living in horror of her own power, and dying at last from having 'seen in the water the lovely Lorelei, her rhine-coloured eyes and her sun-coloured hair'.3

Luckily for the two young foreigners, the Milhaus often left the gloomy luxury of Neu-Glück for their house in the cosy little town of Honnef, on the opposite bank of the Rhine. This was a gayer and more sheltered region, where the hills were terraced with vineyards and the river 'that is supposed to be green, but is sometimes blue and often yellow' (wrote Guillaume to his mother), reflected the vines reddened by autumn. Here there was a synagogue and on Saturday mornings he could see the Jews, wearing their sidelocks and flat felt hats, quarrelling volubly as they wended their way to the service. Immediately he gave them names—Ottomar Scholem and Abraham Loeweren—imagined the oaths they hurled at each other ('so terrible one can hardly repeat them'), and the cause of their quarrel—'Leah with her ewe's eyes and her belly that protrudes a little'—and then, remembering the scraps of Hebrew and Jewish ritual learned from old Léon Cahun and perhaps from the Molinas, he concludes with the *Hanoten ne Kamoth bagoim tholahoth baleoumim*, pronounced before the reconciling Thora.

Occasionally, in the pictures of the Rhineland, there are immediate transcriptions from life, juxtaposed fragments of reality such as the poet was later to use in *Lundi rue Christine* written during his Cubist period. Thus *Les Femmes* employs a photographic technique that resumes in a single evening the long hours of winter spent in the homes of various peasant neighbours:

> The women are serving in the vine-planter's house
> Lenschen fill up the stove and put on water for coffee—
> The cat stretches after warming itself—
> *Gertrude and her neighbour Martin are getting married at last*
>
> The blind nightingale tried to sing
> But the screech-owl's hoot set it trembling in its cage
> *The cypress down there looks like the pope on a journey*
> *Through the snow*—The postman has just stopped

To chat with the new schoolmaster
—This is a very cold winter and the wine will be good
—The deaf vestryman who limps is dying
—The old burgomaster's daughter is embroidering a stole

For the priest's name-day. Out there the forest
Seems to sing with the deep voice of a great organ
Now Herr Dream arrives with his sister Frau Sorrow
Kaethe you haven't mended these stockings properly

—Bring the coffee the butter and sandwiches
The jam the lard a jug of milk

—A little more coffee Lenschen please
—It sounds as if the wind was talking in latin . . .

Occasionally Madame de Milhau piled her family into the de
Dion-Bouton and set off for a tour. Motoring in Germany was
still unorganised and the motorist, as Guillaume explained in
an article he managed to publish in a French review at about this
time, was always in the wrong. When the car broke down or ran
into one of the carts that straggled along the bumpy Rhineland
roads, they would change and take a train. In this way, or on
shorter, solitary excursions, Guillaume managed to visit a considerable number of cities—Düsseldorf, Cologne, Heidelberg,
Munich, Berlin—all of which left their traces in his work. On the
whole, he disliked Germany. Berlin was 'hideous and comfortable'; the women were disappointing ('even the prettiest
always have something wrong about their waists, hands, feet, or
stomachs which latter are often protruding. Those who seem to be
perfect have expressions that are lascivious, servile or insolent,
and look like tarts for a camp of mercenaries. . . .'); the chief talent
of the Germans lay in discovering an *ersatz* for everything. The
second series of *Rhénanes** reflects these cities, with their folklore

---

* Published posthumously in the volume entitled *Le Guetteur mélancolique.*
Apollinaire himself excluded these poems from *Rhénanes,* perhaps because he
considered them inferior in quality, but also, no doubt, because of their
obvious subjectivity, which left too clear a trace both of himself and his
itinerary. Apollinaire's passion for mystification made him dislike publishing
anything that could give his readers a definite hold on his past. Although his
poems were always about himself he was careful to avoid giving himself
away and to divert the reader's attention at a moment when he might have
been able to pinpoint a date or a place, or to give a twist to the poem or story
so that it should appear to have its origins in fantasy.

and their contemporary aspect, their buildings and their citizens; all bathed in a changing light that is purely subjective, so that the great Dome of Cologne, for instance, could inspire one day the delicate and touching *Vierge à la Fleur de Haricot* and on a subsequent occasion, the cynical apostrophe:

> Ton dernier architecte ô Dôme devint fou
> Ça prouve clairement que le Bon Dieu se fout
> De ceux qui travaillent à sa plus grande gloire.*

Early in the following year, Guillaume obtained leave from his employer and set out on a tour of the Hapsburg Empire that was to take him as far as Prague and Vienna. From Prague itself, or immediately following his visit to Bohemia, dates the story entitled *Le Passant de Prague*4 which was accepted by *La Revue Blanche* and to which Guillaume had already contributed his first published short story, *L'Hérésiarque*, written at Neu-Glück, and a critical article on the Pergamon of Berlin. *Le Passant de Prague* begins as a lively reportage in which the writer describes in the first person his arrival in Prague, his first contacts with the population, his search for an hotel and so on. Having settled himself in, and noted the predilection of the Czechs for the French language and people, he decides to explore the town. An elderly passer-by, from whom he asks his way, offers to accompany him. They hold familiar and learned conversation and after a while his guide points out some ancient houses and remarks casually, on noticing the date of one of them, that in 1721 he had just arrived in Munich and found himself in trouble with the Inquisition. This cheerful and—as it soon turns out—libidinous old man, is, in fact, Isaac Laquedem, the Wandering Jew. The visit to ancient Prague evokes a chaplet of memories of other cities and other centuries, and provokes some curious confidences.

'I am used to a life that has no end and no rest', he explains to the narrator. 'For I never sleep. I walk ceaselessly and shall still be walking when the fifteen signs of the Last Judgement appear. But my road is no Calvary and my ways are happy. I

* Your last architect, O Dome, went mad
  Which proves clearly that God gives not a damn
  For those who work for His greater glory.

am the sole and immortal witness to the presence of Christ on
earth, I demonstrate to mankind the reality of the divine and
redeeming tragedy that was played out on Golgotha. What
glory! What joy! But for nineteen centuries, I have also been
a spectator of Humanity, which amuses me immensely. My
sin, Sir, was a sin of genius, and I have long since ceased to
repent it.'

Le Passant de Prague, in fact, already contained all the elements
that were to characterise Apollinaire's future work: the twisting of
myth and legend so as to reveal new meanings of old stories; the
display of learning that was perhaps a form of 'showing off' and
was attenuated as he gained confidence; the obsession with the
glory of God and contempt for the littleness with which men
translate it on earth. Above all, there is the 'simultaneity', which
was the essence of Apollinairean aesthetics and which gradually
developed first into a form of 'Cubism' and then into the system
to which he and the Delaunays gave this name.

It can only be false and dangerous to assign any one source for
an art movement or aesthetic attitude, for these—if they are more
than an artificial grafting on the surface of culture—must correspond to some spontaneous and deeply felt common aspiration.
Yet there can be no doubt that the Cubist movement which
developed in France after 1908 stemmed in a great measure from
Apollinaire's impatience with the limitations of mathematical time
and his almost frantic desire to multiply himself in order to
expand the possibilities of experience. Isaac Laquedem, in
Le Passant de Prague, has conquered the limitations of time;
L'Amphion-Faux-Messie[5] tells of a pseudo-Messiah who has
invented an apparatus, meticulously described by the narrator,
which enables him to transcend the laws of space, and who
thus disappears simultaneously, at the moment of his death,
from eight hundred and forty cities; in *Le Roi-Lune*[6] the narrator
discovers a subterranean kingdom where the mad king Leopold
of Bavaria (a favourite Apollinairean character) has installed
an apparatus of his invention by means of which his subjects can
control or annihilate time and enjoy orgies with men and women
who have been dead for many centuries; and such examples could
be multiplied.

Je suis ivre d'avoir bu tout l'univers. . . .* Ta vie que tu bois comme une eau-de-vie. . . .† J'ai soif villes de France et d'Europe et du monde— Venez toutes couler dans ma gorge profonde. . . .‡ Je suis le gosier de Paris. . . .§ Phrases like these recur so often in the first of the two volumes of poetry chosen by Apollinaire himself for publication, that they cannot be due to chance. Even the title—*Alcools*— is a reference to this obsessive desire to absorb the whole of life, not in logical order or as a neat sequence of events, but all at once, in a single draught. In fact, Isaac Laquadem, Ormesan the false-Messiah, and all the other characters who transcend by magic or pseudo-science the laws of time and space, are simply incarnations of the poet, quaffing life as it comes, with everything it contains, beauty and ugliness, everything, and transforming it into poetry. Later, indeed, lyric inspiration became intellectualised, gave way little by little before the parti-pris of the innovator and the obligations of the visionary; questions of technique became increasingly important. But during this *wanderjahr*, the 'simultaneity' which he was to rediscover one day in Picasso's first experiments in Cubism and later in Delaunay's theories of prismatic colour, was still purely imaginative, a spontaneous response to a twofold and immensely powerful stimulus.

'Cities of France and Europe and the world. . . .' Rome, Nice, Paris, Heidelberg, Munich, Dresden, Prague, Vienna . . . everyone of them was at once grist to the mill of poetry and the water that set the mill itself turning. However, there was a second impulsion, at least as potent. It will be remembered that Guillaume, during his interview with Madame de Milhau in Paris, had been influenced by the presence of the charming English governess who was to accompany them to Germany. Miss Annie Playden was exactly his own age; she had masses of very fair hair, piled high on her head in the fashion of the day, a transparently pale complexion and large, ice-blue eyes. In fact, she was a beauty, and after a short period of friendly sympathy, the tutor was deeply, madly in love with the governess.

---

* I am drunk from drinking the whole universe.
† Your life you drink off like brandy.
‡ I am thirsty, cities of France and Europe and the world.
  Come, all of you, flow down my deep throat.
§ I am the throat of Paris.

The progress of the affair can be traced through the *Rhénanes* poems. There is the early, euphoric period, when the Rhine itself seemed to shimmer with happiness, when the little train that could be heard chugging along the far bank, the songs of the gypsies following their caravans along the river path, even the creaking of the weather-cock in the wind, all seemed to speak of love. The two young people spent nearly all their time together. In the garden, Annie would sit on a stone engraved with the sinister words: 'Gottfried, an apprentice from Bruhl, was murdered here in the year 1860', and listen to Guillaume talking about himself. His stories took as little account of the truth as they had in the past and would in the future. For Annie, he was the son of a Russian general, heir to a vast fortune and scion of the highest aristocracy of his country. The little bourgeoise from Clapham was impressed and consented to kisses in the shadow of the ruined castles that border the Rhine. Sometimes she wondered what he could be doing when he remained shut up for hours in his dark little bedroom at the end of the corridor. He was writing articles for the Paris Press, he told her. It was true up to a point, for he was indeed contributing chronicles on German life to a couple of small reviews at this time. It was typical, though, of his curious reticence and evasiveness about himself, that he never even mentioned that he wrote poetry.*

'At the end of the last century, at Hildesheim, near Hanover,' wrote Guillaume in his room under the overhanging eaves of the house at Honnef, 'there was a young girl named Ilse. Her hair, of a pale blonde colour, had golden shades in it and seemed like moonlight. Her body was slender. Her face was fair, open and smiling, with an adorable dimple in the plump chin and grey eyes which, though they were not specially beautiful, exactly suited her face and moved constantly, like those of a bird. She was incomparably graceful. She was bad at housework, like most Germans and sewed very badly. When her domestic jobs were done, she would sit at the piano

---

* Many years later, when Annie Playden's identity was at last discovered and she was interviewed in America, she was astonished to learn that the 'Kostro' of Neu-Glück had been a poet, and even more so to hear that he had become famous.

and sing, so that she was transformed into a siren; or else she would read aloud, and then she was transformed into a poet.'7

Ilse is, of course, Annie Playden, only partly changed into a German, since Apollinaire is careful to mention that his heroine's mother was English. Her cousin, who becomes mad for love of her, is engaged on a search for the magic treasure of the Three Wise Kings and though the treasure in the story is of gold, we know from many allusions that 'magic', for the poet, was synonymous with the faculty of ubiquity. All through the 'Rose of Hildesheim' there is a feeling of hostile destiny keeping the lovers apart, and in real life, too, Apollinaire probably felt doubts from the beginning, though he refused to admit them, even to himself. Annie was his exact opposite in every respect. Her father, a suburban architect, was so famous for his piety that he was known in Landor Road as 'the Archbishop of Canterbury', and he had brought up his family in accordance with the most rigid principles of Victorian puritanism. Annie had learned from an early age that anything pleasant must be wrong. She distrusted art and, indeed, anything that sprang from the imagination, and vaguely connected Beauty with Sin. Her own beauty, specially, she had been taught to regard as the work of the devil, and she was thoroughly ashamed of it. In fact, she was a terrible little prig and as ill-prepared as any girl in England to cope with the love of an uncontrollably sensual yet deeply sentimental young man with a good proportion of Slav violence and complexity in his make-up.

Yet not even twenty-one years of preaching from Mr Playden had quite destroyed his daughter's natural femininity. At the beginning at least, the tutor had been so charmingly courteous that she almost forgot all she had been taught about the immorality of Frenchmen and the horrors of the Romish Church to which they belonged. When he praised her eyes or her hair, she was half shocked, but half pleased. She would encourage him at one moment, allow herself to be almost carried away, then remember Landor Road and draw back. If she had been trying to madden poor Guillaume with conscious coquetry, she could not have succeeded better. Soon he was completely subjugated, hopelessly in love, and as he grew more and more ardent, Annie grew more and more frightened and retreated further and further into her reserve.

'He was madly in love and I was a little silly who could not allow herself to fall in love because of her puritan education, and also because the Vicomtesse de Milhau had so filled my head with stories about men in general that I could not have any confidence or faith in Guillaume', wrote Miss Playden when, as an elderly woman, she recalled this half-sad, half-sweet episode of her youth, and she added that, 'at certain moments he was violent and impetuous to the point of cruelty, but he could also be very attentive and loving.'

The misunderstanding between the two was complete. Annie believed her suitor's lack of restraint to be a proof of insincerity; Guillaume, who was used to women who knew what they were doing, and had no experience of this type of lower-middle-class Protestant girl, imagined that Annie had been deliberately luring him on and was taking a perverse pleasure in making him unhappy. She was the Lorelei, whose eyes lure men to their death; the 'dark wife' whose love means perpetual mourning. He was already beginning to think of himself as 'ill-loved', a victim of fate, but it apparently never occurred to him that appalling scenes of jealousy, often accompanied by real physical brutality and even threats of murder, were not the best way of endearing himself to a prim and timid young girl. During the first months in Germany, Annie had allowed an affectionate friendship to grow up between them, but before the year had passed, it had turned to fear and resentments, and shame for the few caresses she had allowed him.

Many years later, Apollinaire gave his own account of the affair —or rather, a version arranged in such a way as to spare his self-esteem—in a letter to his friend André Rouveyre. He must have written it in an unusually expansive mood, since he gives himself away to the extent of revealing the true source of the *Chanson du Mal-Aimé*, which:

'. . . commemorates my first love, at the age of twenty, for an English girl I met in Germany. It lasted a year, then we both had to return home, then we ceased to write to each other. Many of the expressions in the poem are unduly severe and insulting for a girl who never understood me, who loved me and then was disconcerted to find she was in love with a poet, that is, a creature of fantasy. . . . Yet she was intelligent and gay and I found it hard to bear her absence. My poems show the state of mind I was in at that time, when I was still an unknown poet among other unknown poets, and she far away and unable to come to Paris. I went twice to London to visit her, but our marriage was impossible and everything was settled by her departure for America. Yet I suffered a good deal, as witness this poem in which I thought myself ill-loved, whereas it was I who loved ill, and also *L'Emigrant de Landor Road,* which commemorates the same love.'

The two visits to London, in 1903 and 1904, were by no means the politely friendly affairs suggested by this letter. Annie seems to have been more terrified than pleased by his reappearance and her family welcomed the unsuitable lover with a marked lack of enthusiasm. As they flatly refused to allow him to stay in Landor Road, Guillaume lodged in various boarding houses in one of which, if we can believe the story entitled *Les Souvenirs bavards,*[8] his sleep was disturbed by the nostalgic dialogues of a ventriloquist, who reproduced the voices of the successive partners of his past, to replay hallucinating scenes of bygone love and jealousy. Perhaps it was true; London boarding houses are certainly frequented by the sort of eccentrics who can be met with nowhere else. Then Guillaume took refuge in the East End, where he lodged with an Albanian named Faik beg Konitza, who sold furs, collected violins and carried on complicated intrigues with his compatriots on the Continent.

From this distant retreat he would make irruptions into Landor Road, where the Playdens received him with cold politeness. Annie would hurry him from the house, take him for long walks, show him Westminster Abbey, the Houses of Parliament, the Tower of London, Madame Tussaud's Waxworks, everything a tourist should admire. This conventional round of sightseeing moved him less than the melancholy sameness of Annie's red-brick suburb, where banality was so intense that it touched the heights of tragedy; or the sinister slums of the East End, where drunken women reeled from the pubs; or the wailing sirens of

the slow steamers on the river; or the play of sombre colours—
black, grey, white, and sudden gleams of red—in the streets . . .

> Au tournant d'une rue brûlant
> De tous les feux de ses façades
> Plaies du brouillard sanguinolent
> Où se lamentaient les façades . . .*

A poet's London, and a London visible only to a poet.

Annie herself was conscious of the charm of these long walks
and perhaps she was sometimes tempted to yield to his pleadings.
'The question of language separated us', she has since confided.
'If I could have spoken and understood French as well as English,
things might have been different, for we sometimes got on very
well.' But even if they had understood each other better, there
would still have been her father to deal with. When Annie
broached the subject of marriage, he categorically forbade her to
think of it and refused even to discuss the matter.

Annie agreed with her father on the whole, and in any case,
she would not have dared to defy him. At last she made up her
mind to put a definite end to the affair and conceived a way of
ridding herself of her irrepressible suitor. When Guillaume
arrived for a second visit to London and made a final effort to
persuade her to marry him, she took him for a walk and confided
that she was engaged and on the point of joining her fiancé in
America. She had under-estimated his tenacity. He demanded
so many proofs and insisted so indiscreetly that the poor girl
finally found herself with a passage booked on a transatlantic
liner. Caught in the toils of her own innocent lies, she ended
by leaving indeed for the States, not as a fiancée, but as a governess. She settled down there, bought a ranch with her savings
and is now, at the time of writing, an energetic old lady in
California.

As for Guillaume, he returned to Paris, and it was after this
second, decisive, visit that he began to compose the *Chanson du
Mal-Aimé* as a long drawn-out act of love and revenge in which

---

* At the turn of a street that burned—With all the flames of its
façades—Wounds bleeding in the fog—Where the façades
lamented . . .

romantic tenderness alternates with brutal abuse, evocations of exquisite lyricism explode into swaggering vulgarity and esoteric images give way suddenly before some verse of heart-rending simplicity. It remained shut away among his papers and notes for six years before it was published, a private monument to grief.

IV

Aesop's Feast

Not one of the joyous band at the *Closerie* or the *Soleil d'Or*, with whom Apollinaire was on such apparently intimate terms, suspected the sadness that underlay his exuberant gaiety. He possessed to an extreme degree the art of disguising reticence beneath a seeming extroversion. Perhaps, indeed, it was a characteristic that many of these apparently intimate friends held in common. An intense loneliness lay behind Moréas' apparent genius for friendship, and Jarry lived in an agony of spirit which his constant companions barely suspected. Perhaps the friendships with which these poets nourished their lives at the beginning of the century were more superficial than their memoirs and reminiscences lead us to imagine. One may guess that the people who really knew Apollinaire were not those who apparently played the leading parts in his life, but others, who remained in the background, like the charming René Dalize, the friend of his childhood at the Collège Saint-Charles, or Louise Faure-Favier, whose discreet and faithful friendship comforted his later years.

In this particular case, at any rate, he managed to protect himself from curiosity by a double-cross so subtle that many of his friends were convinced he had never set foot in Germany and regarded his stories of the Rhineland as fantastic imaginings designed to mislead and amuse them.

The *Closerie des Lilas* was only one of the cafés and bistros adopted by this tireless band that apparently never felt the need of a good night's sleep. There was *Au Père Jean*, where the patron served a special brand of *beaujolais*, brought straight from his own vineyard; the *Caveau du Rocher*; a succession of little places on the Left Bank that would be adopted as temporary headquarters then deserted when someone discovered a still more picturesque

41

establishment. One of their favourites at the time was the *Soleil d'Or* in the Place Saint-Michel, where the review *La Plume* organised 'literary evenings'.

These weekly events were already a tradition. They had their origin in the more formal banquets which the review had been organising for over twenty years and at which such celebrities as Zola, Mallarmé, François Coppée and Verlaine had presided. The famous names had become rare, but a good many promising young writers, and some who had fulfilled their promise, used to meet for dinner at the *Café de Flore* in Saint-Germain-des-Près (which was very quiet and sedate at that time, not at all like the fashionable, sham-Existentialist establishment it has since become). After the meal, they would repair to the cellar of the *Soleil d'Or* for the real business of the evening. There they would be joined by Apollinaire, Salmon and other novices who could not afford to pay three francs for the menu at the Flore and had dined at a wine-merchant's shop in the rue de Seine, where credit was easy. Jarry would be there, presiding when it came to his turn, less as Jarry than as the terrible Roi Ubu; there would be Moréas, drunk and ceremonious, with his impeccable top-hat; Mecislas Golberg, hideous with disease and poverty, and radiant with inspiration and intelligence; the minute Félicien Fagus, a model Civil Servant by day, but by night so intransigent a lover of poetry that he once drew a knife on a huge colleague whose banal verse had exasperated him beyond endurance. There were song-writers, who accompanied their compositions on an upright piano, and the same piano habitually served as a support for the right elbows of poets in full recital. The pose was in the fashion of the day and it was not till several years later that some of them began to suspect it had been a little ridiculous. There were women too. Some of them, like the ancient Maria Kryzinska, who had been connected with the early Symbolists, were poets themselves. Others— the majority—played the role of muse and passed light-heartedly from one aspiring writer to the other.

Perhaps the aestheticism was a little ostentatious. Certainly it annoyed quite a number of people.

'These young men', wrote a literary journalist at about this time, 'seem to take a conceited joy in exiling themselves from the world. They cultivate a peculiar jargon, affect a cynical and mysterious way of life and have their own mythical and sacred gods. They dedicate themselves to an exclusive passion for the most obscure and disquieting figures in modern literature.'

To which *La Plume* replied that, even if it had not 'licked the boots of Messrs Zola, Charpentier and Rostand', at least it had brought Villiers de l'Isle-Adam, Verlaine, Mallarmé and Dierx into the limelight!

Apollinaire and his friends, the youngest and least respectful of the recruits to the 'evenings', considered most of the impassioned reciters of their own verses as mediocre and laughed at the solemn way in which the older habitués laid down the law. This did not prevent them from attending assiduously and reciting themselves whenever they could get a hearing. Like most poets, Apollinaire enjoyed the sound of his own voice and could easily be persuaded to speak one or other of the 'Rhineland' poems, in the strange, husky, slightly chanting voice which André Salmon described as 'muffled yet powerful, almost unearthly and which resembled that of no one else'.

Just at the time when he began to frequent the café, *Le Soleil d'Or* changed its name and became *Le Départ*. Apollinaire, who was superstitious, took the event as an augury. 'Departure' ... a setting out on the road to fame. It was true that *La Plume* could be very useful to young writers anxious to make a name for themselves in literature. The editor accepted a rather bad poem entitled *Avenir*, that recalls the anarchism of the lycée in Nice rather than the lyricism of *Rhénanes,* then a long poem called *Le Larron*, in which recondite words and allusions distract—perhaps intentionally—the attention from an essential bitterness that places it as a post-Annie work.

Perhaps, however, the real importance of the role of *La Plume* in Apollinaire's life was that he made the acquaintance of Jarry at one of its meetings. He has recounted the episode in his own words:

'Alfred Jarry, on the evening in question, appeared to me as the personification of some river, a young, beardless river, dressed in the damp clothes of a drowned man. Everything about him seemed a little spongy—the small, drooping moustache, the jacket with swinging tails, the soft shirt and cyclist's socks; the demi-god was still damp, as if he had only recently risen up from the soaking river-bed.

'We drank stout together and felt ourselves to be friends. He recited poems with metallic rhymes in *orde* and *arde*. Then, after listening to a new song by Cazals, we left in the middle of a frenetic cakewalk. . . .

'I spent the whole night pacing up and down the Boulevard Saint-Germain with Alfred Jarry and talking about heraldic devices, heresies and versification. He told me about the bargemen among whom he lived for a great part of the year, about the marionettes with which he had produced *Ubu* for the first time. Alfred Jarry's voice was incisive, low-toned, rapid and sometimes emphatic. He would suddenly cease speaking to smile, and then suddenly become serious again. His forehead moved all the time, but from side to side, instead of up and down, as one generally sees. At about four in the morning, a man stopped us to ask the way to Plaisance. Jarry immediately pulled out a revolver, ordered the passer-by to step back six paces, then gave him the information. We separated after that and he returned to his *grand chamblerie* in the rue Cassette, where he invited me to visit him.'

Jarry certainly encouraged Apollinaire's natural taste for the bizarre, but his influence went far deeper. He had once said that life was like a walled city. If you lived inside the walls and looked over them at the country beyond, you were perceiving only an incomplete and circumscribed image of reality. But if you destroyed the walls and razed them to the ground, so that the city became part of the surrounding landscape, you got quite a different view and a much truer one. Jarry was too destructive, too much identified with Byzantinism and death to retain his influence over Apollinaire, with his passion for life and 'sane reality',[1] but the conception of the breaking up of the old, formal perspectives in order to perceive life in its full reality became part of the poetry of Apollinaire, André Salmon and Max Jacob, and passed through Apollinaire into Cubism. Besides all this, in Jarry Apollinaire came for the first time into contact with a man who lived utterly and wholly for literature and in literature. That evening in the Boulevard Saint-Germain was one of the land-marks in his career.

The rare contributions to *La Plume*, like those to *Tabarin* and *La Grande France* and occasional 'chronicles' for *L'Européenne*, were gradually bringing his name before the public. However, it was still *La Revue Blanche* that provided the better part of his meagre literary earnings and it was there that he could be sure of a wel-come, nearly every month, for whatever he could offer. After *Le Passant de Prague* he had sent other stories in the same capricious, irreverent and erudite style. The characters were even stranger than the cosmopolitan background against which they evolved: a silk-merchant of Lyons, on whom the Divine Wrath wreaks vengeance in grotesque—and indeed, obscene—form; the in-habitants of a Yugoslavian village, who revolt against barbaric tradition, but soon resign themselves and submit to a custom that finally appears as inevitable as Destiny itself; the 'Latin Jew', who aspires to sanctity, while continuing a career of gratuitous crime; the charming 'Rose of Hildesheim', that commemorates the brief period of happiness before love for Annie Playden turned to rage and bitterness.

The review played an important part in Guillaume's life, and he was not the only one of the band to depend on it. It brought them a little money, and above all, it was a tribune where they could express themselves freely and with the self-conscious audacity of youth. Jarry, for instance, published monthly chron-icles in which he commented on current events with such cynicism and icy humour that he might have found it hard to publish them elsewhere.* Mark Twain's *Roughing It* was published in translation as a serial; all the interesting landmarks in the artistic world were infallibly recognised and discussed: Colette's début at the Music Hall; Mardrus' translation of the *Thousand and One Nights*; exhi-bitions of Impressionist paintings *chez* Vollard and at the *Salon*

---

* A typical Jarry chronicle concerned the massacre, in 1902, of the Euro-pean Mission to New Guinea by the cannibal Papoos. He commented in *Le Mercure de France,* at a moment when the rest of the Press was strangling itself with indignation and crying out for vengeance: 'It would be a grave mistake to imagine that this massacre was due only to base greed or to preoccupations of a purely culinary nature. In my opinion, the event was a manifestation of one of the noblest tendencies of the human spirit—its propensity to assimilate that which it finds good.'

des Indépendants, or of Raoul Dufy, whose earliest paintings the critic describes as 'very youthful, and that is an excellent thing; nothing makes one fear for the future so much as precocious perfection. . . .' In fact the *Revue Blanche* was a sort of mirror of the times and these young writers, who had a keen sense of publicity, naturally liked to find themselves reflected in it.

But one evening Félicien Fagus appeared like a minute messenger of doom on the steps of the cellar of the *Soleil d'Or,* where Apollinaire and his companions were spending the evening, and announced in a sepulchral voice: 'The *Revue Blanche* is about to die.' No one believed him at first, for he was a notorious practical joker, but it was all too true. Times were difficult, in that year of 1903, for avant-garde publications, and the review had come to an end of its resources. Its last number appeared in April, after which its regular contributors found themselves with their work left on their hands. Jarry was almost the only exception: he had a second home in *Le Mercure de France,* where Alfred Vallette and Rachilde watched over him with understandable anxiety, allowed him to write regularly, but forced him to tone his articles down. Apollinaire's final article was entitled: 'Forgeries', and dealt with the faked tiara of Saitapharnès. It contains a phrase that sheds light on much that seems obscure and contradictory in his later career: 'Contempt is a liberating sentiment. It exalts a noble spirit and incites it to great enterprises.' It might have been just one of those paradoxes with which he and most of his friends liked to *épater la bourgeoisie,* but this time it corresponded to an intuitive conviction. No doubt he had it in mind when, ten years later, he launched the 'Anti-Tradition Futurist' manifesto with Marinetti, and hurled at Shakespeare, Hugo, Balzac and all the great forerunners, the traditional, Ubuesque insult: *Merdre!*

Meanwhile, the chief mourners for the *Revue Blanche* had to discover another review that would open its doors to them. One evening, in the *Père Jean,* Apollinaire, Salmon and their friend Jean Mollet decided that the only way out of the difficulty was to found a review of their own. Apollinaire's enthusiasms were so infectious that he could usually persuade people to do what he wanted and he soon discovered two backers to finance the project. One was an Albanian named Thrank Spirobeg, who was connected with a Franco-Albanian publication but whose chief occupation was plotting. No one quite knew why or for what he plotted; he was a natural conspirator in the 'art for art's sake' style. The second was Jean Sève, a young man of comfortable means and literary ambitions. As a reward for his financial help, he was once allowed to sign a short article written by Apollinaire on the subject of modern painting.

A title was found: *Le Festin d'Esope*. The office was André Salmon's one-room lodging in the rue Saint-Jacques. The room was small and the landlord, an upholsterer by trade, was apt to consider it as a store for unwanted pieces of furniture. As it generally contained at least ten people—directors, contributors and just friends—there was hardly room to move and the pallid light of the single oil lamp struggled feebly against a thick haze of tobacco smoke. There, almost every evening, were the 'Baron' Mollet, whose air of authority worked wonders with printers and other creditors; an enormous, blond Swede named Arne Hammer, editor of *L'Européenne* and leader of the Scandinavian colony that was boisterously invading the intellectual life of Paris at that time; there was poor Mecislas Golberg, as obviously doomed as Jarry, whom Stuart Merrill was to describe as

> 'one of the rare Stoics of our times . . . a Stoic because he felt that each of us is alone in the world, each responsible only to his own conscience and that the life each of us achieves is his own personal poem. Situated, as we—as conscious spirits —all are, at the centre of the eternal whirlpool of all things, Golberg found certainty and peace only in himself. . . . '

Then, of course, there was Jarry, the Sacred Monster whom they all venerated for his uncompromising devotion to his own ideal, but who could often prove embarrassing as a friend.

With Jarry anything might happen. Apollinaire, who had been inseparable from him ever since that first, memorable evening at the *Soleil d'Or*, was having a difficult time with him. One evening, notably, he had incautiously tried to rouse his friend from a state of prostration by taking him to the Medrano circus, which was just becoming fashionable among young intellectuals. Jarry, sunk in a sort of stupor, had watched clowns and performing seals without apparent interest. The appearance of a lion suddenly jerked him back to reality. He rose with a wild yell, snatched his revolver from his pocket and was prevented just in time from shooting 'in self-defence'. No one could tell what was in his mind. Did he really imagine himself in danger? Or face to face with a magnificent prey? Or was he simply trying to create a scandal? In any case Apollinaire, who disliked scenes, found the whole affair extremely painful. Yet neither he nor any of his friends ever thought of deserting Jarry. His company enriched them as could no other—except, perhaps, that of Moréas, but he was of another generation.

Sometimes a very young man with a pink, innocent face, came to the rue Saint-Jacques. He had been a worshipper of Verhaeren and was now excitedly discovering the existence of a new and less solemn kind of poetry. This was André Billy, who was later to become one of Apollinaire's closest friends and end up as a member of the austere *Académie française*. He has given us a vivid portrait of his friend as he first knew him during the heroic days of the *Festin*:

> 'In that autumn of 1903,' he tells us, 'Apollinaire wore a moustache and already had a somewhat majestic air. Already he radiated a jovial authority that tended to clownishness. Already in his eyes and lips there was an almost feminine seductiveness that people found impossible to resist. Perhaps he laid down the law a little, but in a way that was his alone, with the good-humour of a talkative restaurant-keeper who will brook no contradiction once he is among his own pots and pans. . . .'

There were naturally a number of different tendencies among this heterogeneous company. Arguments continued far into the night until the air became unbreathable and someone would stumble through the smoke to open the window. Apollinaire, who often surprised his friends by incongruously bourgeois ideas, was anxious to have a 'serious' review. It was he, backed by Mollet, who insisted on a financial column, optimistically signed 'Fortunio'; and a well-known scholar, whose opinions carried weight, was persuaded to write an article on the Naundorff affair, which was much in the public eye at that time. The first number appeared in November 1903, and informed its readers that:

> 'The *Festin d'Esope* will publish works of all kinds, literary

contributions with imagination and ideas. As it does not represent any particular school, its one concern will be to deserve by
the justice of its criticisms and the quality of the work it
publishes, its sub-title of "A Review of Belles-Lettres".'

Nine numbers appeared before the backers, in the capricious
way backers have, withdrew their financial support. To read
them now rouses a nostalgic longing for that charming period
when expiring Symbolism was groping for a new road and experimenting with an anarchy that tried its best to be terrible but
seldom succeeded in being more than gracefully mischievous.
The first number contained a story: *Qu'v'lou*, in which Apollinaire
recalled his stay in the Ardennes, the Walloon dialect that had
enchanted his ears, and the adventures of a drunken and tubercular
poet who had enlivened the torpid atmosphere of Stavelot. The
poems by Moulinas and Nicolas Deniker are distinctly reminiscent of Régnier and Moréas. The old influences were dying hard
and these young revolutionaries referred to Beauty—with a
capital B—almost as often as the Parnassians they despised. But
there was also one of those treasures one sometimes discovers
with such excited joy when leafing through forgotten 'little
reviews': a poem by André Salmon that belongs to a new world
of fantasy and absurdity:

> Elle avait pour aller danser au clair de lune
> Mis son chapeau de lys et de rhododendrons
> Elle avait ses souliers et ses bas de soie prune
> Et des fleurs de lotus brodaient ses pantalons . . .*

Here is the nonchalance, the languid elegance that were to
combine with a passion for life almost as avid as that of Apollinaire
himself, to bring Salmon into the front rank of contemporary

---

* To go dancing by moonlight she had put on
  Her hat made of lilies and rhododendrons
  She had her slippers and stockings of plum-coloured silk
  And her pantaloons embroidered with lotus flowers . . .

poets.* The second number was more audacious, since it included
a contribution by Jarry; a 'Sketch for a Method for Winning the
Applause of the Bourgeoisie', signed by the ineffable Spirobeg;
and a vicious attack by Han Ryner on the sacrosanct Anatole
France. These were followed in succeeding numbers by a translation of Kipling's 'Road to Mandalay' (Kipling and Swinburne
being, at this time, the two English poets in vogue with the
literary avant-garde) and several of Apollinaire's own 'Rhineland'
poems. The review lasted just long enough to publish *L'Enchanteur Pourrissant* in four instalments. Apollinaire, who had always
had a weakness for this first sustained piece of writing, was
delighted to see it in print at last and felt that the *Festin d'Esope* had
fully justified its existence.

*   *   *

Apollinaire once said, in the course of a lecture on the new
poetry: 'None of the young poets I admire, none, I say, holds
himself aloof from the French poetic tradition. . . .' In spite of
their audacities all these young men who liked to pass for revolutionaries were deeply imbued with the Symbolist tradition and
felt they had a mission to continue and renovate it. Their masters
were Vielé-Griffin, Gustave Kahn, René Ghil, Moréas, Henri de
Régnier, Francis Jammes, Maeterlinck, Verhaeren. If they experimented with poetic forms, rejected the stifling alexandrine to
which the Parnassians clung so obstinately, they could refer back
to their elders: to Jules Laforgue, who had proclaimed 'the undeniable charm of a false verse'; to Kahn, Verhaeren, Vielé-Griffin,
Stuart Merrill, who had all at one time or another made use of
blank verse. It is true that these poets, who appeared to the group
of *Le Festin* as respectable ancestors, were still being treated as
enfants terribles by the survivors of Parnasse, who were by no

---

* Apollinaire, who was often—though not always—a generous and
appreciative friend, wrote of him a few years later: 'The surprising aspect of
André Salmon's work, that which reveals all the novelty of this original
mind, is composed of poems in which a lyricism exempt from all vulgarity
seizes on the strangest aspects and characters of our times. Here one encounters gypsies, popes, moujiks, German students, negroes of Africa and
America, sometimes by day, but more often by night, mingling the agitation
of their lives with the cadence of passing trains and the long sighs of sirens
from steamers on the point of departure.'

means inclined to lay down their arms. Catulle Mendès, their spokesman, had just published his very official 'Report on the Poetic Movement from 1867 to 1900' and attributed the propensity to blank verse in the latter three of these poets, to the fact that they were 'foreigners'* and thus incapable of appreciating the French mute *e*. For him, as for all Parnassians, Victor Hugo was a god, unapproachable and absolute; Léon Dierx, Leconte de Lisle and Alfred de Vigny, 'the great white poets of our age'.

Léon Dierx had provided an occasion for a stern reproof to too-audacious innovators:

'He never sinned against dream and ideal . . . he has nothing in common with recent artists . . . who seek a new mode of poetic expression in obscure and fugitive words, in the sonority of imprecise rhythms where the underlying idea is dispersed to the point where the majority of readers can no longer seize it.'

As for Théodore de Banville, Catulle Mendès assured his readers that he had 'never written a verse that did not tremble with its aspiration towards heaven. . . .'

'Thanks to you,' the old Master apostrophised him, 'the Immortals have regained the august heights and are reinstalled on their ivory thrones. . . . But you have done more than reinstate the gods in their glory, you have sought out men and women, people resembling those we know, in the shadows and vilenesses of prose, and forced them also to become gods. . . .'

The little group of Apollinaire's friends could afford to smile. Nothing preoccupied them less than the reinstatement of gods and goddesses, nor had they any desire to idealise their contemporaries as Immortals. For them, Parnasse was a thing of the past, a living corpse. The poets who still followed in its steps were sterile, uncreative, merely trying to resuscitate a system long since dead. They could no longer even claim to follow a tradition, since the chain had snapped. On the other hand, the 'Report' contained some allusions to Symbolism that touched a sensitive point. It would have been too much to expect the obstinate, fanatical old Parnassian to understand or appreciate the later

* Vielé-Griffin and Stuart Merrill were born in the United States; Verhaeren was a Belgian.

manifestations of Symbolism and it was normal that he should speak of 'a poetry inaccessible to natural intelligence'. But when (after, one must admit, a loyal attempt to understand a poet so opposed to himself and his ideal) he summed up Mallarmé as 'the subtle prophet of a Messiah who would never come', it was not so easy to dismiss him as an old fogey. The future of Symbolism was a real and indeed a constant preoccupation for young men who instinctively turned to contemporary life as the direct source of their inspiration. They were too much in love with that life, and too curious of the new era that was just opening before them, to want to transmute or disguise it as the Symbolists had done.

Mallarmé had written:

> 'Abolished is the pretention—an aesthetic error even though it has produced masterpieces—to include in the subtle paper of a volume anything else, for instance, than the horror of the forest, or the mute thunder dispersed among the leaves; not the dense and intrinsic wood of the trees themselves. A few upsurgings of intimate pride, veridically trumpeted out, will evoke the architecture of a palace, the only one that is really habitable, apart from any of those stones on which the pages could not easily close',

but these young disciples were as little concerned with leaves and stones as they were with Banville's 'Immortals'. They found their subjects in Mankind, and generally, indeed, in its less conventional representatives. The Symbolists, like the Parnassians, had worshipped Beauty and held it to be the essential matter of poetry. Sometimes, they discovered and chanted, as Baudelaire had taught them to do, the fascination of things horrible or hideous. Yet even then, beauty was the essential matter of the poem, an inescapable presence. When Baudelaire had written *Une Charogne*, it was not really of the putrefying corpse that he was writing, not of horror and ugliness for themselves, but of the will-o'-the-wisp, the phosphorescent flames of beauty that dance on the surface of corruption. Corbière's *Crapaud*, or his *Paysage Mauvais*, where:

> Bone-white, bane-white, throttles tight
> The choking wave's death-night . . .
> Pale miserable marsh, where great
> Worms tickle the moon's appetite . . .[2]

Pablo Picasso: *Les Demoiselles d'Avignon*

Annie Playden in 1901

Madame de Kostrowitsky

Apollinaire
and Madeleine Pagès
in Oran

Paul Fort
in the days of
the *Closerie des Lilas*

Laforgue's graveyards, the 'Songs of Maldoror', were all written in the same romantic mood, with the same delectation in horror that finally reveals itself as Beauty.

For Apollinaire, Salmon and their friends, the question of Beauty presented itself in quite a different way. Is a telephone, a motor-car, a camera, beautiful? The Symbolists, who had seen the birth of these peculiar objects, had sidestepped the question by ignoring them. But by 1904, they had become part of daily life and, so far as the younger generation were concerned, a welcome part. They were a pointer to the future, the forerunners of a new world in which science would be king. To the group of *Le Festin*, the prospect seemed attractive and exciting. The motor-car, telephone, and so on had nothing to do with beauty or ugliness. They simply existed, and because they existed, they were part of life, and thus part of poetry.

It was this consentient, affirmative attitude to the future, this lucid acceptance of all the manifestations by which it was heralded, that set men like Apollinaire and Salmon apart from their immediate predecessors. When Salmon wrote:

> Et l'on serait triste à mourir
> Si les libellules ne dansaient
> A la gloire des mondes cassés
> Le ballet des temps à venir . . .*

he was expressing an essentially new attitude. Apollinaire himself was perhaps even more fascinated by the future, as he saw it taking shape in the present. 'We should love our own times', he explained once to a friend. 'It is quite wrong to decry them by comparing them with the past. We are living in a marvellous age, full of burning imagination and fascinating progress. The twentieth century is far more exciting than the nineteenth.'

From the perspectives of fifty-five years later, it is clear that the rupture with Symbolism was already consummated. At the time, however, it was not so evident, and these young men

---

* And we should be deathly sad
  If the dragon-flies were not dancing
  The ballet of future days
  To the glory of broken worlds. . . .

continued for several years to consider themselves as Symbolists, but uneasily, as if aware of an ambiguity.*

On April 15, 1905, *La Plume* held a banquet to celebrate its seventeenth anniversary. The review had always been sensitive to changing tendencies and had the honourable reputation of providing a neutral ground on which representatives of the different literary movements could meet in more or less friendly rivalry. On this occasion, the discussion that followed the dinner evidently produced a definitive clash of ideas between the old and the new. Apollinaire, who was one of the less distinguished guests, was certainly incapable of respectful silence when an argument of this sort was in course and one may suppose he contributed his point of view. At any rate, the next number of the review contained an editorial which he might have signed himself and in which it seems permissible to detect his influence. The text is worth quoting as an indication of a new spirit in art and literature—the spirit of the twentieth century:

'There are moments in every existence, whether it be that of an individual or of a community, when life seems to stand still, feverish, astonished, pregnant with the unknown. We are waiting impatiently for that unknown which will lead us back to a road that has been lost in fog. This is the moment when Habit is in its death-agony and the torrent of Renewal—occult or already revealed—flows implacably over regions that have hitherto appeared untouchable. Venerated names are forgotten, men and works that used to be constantly evoked suddenly appear insufficient, even insignificant. One rebels against one's masters, slays one's gods. . . . It is then that we wait impatiently for the Word that is still unrevealed. For the individual, such moments represent a turning point in the life of the mind; they assemble and discipline certain forces, and the individual renews himself and enters into a new phase of his existence. As for the collective life, these moments of waiting are a preparation for great renewals of ideas and forms.

'We have come to such a moment of waiting. We feel it and we know it. We are anxious, unsatisfied, blasé about everything

* Paul Fort, who was so intimately connected with Apollinaire in his youth, followed a very different path and never ceased to consider himself as a Symbolist.

we are shown, for everything bears the stamp of a past we no longer love and of which we wish to retain only certain aspects . . . those that will help us to live, and to prepare the future. We are detaching ourselves more and more from those ephemeral things of the past that have now become official or scholastic. We hope for a profound renewal, that will be more than merely formal, of societies, myths, the arts, philosophy, science. And as our great desire is of an active nature, we are un-consciously preparing the expected Coming by our dreams and the very strength of our hope; and then the fine sonority of the awaited Word will break at last through all the fog and fill every breast with enthusiasm.

'Several of us recognised this truth on the evening of our Banquet. There were present certain significant elements of the preceding generation and a whole phalanx of our own. . . '

The manifesto was signed by "the editors", who were Ricciotto Canudo and André Tudesq, but it represents so exactly Apollinaire's own attitude at this point that one cannot but wonder whether he had a hand in it.

Perhaps this is the moment—when *La Plume* has at last pointed a precise and surgical finger at the mortal malady of Symbolism—to return to *La Chanson du Mal-Aimé*, which Apollinaire probably finished towards the end of this year of 1905.

It should be remembered that, at this date, he had not yet been metamorphosed into the theorist of aesthetics we shall meet in the *Bateau Lavoir* and then in the cafés of Montparnasse. It is safe to suppose that anything he wrote up to, roughly, 1907 was a spontaneous expression of his feelings—and though his feelings were often modified by his reading and his friends of the moment, they were none the less real and unintellectualised. The *Chanson du Mal-Aimé* is simply himself, uninfluenced by any conscious search for novelty. If one recognises in it a note that is unmistakably new, that is simply and directly due to the fact that Apollinaire was writing as a man of the twentieth century and no longer, in spite of what he believed himself, as that typically fin-du-siècle phenomenon, a Symbolist. He is directly present in this major work. The very evasiveness that breaks short a too-personal phrase, a too-revealing cry, corresponds exactly to a personality by turn confiding and elusive. When he apostrophises himself directly, as he did in so many poems,* he is not being any more 'real' than when, in the *Chanson*, he breaks off a verse as candid and pathetically simple, as pregnant with pain and nostalgia as:

> Mais en vérité je l'attends
> Avec mon cœur avec mon âme
> Et sur le pont des Reviens-t'en
> Si jamais revient cette femme
> Je lui dirai Je suis content.†

to launch into a series of allusions to satyrs and pyraustes, to Faust and the Burghers of Calais.

This 'presence' of the poet in the poem goes much further and deeper than the 'presence' of the Romantics or Symbolists in their work. It is directly attached, not to any single mood, not to some irrepressible or consciously chosen moment of joy, sorrow or love that seeks an outlet in poetry, but to a whole psychological process. Subjectivity in poetry had meant till then the Romantic *moi*, more or less invented by Chateaubriand. It was the crystallisation of a certain mood, that was most often one of melancholy or despair. It was Alfred de Musset's:

> J'ai perdu ma force et ma vie
> Et mes amis et ma gaîté
> J'ai perdu jusqu'à la fierté
> Qui faisait croire à mon génie.‡

But Apollinairean subjectivity, which the *Chanson* perhaps reveals in its most complete and perfect form, is a direct transcription of the psychological discontinuity which we all recognise in our-

---

* Un jour je m'attendais moi-même—Je me disais Guillaume il est temps que tu viennes.... Guillaume qu'est-tu devenu?... 'Je suis Guillaume Apollinaire—Dit d'un nom slave pour vrai nom, etc., etc.

† But truly I await her
With my heart with my soul
And if ever this woman returns
On the bridge of Come-back-to-me
I shall tell her: I am glad.

‡ I have lost my strength and my life
And my friends and my gaiety
I have even lost the pride
That seemed to prove my genius.

selves but which had not, for many centuries, found its way into poetry.² This does not mean that it was not in the French poetic tradition. Four and a half centuries earlier, Villon had followed the oscillations of his mood as closely as Apollinaire was ever to do. One has only to re-read the *Testament* to find the same alternation between gaiety and bitterness, the same apparently gratuitous insertion of lyrics, the same feeling of passing time and shifting sentiments, that are among the marks of Apollinaire's 'modernity'.

The subjectivity of Apollinaire, like that of Villon, is continuous, mobile and many-faceted, like human nature itself. Romantic subjectivity separated a moment from the stream of time out of which it was formed and presented it as complete in itself. Apollinaire follows the stream wherever it goes. As the months pass, his attitude towards Annie Playden is continually changing. Sometimes he remembers with infinite tenderness the happiness she once brought him. Sometimes the humiliation of his defeat overwhelms him and he reviles her with violent and almost obscene abuse. At one moment, he recognises her in the slinking figure of a petty criminal in a London stream, then in the 'inhuman gaze' of a drunken slut in an East-End pub. Sometimes she is the sinister 'dark wife', then she becomes 'my dove', 'my white harbour', 'my distant island', 'my Desirades'. Sometimes the lover seems to forget her in his absorption with his own sorrow—a sorrow that becomes universal, mingling with the loves of ancient kings, or part of the whole of humanity led in a frantic round by 'the demons of chance'. There are moments of truculent humour, as if he were bent on proving to Annie that she is of no importance . . . and then he is back, alone, in Paris, where the evenings are 'drunk on gin, flaming with electricity', and where, in an ultimate surrender:

> Les cafés gonflés de fumée
> Crient tout l'amour de leurs tziganes
> De tous leurs syphons enrhumés
> De leurs garçons vêtus d'un pagne
> Vers toi toi que j'ai tant aimée*

* The cafés swollen with smoke
 Cry all the love of their tziganes
 Of all their wheezy syphons
 Of all their aproned waiters
 Towards you you whom I have loved so much.

Surely, anyone who has had a similar experience, will recognise in this very incoherence and disorder, the deep truth about unhappy love.

V

The Meeting with the Magician

At about the same time that Guillaume de Kostrowitsky had arrived in Paris with his mother, another youth, a few months younger than himself, had disembarked from Spain. Pablo Ruiz, who was soon to be known as Picasso, was a native of Malaga and had been studying at the School of Art in Barcelona, where his father was a teacher. By the time he was fifteen, he was considered a prodigy. He drew as no one else could draw, with the sureness and subtlety of the ancient masters and the audacity of his idol, El Greco. Naturally, he had dreamed of Paris—the centre of the world for artists. Several times he had almost succeeded in breaking away from the grim yet insipid traditionalism of nineteenth-century Spain. At sixteen he had held his first small exhibition in a gallery in the Place Clichy. It had been a success that had passed all his hopes. And after that, there had been nothing. There were too many clever artists in Paris, and too many successful exhibitions. Paris had a short memory and often forgot one day what it had acclaimed the day before.

The young Spaniard made several more visits to France, and each time he had the same false success that left him as unknown and penniless as before. And each time, the atmosphere of Barcelona seemed more unbearably provincial. So in 1899 he burnt his boats (or thought he did, for he was to be driven back several times to Spain) and came to settle in France.

Guillaume, too, had sustained wounds in his first encounter with the capital, but those of Picasso were infinitely more terrible. He knew practically no French and, like so many of his compatriots, had little gift for languages. He had started out with a small sum of money, but a precocious passion for red wine and pretty women soon left him penniless. The Paris he discovered in these conditions was a sordid underworld and his friends were foreigners, living like himself on the edge of starvation in wretched bedrooms in slum hotels. Spanish anarchists were numerous among them and many of them lived on a rather vague dividing line between the world of art and that of crime. The chief link between these two worlds was Manolo—the same impecunious painter and writer of verses in pidgin French whom Apollinaire had met at the *Closerie des Lilas,* in company with Moréas. He was to render some important services later, though his proclivity for petty thieving sometimes made him an embarrassing companion.

Various owners of small galleries were glad to show Picasso's paintings and among them was Ambroise Vollard, who prided himself on being a discoverer of new talent. One day an unsuccessful painter dropped into his shop in the rue Lafitte, where a number of canvases from Barcelona were hung in a rather bad light. This young man was Max Jacob, and like many neurotics he was abnormally sensitive and responsive. At any rate, he realised in an instant that he was in the presence of genius. In a state of feverish excitement, he scribbled a note to ask for an interview. Picasso replied and soon after the two met—and never separated again.

Max Jacob was several years older than Picasso—a curious mixture of Jew and Breton, so that it was always as if two conflicting forms of mysticism were at war within him. His childhood had been difficult. His father, a tailor by profession, had shown little understanding for his son's inexplicable passion for words and colours; his schoolfellows had persecuted him on account of his race. He had tried, during his teens, to commit suicide, but even at that early age poor Max's most dramatic gestures were fated to take a grotesque turn. The tie with which he had attempted to hang himself from the window bar had broken, landing him safe and sound on the floor below, where his father received him with the words: 'Aren't you ashamed to play like a child at your age?' while his mother added briskly: 'You've still got plenty of time before you need think about dying!'

Max had been a brilliant scholar and seemed destined for a successful career. But nothing came of all the studies and all the honours. He was one of those exceptions among the human race who can breathe only in a climate of instability and mystification, who are at ease only in a world of dream created by themselves. He came to Paris, painted, suffered from a single, unhappy love affair (which disgusted him with women for the rest of his life) and turned to poetry. When his family cut off his small allowance, he moved into a room in an hotel in the Boulevard Barbès and decided to live on bread (borrowed from compassionate bakers) and to devote himself to writing. Thus, by drinking water and going to bed at dusk to avoid the cost of light, he could live with no expenses apart from rent.

It was at this point that he met Picasso and recognised a part of himself in paintings such as he had never seen before. He brought the young Spaniard back to his room and read him his poems through an entire night. Picasso understood not a word, but he had immense respect for poetry and those who wrote it and it was enough for him to listen to Max's voice to be sure he was a genuis. When the recital was finished he rose and declared solemnly, with his harsh Spanish accent: 'You are the greatest poet of our times.'

Of all the words in the world, they were those Max most needed to hear. Constantly anxious and unsure of himself to the point of neurosis, he had found the friend, the champion, who would sustain him and give him courage. From that time on, the two were inseparable. They communicated mostly by signs, but understood each other perfectly. Picasso, who was penniless at this time, moved into Max's room and his new friend decided to work for the two of them. He found various sordid and more or less humiliating jobs, drifted from one to the other and created a rocky yet childlike poetry out of his trials:

> M'as tu connu marchand de journaux
> A Barbès et dans le métro?
> Pour insister vers l'Institut
> Il me faudrait de la vertu.
>
> Mes romans n'ont ni rangs ni ronds
> Et je n'ai pas de caractère.
> M'as-tu connu marchand de marrons
> Au coin de la rue Coquillère?*

* Have you seen me selling papers
  At Barbès or in the Metro?
  It would take a lot of perseverance
  To get elected to the Institut
  My novels make no sense
  And I have no will-power
  Have you seen me selling chestnuts
  At the corner of the rue Coquillère?

In point of fact, such romantic and independent jobs as the selling of newspapers or chestnuts were not nearly so displeasing as certain others he exercised—for instance, that of counter-jumper in the shop of a rich and contemptuous uncle, who soon degraded him, in view of his remarkable incompetence, to the rank of floor-washer. Each day, he would leave at seven and walk to work, never failing to call at the Cathedral of Notre-Dame on the way. Hunger and misery had brought to the surface a mysticism that, like everything he did, was at once comic and touching, and each morning the little Israelite would kneel to recite his unique prayer: 'Oh, God, if by any chance you exist, let me be not too unhappy!'

As for Picasso, he worked at night and slept when Max got up. He was painting with a sort of despair. The neo-Impressionists he had so passionately admired in Barcelona seemed false and unreal in face of the violent, sordid existence he had discovered in Paris. The rosy-tinted flesh of Renoir's bathers, the play of light in Manet's boating scenes, even the furious romanticism of Van Gogh, had nothing to do with the human condition as he had discovered it in the last few years. Only Toulouse Lautrec, who had dragged out a miserable existence in the same equivocal underworld as himself, had a sort of relevancy for the young Spaniard. There, at least, was an atmosphere he could recognise, a world whose frontiers lay close to his own. The discovery of Toulouse Lautrec was an encouragement that came at a moment when he badly needed it, but it could not solve his problems or even help him to discover a personal style in which to render the cruel, fascinating world that had been revealed to him. His prodigious talent for drawing had become a useless encumbrance. He no longer knew what to do with it, or why he possessed it. So he worked desperately, drank even more desperately and spent his energy in a furious passion for women, waiting for the revelation he knew would come. His friend Max wrote more and more poetry and peered into the future by means of horoscopes and all the tricks he could pick up from the seedy fortune-tellers and occultists he frequented, struggling with a furious desire for God that disconcerted and amused his friends. Poor Max's moments of religious fervour were expressed with such exaggerated emphasis and gave rise to such long-winded and picturesque descriptions of a comically unorthodox relationship with the divinity that no one took them very seriously. It was not till many years later that his friends understood all the sincerity that lay beneath the clowning.

Once more Picasso was forced to return to Barcelona. Max remained in the Boulevard Barbès, more lonely than ever, writing poetry feverishly in the room encumbered by his friend's canvases. He wrote about anything that came into his head, about his own life, his misery, about God, about the phantasms of his imagination that gradually invaded the inhabitants of the material world around him. He took odd jobs, one after the other, and was generally dismissed after a few days, either for incompetence or eccentricity.

Picasso, in Spain, was going through a period more of spiritual misery than material difficulty. There seems to have been at this time an outbreak of a sort of collective neurosis among the artists who, like himself, lived in Paris on the brink of starvation and returned to Spain when it became impossible to do otherwise. There were a number of suicides; one of his closest friends became mad and had to be removed to an asylum. He himself was in a state of anxiety and depression caused by the atmosphere of catastrophe that surrounded him. Yet it happened that his physical and creative vitality was so great that he was able to make use of all this wretchedness, transpose it into art and finally discover his own personality.

When he returned to Paris in 1904, the pictures he brought with him were no longer brilliant, cruel gropings in the style of Toulouse Lautrec, but the tragic canvases of the Blue Period, with its lamentable, diaphanous Jews; its series of 'Maternities'; 'The 'Blind Man's Meal'; 'The Sick Child', painted in blue gouache; the 'Mistletoe Seller', in which the child and man are pressed so close together that 'they form a single column of desolation'.[1] And all these were bathed in a strange, blue twilight that seemed like the colour of sadness itself, yet with forms so noble in their fragility that they evoked no sentiment of pity.

The room in the Boulevard Barbès was too small for such a large collection and Picasso, who had saved a little money, moved into a chaotically constructed wooden building in the rue Ravignan, just below the Sacré-Cœur, on the hill of Montmartre. It was built on two levels, so that the ground floor on the rue Ravignan was at the same time the fourth floor if one approached the building from the back, opening on the Impasse Cottin. It contained a complicated maze of narrow passages, on to which opened a number of draughty uncomfortable studios, inhabited chiefly by impecunious artists.

Almost immediately, Picasso became a personality in Montmartre. He was still very young, almost childlike in some ways, but it was impossible not to notice him. He was small and stockily built, his forehead always barred by a lock of jet-black hair, and always dressed in workman's overalls in a shade of electric blue. He had extraordinary eyes, which many people found frightening. Berthe Weill, who had been the first dealer to buy a canvas from him, had visited him during his early days in Paris and has recalled that, when he opened the door, she had been so struck by a kind of 'terrible pride' in these eyes, that she had recoiled for a moment and only entered with reluctance. Someone else described them as being like black currants, and Apollinaire, who soon became a friend almost as intimate as Max Jacob, always said they were like the eyes of a bird, constantly shifting. He adored animals and was always surrounded by cats and dogs. He was so easy-going at this time that he could never prevent his studio being overrun at all hours of the day by a continual procession of his compatriots, who sat about, talked endlessly and wasted his time. He solved the problem by working at night, and the pile of canvases stacked against the wall grew and grew, although anyone who was interested had the right to take away anything that pleased him.

Very soon the house in the rue Ravignan became a centre of attraction for young artists and writers. Picasso had brought Max Jacob there as soon as another studio became free, and he soon became intimate with another lodger, a large, lethargic girl named Fernande Olivier, with whom he lived for a number of years. She was twenty-five at the time and Picasso was rather ashamed of her age and used to prepare his friends before they met her with the explanation: 'She is rather old, but she is very beautiful.' Manola was another lodger there, so was the painter Van Dongen, and the young Pierre Mac Orlan, who was not yet a novelist, but a caricaturist, with a taste for picaresque adventures. Others came and went and presently the house became known as the *Bateau*

Lavoir. The name came from the long, boat-like shape of the building that recalled the washing-barges on the Seine and from its mazy, cobwebby womb were born a good many of the ideas and theories that, for good or ill, have made the art of the twentieth century what it is to-day.

*   *   *

Apollinaire was living at this time with his mother, brother and Jules Weil in the fairly distant suburb of Le Vésinet. Madame de Kostrowitsky had rented a large house standing in its own garden. The furniture, so far as the rare visitors could see, consisted of a billiard table, surrounded by a number of baize-topped card tables, so that the place seemed more like a gambling house than a normal dwelling. A few intimates were admitted, however, to her *salon*, which was a faithful imitation, executed by a leading department store, of the tent of Abd-el-kadar, the Algerian rebel leader. She had celebrated her arrival by cutting down a fine tree in the garden, and when the owner called to protest, he was met with such a torrent of abuse that he beat a terrified retreat and hardly dared thereafter to insist on payment of the rent. Guillaume returned there each night, as late as possible. After the failure of the bank in which he had been, strangely enough, a model employé, he had been engaged as editor of a small financial review called *Le Guide du Rentier*. The job was not very demanding and left him plenty of time to compose odd articles, and write poems and stories. On the other hand, the pay was too small to allow him to be independent of his mother and the necessity of taking the train each evening at the Gare Saint-Lazare seriously restricted his social life.

Perhaps this accounts for the fact that it was not till the end of the year 1904 that he met Picasso. They had several friends in common—Jean Mollet, Manolo and others—and Picasso, who had at last learned a certain amount of French, had immense intellectual curiosity and liked to know everything that was going on among the young generation of poets and writers. It was 'Baron' Mollet who guessed that an encounter would be fruitful and insisted they should meet. One evening he brought Picasso to a bar in the rue Amsterdam, where Apollinaire was accustomed to wait, in varied and picturesque company, till it was time to take the last train.

They found him playing dice with a stout, red-haired Englishman and two negresses wearing cartwheel hats adorned with multi-coloured ostrich feathers. The spectacle enchanted Picasso. As for Apollinaire, he later described how Picasso struck him at the first rapid meeting as 'an adolescent with unquiet eyes, whose face reminds one of Raphael, and at the same time of Forain'. There was no time to talk, since Apollinaire was greatly absorbed with his negresses, but a rendezvous was arranged. At the next meeting, Picasso brought Max Jacob, who has given his own account of the occasion:

> 'Without interrupting a speech at once gentle and violent on the subject of Nero, and without looking at me, he held out a short, wide hand (it made one think of a tiger's paw). When he had finished his speech, he rose and led us out into the night with great bursts of laughter, and then the finest days of my life began. . . .'

The three men could hardly bear to separate and Apollinaire was invited to lunch next day. When he arrived at the *Bateau Lavoir* he discovered Picasso in an inadequately heated studio; the stove was also used for cooking, but water could seldom be persuaded to boil on it. There was a mattress-less divan and a rickety table, in the drawer of which Picasso kept a white mouse. A yellow earthenware basin was balanced on the stove, with a towel and piece of soap nearby, and the furniture was completed by two shaky chairs and a black japanned trunk that could be used as a third seat. The skylight had been partly painted over in blue, so the room was dimly illuminated by a weird, underwater light and looked rather like one of Picasso's own paintings.

He was a charming host, though it was not always easy to understand his voluble, hispanic French. Fernande was there, and she decided at once that Apollinaire, though kindly and not without charm, was above all childishly vain and preoccupied by the effect he was producing. Max Jacob, however, made no such reservation. Apollinaire's radiant good will reassured him and soothed his exacerbated sensibility. With him, as with Picasso, he sheathed his biting tongue and made none of the wounding remarks that sounded like unjustified attacks, but were really a defence against the attacks he imagined were being prepared against him. Guillaume, on his side, was subjugated by Max's subtle, punctilious charm. The bald little man, with his pince-nez and air of precocious maturity that contrasted with Picasso's almost childlike appearance, was a genius in conversation. He could improvise brilliantly on any subject. His greatest pleasure was to astonish his listeners by carrying his own arguments to the limits of absurdity, forcing them to follow him, then, by suddenly reversing his point of view, teaching them 'the secret of objectivity'. Many people found this method exasperating, but Guillaume, who himself practised and enjoyed the art of verbal volte-face, was exactly the right partner for him. By the end of the afternoon a solid and, as it turned out, lifelong friendship had been established between them. Only Fernande was dissatisfied. She had been left out of the conversation, for Max Jacob frankly detested women and Picasso and Apollinaire, who adored them, had no desire to hear their opinions on art and life.

As it turned out, it was more than a friendship that had been founded that day. The core, and indeed the essential originality, of Apollinaire's character was a quite extraordinary faculty for immediate assimilation of novelty. His mind was constantly open to new impressions and he was able to talk and write brilliantly on anything that happened to stimulate his imagination, without necessarily having more than a superficial knowledge of his subject. Just as stories like *Le Passant de Prague* often give the impression of a long intimacy with cities where, in reality, he had spent only a day or two, so he could inflate mere snippets of information on almost any subject, into an appearance of profound learning. The basis of the performance was often, in fact, extremely flimsy, yet it would be a mistake to imagine that he was a charlatan. His intuition was so acute that he was able to create and construct works and theories that were perfectly valid in themselves, even when their roots could not bear close examination.

The first contact with Picasso's paintings produced a cerebral shock that set Apollinaire's mind working in an entirely new direction. Although he *knew* very little about painting and had not been specially interested in it till that time, he *understood* immediately. In fact, he understood better than the painter himself, who had been working instinctively, without analysing himself.

First of all, Apollinaire saw with the eyes of a writer; that is, he understood the poetic potentialities of the subjects of the Blue Period. His early articles are like recreations of these canvases in a different medium. In his translation, they become:

'... children who have wandered about on their own and never learned the catechism. They stand still, and the rain stops at the same moment. "Look! There are people living in those houses and they wear shabby clothes!" These children, who have no one to caress them, understand everything.

'These women, whom no one loves now, are remembering. ... They do not pray; they are the pious guardians of their memories. They shrink back into the shadows as if into some ancient church. These women have made their act of renunciation and their fingers move as if they are weaving wreaths of straw. They disappear at daybreak, having attained consolation through silence.

'Old men stand about, wrapped in icy fog. They do not meditate, for only children know how to meditate. ... These old men have the right to beg without humility. ...'[2]

At the same time, though, he saw from a new angle—that of a theorist of aesthetics. From that time on—perhaps from the very moment when Picasso first turned the canvases stacked against the wall and revealed the graceful, blue columns of human misery—Apollinaire became an art critic. Without any previous experience or knowledge, he understood why Picasso painted as he did. Day after day, he climbed the steep streets that led to the rue Ravignan, watched Picasso as he painted and explained the painter to himself.

Picasso was changing, and Apollinaire watched the change and reported it in his own manner:

'For a year, Picasso lived these fluid paintings, that were blue like the liquid depths of the sea, and pitiful.

'Pity rendered Picasso more bitter. In his open spaces one can see a hanged man, stretched out above the houses, over the heads of oblique passers-by. These tortured creatures were awaiting a redeemer. The rope stretched miraculously above the garrets; the window-panes flamed with flowers. ...

'This frenzy was succeeded by calm.

Pablo Picasso: *Self Portrait, 1906*

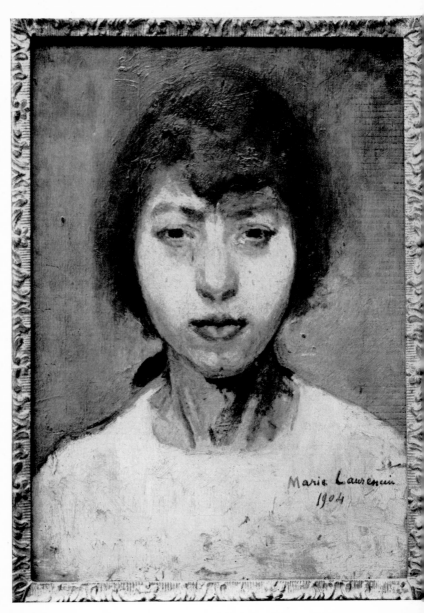

Marie Laurencin: *Self Portrait*

'Here are harlequins who dress in rags that the painting gathers up, intensifying or blanching their colours in order to express the force and duration of passion, while the lines, delimited by the form of the tights, intersect or thrust outwards.

'The harlequin in his square-shaped room is transfigured by paternity, while his wife splashes herself with cold water and joys to see herself as slim and fragile as her puppet husband. Nearby is a neighbouring family, snug in its caravan. Sweet songs mingle together and elsewhere, soldiers pass by, cursing the day.

'Love is a fine thing when it is dressed up, and the habit of living at home strengthens the sentiment of paternity. The child draws the woman closer to its father. Picasso would have woman glorious and immaculate. . . .'

Under the lyric, subjective style, there is an attentive observation of the painter's evolution and the improvised critic concludes:

'His persistence in the pursuit of beauty has led him far. He has become morally more Latin, and rhythmically, more of an Arab.'[3]

At the time when he met Apollinaire, Picasso was, in fact, entering into what has become known as the Harlequin Period, that was to be succeeded almost immediately by the Pink Period. His forms, that had been fragile and elongated, were becoming more massive, almost sculptural; the colours tended more and more towards pink and reddish-brown shades. Apollinaire divined the trend towards a greater objectivity, that was to lead to Cubism, and to so many and varied experiments.

'Picasso', he explained later, 'used to be one of those artists who are not men, but instruments of art. Their reason is powerless against themselves. They do not struggle, and their work bears no trace of struggle. . . . It is as if they are a prolongation of nature and their work does not pass through the medium of their intelligence.'

This was the Picasso of the Blue Period; to some extent, that of the Pink Period. But a new Picasso was evolving; he was turning into one of those artists who 'strain towards Nature and have no direct contact with her. They must extract everything out of themselves and there is no demon, no muse, to inspire them.' And

Apollinaire added: 'There has never been a spectacle more fantastic than that of the metamorphosis he has undergone in becoming a painter of the second type.'4

One may wonder how far Apollinaire himself was responsible for that metamorphosis. Picasso, speaking of his youth, once told a reporter that 'in those days, painters and writers influenced each other mutually', and one can hardly doubt that he was thinking of Apollinaire, massively and attentively installed on the black japanned trunk, watching his movements, observing his brushstrokes and prolonging in his own mind all he saw.

Soon after the meeting in the *Bateau Lavoir* Apollinaire was writing his first article as an art critic, in his own review. Through *Le Guide du Rentier*, he had come into contact with yet another of the more or less wealthy men with literary ambitions who still existed in those happy days and could often be persuaded to help promising young writers. Henri Delormel provided the funds for a small review with the promising title *La Revue Immoraliste,* and contributed, as he had earned the right to do, the opening article. It was an elegantly expressed little essay in praise of prostitution, and his friends in the world of finance concluded, as they were meant to do, that he was no end of a dog. André Salmon contributed a curious short story entitled 'The Manuscript discovered in a Hat', and Apollinaire reserved the 'Notes of the Month' for himself and took advantage of the occasion to express some of the new ideas that were preoccupying him:

'It has been said that Picasso's work shows a precocious disillusionment.

'In my opinion, the contrary is true.

'Everything he sees enchants him and it seems to me that he uses his incontestable talent in the service of an imagination that mingles delight and horror, abjection and delicacy.

'His naturalism, with its loving precision, has a counterpart in the mysticism which, in Spain, is to be found deeply rooted in even the least religious mind. We know that Castelar used to carry a rosary in his pocket and though I imagine that Picasso is not religious, I wager he still keeps a cult for St Teresa or St Isidore.

'In Rome at carnival time, certain masks (Harlequin, Columbine or *cuoca frances*) after a night of orgy that sometimes ends in murder, go at dawn to St Peter's to kiss the time-worn toe of the statue of the Prince of Apostles.

'Such beings would delight Picasso.

'One feels that his slender acrobats, glowing in their rags, are true sons of the people: versatile, cunning, dextrous, poverty-stricken and liars. His mothers clench delicate hands such as one often notices in young mothers of the working classes, and his nude women are grafted with the fleece that traditional painters despise and which is the shield of oriental modesty.'

The *Revue Immoraliste*'s lack of success was attributed to its title, which might have put off respectable readers, and the second number was re-baptised *Les Lettres Modernes*. It contained a poem by Max Jacob, which delighted Apollinaire by its mingled eccentricity and simplicity. It was the first poem Max had ever published and Apollinaire had been obliged to wrest it from him practically by force. Max Jacob practised a strange and rather twisted form of humility—which his friends believed to be the other face of an immense pride—and refused to consider himself on the same artistic level as themselves. As he was also extremely superstitious, he was inclined to believe that it was some obscure form of bad luck brought by himself, which caused the review, in spite of its new name, to die after the second number.

VI

The Cubist Years

*L'art des peintres nouveaux prend l'univers infini
comme idéal.**

At about this time, Montmartre in general and the *Bateau Lavoir*
in particular, was becoming a sort of magnet to the advance guard
of art and literature in Paris. More and more young writers and
artists were coming to live there. Roland Dorgelès and Francis
Carco had joined Pierre Mac Orlan; all three have become famous
novelists, but were then struggling poets. André Salmon, who
had taken a room in the rue Vincent, was composing his first
volume of verse: *Tout l'Or du Monde*. There was the whole group
of Spanish painters, the original inhabitants of the *Bateau Lavoir*
and the new arrivals who had come to join them. There was the
rugged young Flemish painter, Maurice Vlaminck, who at heart
detested this bohemian society and escaped to the country whenever he could. Soon he was quarrelling with Picasso, whose
intellectualism he despised, and he has remained his most hostile
critic ever since. 'Painting is like cooking', he used to say con-
temptuously. 'It should be tasted, not explained.' He had brought
his friend André Derain to Montmartre—Derain, whose conception of painting was exactly the opposite of his own and whom
Salmon accused of trying to force his friends to speculate on the
whole problem of art every time they took a brush in their hands.
There too came the young Dutchman, Van Dongen, who was
still far from the fashionable painter of chocolate-box portraits
he was later to become; and Maurice Raynal, who was to develop
into one of the leading critics of his time. And finally, there was
Apollinaire himself. He was still too much afraid of his mother
to break away from her entirely, but he rented a tiny flat in the

* Apollinaire: *Les Peintres Cubistes*.

rue Léonie (that was soon to become the rue Henner) and spent more and more time there, in spite of scenes at Le Vésinet.

There were other painters in Montmartre besides what the incensed bourgeoisie of the quarter were soon calling 'Picasso's gang'. One of them was the handsome young Italian Modigliani, who had not yet discovered his own unique style and who was considered in the *Bateau Lavoir* as rather an amateur—a fake bohemian, too good-looking, too well dressed and who drank too much for a serious artist. Even less seriously did they take poor Maurice Utrillo, son of Suzanne Valadon, who, before becoming a painter herself, had been Toulouse Lautrec's model for *L'Écuyère*. Utrillo drank even more than Modigliani, lapsed occasionally into fits of madness, and painted with loving care exact reproductions of the streets and houses of Montmartre. He was generally to be seen installed with his easel, a bottle of red wine beside him on the pavement and quite impervious to the children who hurled insults and lumps of mud at the 'madman'. Picasso, who would never have dreamed of painting out of doors, apparently never troubled to make his acquaintance.

All these painters, whether they frequented the *Bateau Lavoir* or not, retained their individuality, and there was never, as some writers have made out, a 'school' of Montmartre. There was, however, a deep feeling of solidarity among them, perhaps because they were all very young—nearly all in their early twenties—all poor, all single-heartedly preoccupied with their art. Picasso and Apollinaire were two poles of attraction around which most of the *Montmartrois* gravitated, but this was because of the strength and attractiveness of their characters, and not necessarily because everyone agreed with their ideas.

This was the heroic period of bohemianism and for a few years it was not a pose or a retreat from reality but a necessity. The bohemians disliked being poor, but at least poverty had a picturesque quality in those days, that disappeared after the World War and never returned. Credit was easily obtained and the restaurant and bistro-owners of Montmartre had a great respect for the arts. It was easy to move them to pity; and most of them were ready to chalk up the price of a good many meals and then, when the total became really impressive, to accept a canvas, or even a few manuscript poems in payment. Fernande Olivier has recalled how it sometimes seemed absolutely necessary to Picasso and herself that they should give a luncheon party, even though there was not a *sou* in the house. The device then was to order the meal from a cooked-food shop, specifying that it should be delivered at a certain hour. When the time came, they would wait in hiding when the bell rang until the delivery man—determined not to have dragged his basket up the steep hill in vain—would leave it at the door. As soon as he had disappeared the basket would be whisked inside and the feast prepared—with the question of payment put off until better days.

Montmartre was still almost a village in those days—half-town and half-country and more or less ill-famed. The *Bateau Lavoir* was the centre of its purely intellectual and artistic life, but there were also certain cafés and bistros that were considered as regular meeting places, and above all the *Lapin à Gilles* that served as a sort of village inn, where the different categories of Montmartre's citizens met and fraternised. The establishment still exists, though it has been known for a long time now as the *Lapin Agile* and has become an attraction for tourists 'doing' Montmartre. In those days it was already a sort of cabaret in which the patron, Frédé, provided the attractions. These consisted in recitals from Ronsard, Verlaine and populist poets of the day—half-sung, half-chanted in his strange, deep voice. Sometimes the entertainment was varied by poets brave enough to recite their own works to this critical and noisy audience, and sometimes there were songs by Pierre Mac Orlan, Francis Carco or Jehan Rictus, who were glad to be offered a free drink by the patron in return for their efforts. There was also a whole band of more disquieting characters who were to be met there—petty criminals, pimps and prostitutes who formed a sort of parallel world to their own. They exercised a disquieting fascination on nearly all the writers and nearly all have reflected at some time or another the sinister and pathetic underworld with which they came into contact at this time.* This romantic taste for vice and wretchedness was an intellectual fashion in the early years of the century, and was part of the general tendency towards the bizarre that was typical of the

---

* Some of the famous novels inspired by the underworld of Montmartre are Francis Carco's *Les Innocents* and *Jésus-la-Caille*, and Mac Orlan's *Quai des Brumes*.

times and so deeply ingrained in both Jarry and Apollinaire. It is significant that the circus, where everything is bizarre and unexpected, was the favourite entertainment among intellectuals during these years.

The lives of the tenants of the *Bateau Lavoir* and their friends who lodged in cheap hotels or furnished rooms on the hill were regulated in proportion to their poverty. Each day's meals were a problem and there was more drinking than eating at the *Lapin à Gilles*—as Mecislas Golberg used to say in the days of the *Soleil d'Or*, 'There'll always be someone to pay for a drink; a sandwich is more difficult.' Nobody except Modigliani would have dreamed of spending money on clothes, although Fernande talked endlessly about the hats she could never buy. When one of the band was obliged to present himself in respectable attire to a prospective client or employer, he would have recourse to Apollinaire and Apollinaire would raid his brother's wardrobe. Albert de Kostrowitsky was a model employé in a bank and always neatly turned out. Luckily he was a good-natured young man, as well as respectable, and he never seems to have protested when his trousers and waistcoats were loaned to Guillaume's rapscallion friends.

Nearly all the young poets of Montmartre found themselves obliged to earn their living in some secondary way, at least at the start of their careers. They solved their problems in various ways —André Salmon used to compose novelettes for romantically-minded shop-girls, and became so skilful that he was able to produce a completed work for his publisher in a bare eight days; Dorgelès worked as a journalist; Mac Orlan as a caricaturist; Max Jacob, as we have seen, had been a shop assistant and had had a long series of desultory jobs that led nowhere. As for Apollinaire, he had specialised for a time in banking. It is true that he had not the slightest aptitude for or interest in the subject, but Madame de Kostrowitsky had connections through Jules Weil and was in the habit of placing her sons, without consulting them, in jobs chosen by herself. André Salmon, who knew her quite well, was struck by the fact that the banks she chose for Albert were always solid, respectable establishments that were likely to last for ever, while her elder son was directed into affairs that were obviously destined for bankruptcy, with a good prospect of prison for the directors.

However, Apollinaire had discovered for himself, early in his career, that erotic literature was much better paid than literature *tout court*. When he was really hard pressed, there was always a market for the kind of novel that is sold only under the counter. He could write them very quickly, and probably enjoyed himself doing so, since he had a distinctly Rabelaisian side to his character. Actually, the poet always remains present in his erotic works, and the humorist too. The themes, indeed, follow much the same pattern as Sade's *Les Cent Vingt Jours de Sodome,* but the tone is full of a joy of life that is a direct contrast to the tragic gravity of the Sadian nightmare. Nor was he the only one of the band to balance his budget by occasional incursions into the realm of erotica. Several young writers of Montmartre, who have since become as respectable as they are famous, supplemented their incomes in the same way but with less talent.

As for the painters, they relied in times of difficulty on the picture-dealers who played an important part in the life of Montmartre at this time. In the quarter surrounding the rue Lafitte there were a number of shops or little galleries that served much the same function as cafés, since people could meet there and talk for hours, without having to pay for a drink. These dealers would often come to the rescue of an unknown artist in a time of financial crisis, by buying a canvas for a small sum. Many of them were sincere lovers of art; some, it is true, later made a handsome profit out of these purchases. Yet the fact remains that they had risked their purses and reputations by encouraging painters whose work could not at the time be judged by established standards.

There was Berthe Weill, who, with Clovis Sagan, had been the first to buy Picasso's pictures when he was still a boy fresh from Barcelona. It is true that she bought almost anything, with what seemed like total lack of discrimination but was perhaps a hit-or-miss intuitiveness. She had a shop in the rue Lafitte, where she sold books, bric-à-brac and pictures and among the extraordinary medley of objects could be found—if anyone had cared to look for them—dusty canvases of most of the coming young painters of the period. Nearby there was Durand-Reil, who organised audacious exhibitions of paintings no other gallery would touch; and near him was the shop of Ambrose Vollard—a huge, dark, gloomy man with a lisp and big, round eyes in a big, round head, who had

done more than anyone else to impose Impressionism on the
public and was soon to become one of the central figures in the
world of art. He was the friend and adviser of every young painter
of the avant-garde. Perhaps he helped them, perhaps he exploited
them, perhaps he did both at once. They themselves were never
quite sure of the truth. He disconcerted painters and clients by
watching them with a look of immense cunning from beneath
thick, half-shut eyelids; often he seemed to be sunk in a dream,
listening without seeming to hear what was being said, then
suddenly putting a question that had nothing to do with the
subject on hand: 'I say, do you believe that women . . . ?' or some
such irrelevancy. He often invited friends to lunch in his cellar
dining-room and as soon as the last mouthful was swallowed, he
would sink into a deep sleep.

Apart from such eccentricities—many of which were borrowed
from his friend Jarry and the still ubiquitous *Père Ubu*—he was a
curious combination of a fanatical art lover and a mercilessly
astute dealer. He loved many and diverse painters, but his real
idol was one in whom no other French gallery took any interest at
that time—Paul Cézanne, whose recent death had passed almost
unnoticed, and who was still practically unknown, not only to the
general public but even to other painters. Cézanne had been an
unpractical, unsociable man, living chiefly in Provence, far from
perspicacious dealers on the lookout for likely investments.
When he had exhibited a collection of canvases in Paris in 1895,
there had been a storm of mockery and abuse. Only a few people
had understood that what appeared like incoherence was really a
groping for a new vision—the vision that was gradually to spread
wider and wider until it became the vision of Reality itself as seen
through the eyes of the twentieth century.

'We must learn to discern in nature the cylinder, the sphere, the
cone', he had written to Emile Bernard. He had realised that the
structure of objects can be modified by changing their colours or
by juxtaposition with other objects, and perhaps he divined that
the study of volumes was to become a key to what his successors
would consider as the New Reality. For him, painting was not
limited to the imitation of objects by means of line and colour,
but a means for creating a 'plastic conscience', and towards the
end of his life he had tended to create an Impressionism that was

concerned no longer with colours, but with shapes and forms. The result was a kind of painting that seemed outrageous even to people who had become used to Impressionist art. It is doubtful whether Vollard himself realised exactly what Cézanne was trying to do or understood his full significance, but he loved him in an instinctive way and foresaw that he would have importance in the future.

It happened that Gertrude Stein had just come to settle in Paris with her brother. She was then still a young woman, fresh from the Medical School in Chicago, short, stout and massive, with a fine head, large features and a deep masculine voice. She liked to say of herself that she was too intelligent to fear ridicule and too sure of herself to care what other people thought of her. Both the Steins were interested in painters and painting, and as they were rich they could buy the paintings they liked. Leo Stein had been in Florence and it was there that he had come across some landscapes by Cézanne and had promptly fallen in love with them. He had enquired about them and about how he could see more of the painter's work and was told that Vollard was the only dealer in Paris to possess any of it. So he and Gertrude arrived one day at the shop in the rue Lafitte and succeeded, after considerable difficulties—for Vollard was not always in the mood for selling—in persuading him to part with a small landscape. After that, they gradually bought several more Cézannes, than a small Manet, two Gauguins and two tiny Renoirs. All these were quite cheap at the time and formed the beginnings of a collection of modern paintings that the two Americans hung in their house in the rue de Fleurus. Soon they had quite a reputation throughout Paris as connoisseurs of modern art.

The rue de Fleurus quickly became a centre for rich amateurs and painters. The Steins were born hosts and knew how to bring people together and make them like each other and profit from each other. (At one dinner-party, where most of the guests were painters, each of them was surprised to feel in such good humour and to find himself talking so brilliantly. It was only at the end of the evening that someone noticed that each had been placed in such a way that he was facing one of his own canvases, hung on the wall exactly opposite his place.) At the same time, the brother and sister were interested in everything new and Gertrude Stein herself was writing her first novel, which was to be given the title *Three Lives,* and studying the technique of the young Irish-man, James Joyce, who was just becoming fashionable among Parisian intellectuals. At first, both she and Leo had considered neo-Impressionist painting as the newest and most daring adventure in art, but soon they began to discover a new generation that was reacting against Impressionism and creating a new style.

The first of these painters was Georges Matisse, who was then about thirty-seven years old and was living with his wife and children on the Quai Saint-Michel. He was associated with a number of young painters—Derain, Vlaminck, Marquet, and others—in a group which called itself *Les Fauves.* They were attempting to introduce—or reintroduce—pure colour into painting and had exhibited for the first time at the *Salon des Indépendants* in 1905. Their efforts had been ill-received and described by hostile critics as 'an orgiac debauch of colours', and 'appalling lumps of ochre, red, chrome, blue, mauve and orange, which they pass off on us as landscapes or seascapes'. The Steins were interested in this crude, violent painting and Matisse soon became an intimate friend of their household.

Then, at almost the same time, Leo Stein discovered in Clovis Sagan's shop a painting of a nude girl with a basket of red flowers. It was signed by Picasso, and though he had never heard the name, the picture interested him and he bought it for 150 francs. Gertrude was interested too and one day they climbed up to the rue Ravignan and knocked at the door of Studio No. 7. Picasso admitted them, rather unwillingly, and they found themselves in the dim, smoky-blue room, among a number of dogs and some lounging Spaniards. Picasso showed them his canvases, while visitors came and went and Fernande looked on without much interest. This was the beginning of a friendship that was never easy, since Picasso was violent, uncivilised and susceptible and quite unused to rich bourgeois, specially if they were American. However, they became very devoted to each other and Picasso often came to the rue de Fleurus—where Gertrude's friends decided that he looked like a handsome shoe-black—and painted a large picture of his hostess. She was rather disappointed in the result and complained that it was not at all like her, but Picasso said to her earnestly: 'But you will become like it', and strangely enough that is exactly what happened.

sentence

It was thus at Gertrude Stein's house that Picasso discovered Cézanne. He had seen a few of his paintings before in Vollard's shop but he had probably not been ready for them. It was in the rue de Fleurus that he really studied them and came to understand what they meant for him personally. The discovery came at a moment when he himself was groping towards a more sculptural style of painting, in which structure and volume were becoming increasingly important and in which intelligence—as Apollinaire had so quickly understood—was gradually gaining predominance over sensibility. This encounter of Picasso with Cézanne was no doubt one of the important landmarks in the history of modern painting and it was at this time that the art of the twentieth century began to take a decisive turn in the direction of objectivity.

It was natural that Gertrude Stein should bring Picasso and Matisse together and soon Matisse too was living in Montmartre, near his young friends, Derain and Vlaminck. He was not, in fact, very happy there. He and Picasso had very different temperaments. He was older than most of the group and could not understand the mixture of morbidity and love of fun that was characteristic of Montmartre's bohemia. At the same time, he was strangely lacking in self-confidence and rather solemn and direct, so he was not at all the sort of man to enjoy the joke when chalked slogans began to appear on the walls of the *Butte*: 'Matisse drives mad!' 'Matisse is worse than war!' and so on. He suspected Max Jacob, but never succeeded in unmasking the culprit. He was there, however, long enough to participate in the collective discovery of negro art and to come under its influence in his own painting.

It was Vlaminck who made the first discovery.* One day he noticed in a suburban café, three roughly sculptured figurines on a shelf behind the bar, which he persuaded the *patron* to give him in exchange for a round of red wine for all the customers present. He took the statues home and showed them to his friend Derain. Both of them were more moved than they could explain, even to themselves, and felt obscurely that the figures were connected in some way with their own gradually evolving ideas about painting. At that time it was easy to discover African masks and figurines,

* A great many people have claimed to have 'discovered' negro art, but Vlaminck's own testimony and that of Apollinaire seems to confirm the priority of Vlaminck and Derain.

neglected as worthless junk in the curiosity shops. Vlaminck and Derain bought a few more examples of this disconcerting form of art, and one day they took their collection to Picasso's studio to see how he would react to it. Matisse was there and the two men stared in silence for a long time at these curious objects which were so strangely, so inexplicably close to their own most intimate preoccupations. The unknown makers of these curious objects had, in fact, succeeded in doing something towards which they themselves had been vaguely groping, for longer perhaps than any of them except Picasso realised. These representations seemed to come from a purely plastic world, 'far from the avatars of time and space, where nothing counts except supple, interpenetrating combinations of elementary solids such as are found in nature and in geometry'.* They had a moving simplicity combined with a mysterious intensity that came partly from their unknown origins, since it was impossible to do more than guess at their age or their real significance in the eyes of the unknown men who had created them. They often combined elements which, according to Western tradition, had nothing to do with art—feathers, tinsel, bits of metal, renewed or added throughout years and perhaps centuries —which seemed like a challenge to the 'solemnity' of the post-Renaissance attitude to art that annoyed the young *Montmartrois*. Altogether, this almost chance confrontation with a totally different conception of art was of the utmost importance to a whole generation of painters. 'Maurice Vlaminck's taste for negro sculpture and the meditations of André Derain, at a time when Impressionism had at last delivered painting from the chains of academism, were to have a decisive effect on French art', wrote Apollinaire later, looking back on this period of discovery.

The results soon became evident. In the summer of 1907 Picasso, who normally hated the country and declared that every-thing smelt of mushrooms there, decided to take a holiday at Sorges in the Vaucluse. Perhaps he was already tiring of the promiscuity and constant interruptions of life in the *Bateau Lavoir*. At any rate, he remained absent for several weeks and when he returned, he brought with him an astonishing canvas which resembled nothing he had done before. Once the first shock of surprise was over, his ribald friends christened it 'The Philosophic

* André Lhote.

Brothel' but Apollinaire and Salmon felt sure that it heralded something new and that it had an importance which they themselves could not yet define. They came every day to the studio to look at it and each day they found that Picasso had retouched and modified it during the night. Then one morning they saw that the five figures in the composition had been definitively deformed, and Picasso told them that the picture had been renamed *Les Demoiselles d'Avignon*. The first Cubist picture had been born.

Every serious historian of modern art has insisted on the importance of the *Demoiselles d'Avignon* as a turning point. The picture contains all the elements we recognise to-day as characteristic of twentieth-century painting. It is entirely objective, there are no reliefs; curves have been almost—although not yet quite—eliminated; the forms are arranged in geometric patterns that reflect the painter's preoccupation with negro sculpture. In fact, it constitutes an almost complete break with traditional Western art. As one of Picasso's most astute critics has pointed out: 'From this year 1907 on, painting was never to be the same again. There is no example in the history of art, of such a total rupture or such a far-reaching renewal.'[1]

None of the people involved has been able to explain how the term 'Cubism' came into being, but after the *Demoiselles d'Avignon* the movement crystallised and became a recognisable 'school'—although the Cubists themselves disliked this term and always worked as individuals, each according to his own conceptions. What it was worth artistically is a matter of opinion. A Cubist picture certainly has very little relation to art, as the word was understood before 1907. Ever since the Renaissance it had been taken for granted that painting and sculpture were concerned with the visual representation of Beauty, just as poetry was concerned with its verbal representation. Quarrels over aesthetics had sprung solely, until then, from differences of opinion as to what was, or was not beautiful; whether a certain mode of expression did or did not serve the cause of Beauty. Painting and poetry had been a matter first of sensibility, then of techniques for communicating that sensibility through a chosen medium.

Apollinaire's poetry was still, at this point, an affair of sensibility. Indeed, it was to remain so to a great extent, since he was essentially a man of sensibility rather than of intellect; his intellect came to the fore where other people's art was concerned, rather than his own. Picasso, on the other hand, was first of all an intellectual, or rather, as Apollinaire himself had guessed two years earlier, he had been gradually recreating himself, casting off his natural sensibility and cultivating an intellectual attitude towards his art.

Les Demoiselles d'Avignon had nothing to do with Beauty and could not have been called beautiful by any standards. When he painted the picture, Picasso had been trying to achieve something else, something quite different. For the first time, perhaps, since the Renaissance a painter had refused to content himself with remaining in front of his subject and considering it from a single angle. He had treated the five figures in the picture as palpable objects, with numerous surfaces or facets, all of which could be 'possessed' by the painter, merely by changing his own position instead of remaining immobile at a respectful distance. In this way, he had shown the component parts of the whole, instead of just those which would have come within a single angle of vision. The picture represented for the first time, instead of a desire to create Beauty, a conscious triumph of Will over Taste. It had been conceived out of the painter's desire to discover the truth about a given object by revealing simultaneously all its aspects or angles, as if he was placed, not in front of his subject, but at its very centre. This has, indeed, proved to be the lasting, durable element that has remained to dominate visual art long after Cubism, its first vehicle, died a natural death.

The comparatively brief history of the Cubist movement raises some curious questions. How far, for instance, was the Cubist myth an artificial creation? No doubt the inspiration behind it was largely cerebral and a rather amateurish knowledge of and interest in mathematics played a certain role in its development. There was also a very conscious determination to break with the past and do something new. Max Jacob, at each new canvas of Picasso, would cry: 'Still too Symbolist!' spurring the painter on to ever greater objectivity. Apollinaire, attentive and assimilative, was elaborating the theories he was to publish later, together with studies of individual artists, under the title: *Les Peintres Cubistes. Méditations Esthétiques*. Picasso, as Apollinaire himself remarked, was still unsure of himself and extremely sensitive to criticism.* His search for a new form of art undoubtedly gained momentum from the theories which his friends, especially Apollinaire, based on his own work.

'Verisimilitude is no longer of any importance,' wrote Apollinaire, in *Les Peintres Cubistes* (and proclaimed it long before the book appeared), 'since the artist sacrifices everything to truths inherent in a higher form of Nature, which he divines although he has not yet discovered it. The subject is hardly, or not at all, taken into account.

'Generally speaking, modern art rejects most of the ways in which the great artists of the past have sought to please.

'Though the aim of painting is now, as ever, to please the eye, the art-lover is invited to take in it a pleasure different from that which he takes in the sight of natural objects.

'Thus we are progressing in the direction of an entirely new form of art, which will have the same relationship to painting as the term has been understood till now, that music has to literature.

'It will be pure painting, just as music is pure literature.

'The pleasure a music lover takes in a concert is quite different from that which he feels when listening to natural sounds such as the murmuring of a stream, the crashing of a torrent, the whistling of the wind in a forest or the harmonies, founded on reason rather than aesthetics, of human language. . . .

'Picasso studies an object in the same way that a surgeon dissects a corpse. . . .'

Then the writer sums up:

'The social function of great poets and great artists is constantly to renew the manner in which nature appears to the eyes of Mankind.'

Other influences can be discerned in this early stage of Cubism —Jarry's, for instance. The 'Super-male' had died, raving and destitute, in hospital, just at the time when the *Demoiselles*

---

* When Braque exhibited the first Cubist picture at the *Salon des Indépendants* in 1908, Apollinaire surmised that if Picasso, with his more impressionable nature, had exhibited at the same time, he would have been discouraged, perhaps for ever, by the mockery of the critics.

d'Avignon came into being. But Apollinaire had often brought him
to the *Bateau Lavoir* and Picasso and Max Jacob had been deeply
impressed. There, as in Salmon's room in the rue Jacob, he had
spoken of the razing of the city walls, with the resulting change of
perspective, and Picasso's eager mind had seized on the image. A
change of perspective, the visual exploration of volume instead of
light, the assimilation of science with art, all this was infinitely
attractive and all of it was part of the Cubist idea. The mathe-
matician Princet played his part too in the creation of the new
theories; so did Georges Braque, who had begun to paint in the
Cubist style at the same time as Picasso, so that each owed much to
the other and neither, perhaps, would have been completely
himself without the other. Braque was already beginning to seek
'poverty in the means of expression' imposing on himself a
deliberate asceticism in order to concentrate ever more intensely
on essential form. It was already becoming evident to initiates
that Cubism, in one form or another, would prove to dominate all
the other pictural experiments of the twentieth century. As for its
origins, Maurice Raynal—an objective observer who was present
during the whole time it was being elaborated—has affirmed that
'though the glory of its discovery belongs to Picasso, the codifica-
tion of Cubism was the result of teamwork in which the exchange
of views between partisans and adversaries bore fruitful results'.

*   *   *

That the Cubist movement was cerebrally conceived, consciously
developed and then cleverly publicised, cannot be denied. Yet
no movement in art can be entirely artificial or completely dis-
sociated from a general, contemporary current of feelings and
ideas. That current may flow beneath the surface and only become
evident in later years, but it exists, latent, and often manifests
itself prematurely in poetry and painting, so that it appears like a
foreign excrescence erupting among other trends which are in
harmony with the more obvious psychological characteristics of
an epoch. Both Apollinaire and Picasso were extraordinarily
gifted for that divinatory function of the artist, which consists of
translating, verbally or visually, currents which have not yet come
to the surface and of which he himself may be aware only sub-

7

consciously. There is no reason to suppose that the Cubist movement, or the trend towards abstraction, were unique in the history
of art, or in the history of humanity. Like every other art, it was
based on the evolution of the thoughts and feelings of Mankind,
and these thoughts and feelings have often been provoked by
material facts of everyday life. This was specially true of all the
tendencies during these first decades of the twentieth century, a
century in which man's existence suddenly became far more
condensed as well as far more complicated. The invention of trains
and motor-cars meant that modern man was already registering
impressions at an infinitely greater speed than a man of the eight-
eenth century could ever have done. This resulted in a rupture of
forms, which had been brought about first by scientists or en-
gineers, and was next translated into visual art and later into
literature, and then, finally, recognised as true by men in general,
and taken more and more for granted. The *Demoiselles d'Avignon,*
like Braque's *Grand Nu* and *Marine*, painted almost at the same
time, were hints in visual form of a change in man's general
outlook, or cosmic attitude, which would demand more and more
urgently as time went on to be translated into a new kind of art.

'The Fourth Dimension', wrote Apollinaire, 'has found its
place in art, just as it has in science. Painters are forsaking the old
art of optical illusions and local proportions in order to express
the magnitude of metaphysical forms.' Apollinaire's writings on
art were lyrical and elliptic, but a few years later Albert Gleizes,
who was to become one of the principle theoreticians of Cubism,
explained how this fundamental Cubist idea applied to the actual
painting of a picture:

> 'Cubism goes beyond externals in order to get a better hold
> on them. It no longer suffices to look at the model, the painter
> must re-conceive it. He will transport it into a Space which is
> at once spiritual and plastic in nature—a Space in regard to
> which we may perhaps allow ourselves to speak of the Fourth
> Dimension. Here, proportions become qualities, sensations
> are no longer linked to a rigid system of axes and their value in
> terms of expression is the sole factor that determines the order
> in which they are transcribed. The exact placing of the parts of
> a face or a landscape no longer depends on that of the other

parts. It depends instead on their place in the artist's mind, on their true place. When we evoke the image of a face, or a city, we do not imagine it in full-face or profile, nor think of its exact topography. Yet the image of that face or that city is more real than any portrait or a hundred post-cards could ever be.'

There is no reason to suppose that Apollinaire—or Gleizes, for that matter—understood the Fourth Dimension better than anyone else. Apollinaire, who was always ready to change his position and contradict himself, remarked a few years later that it meant nothing more than 'a manifestation of the aspirations and disquietude of a number of young artists who had been studying negro and South Sea Sculptures, meditating on scientific works and hoping for a sublime Art'. The fact remains, however, that Cubist art was based on a conception of Space-Time that is gradually becoming almost a commonplace.* In the early years of the century, though, it was still a novelty and Einstein's name was almost unknown. Yet the problem had been one of Apollinaire's essential preoccupations—though he was far from being a scientist or a philosopher—even in his very early writings. It had resulted in the 'simultaneity' in poems like *Vendémiaire* and to some extent in the *Chanson du Mal-Aimé*, as well as in *L'Enchanteur Pourrissant* and many of his short stories. Though the *Enchanteur,* like the *Passant de Prague* and *Amphion-Faux-Messie,* can be explained to some extent by a natural taste for everything strange, curious and irrational, it remains that they appear to-day as corresponding to a necessity, forming part of—or rather, symbolising—a subterranean current which is only now becoming universally apparent. Though Cubist technique can be analysed and explained in relation to a new preoccupation with volume rather than light, we can see it to-day as a visual translation of the new preoccupations that were being forced on men by their sudden precipitation into the Age of Science, and Age of Speed.

So at the root of Cubism—and thus of all abstract art to-day—

* For instance, Dunne's *Experiment with Time* and P. Teilhard de Chardin's *Le Phénomène humain*. Teilhard de Chardin remarks that a 'modern' man is distinguishable by the fact that he has become capable of seeing the world not only in terms of Space, nor of Time, but of biological Space-Time; and moreover that he finds himself unable to see anything in any other relation, and himself to begin with.

we find Picasso's genius for visual invention and, looking a little further, Apollinaire's innate taste for mystery and mystification.

*   *   *

Mystery and mystification. . . . Apollinaire's legacy to the future consists partly of his creative work, but also to a great extent of myths created by him. These myths, of course, were never wholly gratuitous, for if they had been, they would not have been myths at all, but merely inventions. The essence of myth is that it grows from roots struck deep in hidden currents that swell beneath the surface of human thought. So all 'movements' in art are in the nature of myths, though all myths do not necessarily find expression in art. Apollinaire's unique talent lay in the divining of such currents and discovering vehicles through which they might be incarnated. Once such vehicles had come into being, once the *mystery* had taken formal shape, his taste for *mystification* became uppermost. And mystification is always more easy to discern than mystery—hence the accusations of charlatanism that were to pursue Apollinaire all through his life and throw him into such homeric rages.

There can be no doubt that both Apollinaire and Picasso, as well as many of their friends, had an acute sense of publicity. The launching of Cubism was an inextricable tangle of serious research, opportunism and hoaxing. The two latter elements were naturally more evident to spectators than the first, and plenty of people, then and since, have concentrated unduly on them. This aspect of the affair appears in a conversation that was noted and later reported by Madame de Kostrowitsky's landlord. This sorely-tried man, although he knew his tenant only too well, had never met her son and set eyes on him for the first time when a certain minor artist named Gottlieb brought him to a café frequented by painters and pointed out the habitués:

> 'The fat one is a certain Apollinaire . . . a bit dotty, but he knows how to get on in life. They're launching 'Cubism' now, together with the picture-dealers, and Apollinaire does the bluffing.'
> 'And it takes?'
> 'Yes, that's the funny thing about it. It's a whole mutual-

admiration clique. Even the Sar Péladan is in it. We've just come from a bistro in Belleville. It's a set that wants to renew art, literature, customs. . . . What a mix-up! Some of them go in for spiritualism and they have another meeting-place in the rue de la Boule Rouge. I went there once and it was there I met Apollinaire. He pretended to be a magician and goodness knows what else.'

'What does he do apart from that?'

'No one knows. One sees him in all the newspaper offices and in the libraries and at the Stock Exchange. He'll accept all the invitations he can get, but he never invites anyone in return.

'At any rate, he seems to thrive on it. Lord! What jowls he has!'

Cubism was, indeed, being launched on the market with some fracas. Painters, after all, have to live and writers have to interest their readers if they are to make both ends meet. André Salmon had recently become art critic on the staff of an important daily paper and was able to bring the work of his friends to the notice of a wider public than it could normally have hoped to reach. Apollinaire was writing in smaller, but often influential reviews; the Steins had publicised Picasso among rich amateurs (although they themselves refused to buy any more of his paintings once they had become 'Cubist') and the dealers and art-galleries were beginning to suspect that they were on to a good thing. Exhibitions were organised, in France and abroad, and the catalogues were nearly always prefaced by Apollinaire. Some of these prefaces, indeed, were written for painters whom he held in little esteem, since as he explained a little later, when he had begun to worry about his reputation, they were often written for the sake of the movement in general rather than for its members.

Meanwhile Cubism was organising itself, discarding some members and attracting new ones. Derain and Matisse had withdrawn as soon as it ceased to be a sort of exaggeration of *Fauvisme*. Georges Braque, who was a serious, sensible young man, was the first to exhibit a Cubist picture at the *Salon des Indépendants*, in the same year. Metzinger painted the first Cubist portrait—that of Apollinaire himself, and exhibited it in 1910. Another young Spaniard, Juan Gris, arrived in Paris, discovered Cubism and was transported with enthusiam. 'Here is a new language in which to describe the world!' he cried, and was soon carrying that language into its scientific phase. His painting rather annoyed Apollinaire and Picasso, since they were obliged to recognise in it their own theories taken, so to speak, out of their hands and carried further than they were yet prepared to go. 'This is a profoundly intellectual art,' Apollinaire wrote of him, 'in which colour has only symbolic significance. [It springs from] a scientific conception of purity.' Gleizes, Delaunay, Francis Picabia, were beginning their experiments. The second stage of Cubism was in sight.

Meanwhile, the results of all the scandal caused by Cubist painting, and the publicity the movement was receiving, were becoming evident in Montmartre. The *Butte* was becoming fashionable. Rich amateurs and curious foreigners arrived in the rue Ravignan, invaded Picasso's studio. Some of them even bought canvases. Unfamiliar faces began to appear at the riotous banquets these bohemians sometimes organised among themselves. The visitors brought a relative prosperity and already the face of Montmartre was beginning to change.

Above all, Picasso was changing. His friends noticed how sombre and unsociable he was becoming, how he was retreating further and further into himself in the search for *the next stage*. He was obsessed at this time by technical problems which he feared he might never be able to solve. His comrades had accepted Cubism rather as if, seeking a house in which to live, they had discovered one suited to their needs and moved into it as a permanency. Picasso, an eternal nomad, could never feel himself at home between the four walls of a system and he had hardly invented Cubism before he was looking for a way to go further along this strange new road. The enthusiasm of the dealers could not hold him back for a moment. He withdrew into himself, thinking about Cubism, and thinking beyond it. People sometimes interrupted his long silences to enquire whether he was ill or sad. Then he would look up in surprise to say, 'I was thinking about my work', and relapse into his intimidating muteness. For the first time since he came to the *Bateau Lavoir,* his friends found they were no longer welcome at all hours of the day and night in his studio. Admirers, and even possible clients, often got a cool reception. One evening, a band of young German artists who had come to Paris specially to visit him, discovered him spending a quiet evening at the *Lapin Agile*, and carried him in triumph, singing sentimental German songs as they went, to the Place du Tertre. Picasso suddenly felt he had had enough of them and, snatching a revolver from his pocket, began firing wildly in the air. The Germans melted away; the Place du Tertre was a desert; and Picasso, tucking his revolver back in its place, returned morosely to the *Lapin Agile*.

He had, in fact, outgrown Montmartre. In 1910, still attached—though insecurely—to Fernande Olivier—he left the rue Ravignan and moved into a handsomely furnished studio with modern comforts, in the Avenue de Clichy. André Salmon had married a few months earlier and removed to the Left Bank, at the same time as Modigliani. Apollinaire had already transported his mother's Breton sideboards and cupboards from the rue Henner to the rue Gros, in distant Auteuil. Like Picasso, he knew when it was time to move, and time to seek new horizons. He was twenty-eight and had outgrown many things.

> Belles journées, souris du temps,
> Vous rongez peu à peu ma vie.
> Dieu! Je vais avoir vingt-huit ans,
> Et mal vécus, à mon envie . . .*

Inevitably, the verse recalls Villon, who had lived the bohemian life (and worse) a little too long and, like Apollinaire and many of his friends began to feel, at the approach of his thirtieth year, a desire for stability and a certain irritation with things that had seemed so joyful in the past.

* Joyful days, time's mice,
  Little by little you gnaw my life away.
  God! I am going to be twenty-eight years old,
  And the time ill-spent not as I desired. [*Le Bestiaire*]

VII

Rocket-signal

*Quel est ce fusée-signal?**

Back in 1905, when Montmartre was not yet a legend but still a living reality and 'Picasso's gang' still had all the illusions of youth, Paul Fort had founded the review *Vers et Prose*. He was thirty-three years old at the time and the *Mercure de France*—that Mecca of young writers—was publishing his *Ballades françaises*, so his name was known to a much wider public than any of the group of the defunct *Festin d'Esope* had attained. One could have foreseen, even then, that 'the cricket of the North', as Mistral had called him, would one day be elected 'Prince of Poets'.† He had never allowed himself to be deflected, like Salmon or Apollinaire, into the profitable and amusing byways of journalism, but remained immutable, a sort of ideal figure of the pure poet, dedicated to his ideal. His work was already considerable and Apollinaire was right when he prophesied that the series of *Ballades* would terminate only with his life.

'Each series of the *Ballades*', he wrote of his friend, 'is a renewal of nature and of mankind. Here, art is synonymous with creation. Paul Fort creates history, legend, joy, melancholy and love. He creates all these in such an orderly and reasonable way, that probability, or, I should say, truth, is never outraged.'

Paul Fort remained faithful to old loves, though he was always willing to acquire new ones. He still lived on the Left Bank, which most of his friends were deserting for Montmartre, still adored Moréas and remained true to Symbolism, in which he saw the very spirit of poetry. The movement was increasingly

* Apollinaire: *Fusée-Signal*.
† Paul Fort was elected 'Prince of Poets' in 1912, succeeding Léon Dierx.

under fire, from the old guard and the new. Ever since the Dreyfus case, chauvinism had been in the air. Now it was invading literature. Certain critics were beginning to insist on the national aspect of French writing, and protest against foreign infiltration. Catulle Mendès had confined himself to condemning blank verse as an importation by foreign-born poets whose ears were not attuned to the refinements of the mute *e*. Now the *Revue des Poètes* was proclaiming open war against Symbolism itself: 'Our national good sense, in the person of our most glorious writers, protests against this enervated byzantinism! The whole of this movement is infested with exoticism. . . .'

The mood of the day subscribed to this view. 'Naturism' was still in vogue. Barrès, Maurras, Léon Daudet were demanding, as Bouhélier had done in Brussels, 'a renewal of the national spirit', of logical thought and precise language. 'Mystery', which was still the essence of poetry for Symbolists, was on the way to becoming a pejorative term, meaning something vague, obscure and lifedenying.

It was not just a mode of expression, an intellectual fashion, that was in danger, but a way of life. Mallarmé had opened windows on to a new world, a world in which silence was more eloquent than speech, music unheard infinitely sweeter than any perceptible chords, and where suggestion widened limitlessly the boundaries of statement.

'Perhaps it is impossible', wrote Jacques Rivière, looking back on his youth, 'to make people understand what Symbolism meant for those who *lived* it. A spiritual climate, an enchanting place of exile, or rather of homecoming, a paradise. All those images and allegories, most of which appear to-day like limp, worn-out garments, seemed to speak to us, to encompass us around, to help us ineffably. . . .'

Paul Fort had been one of those 'secret young men'* who had *lived* Symbolism, as others would soon begin to *live* Cubism. He had talked with Mallarmé in his old age, had perhaps heard him

* 'Do you realise that in every town in France there lives some secret young man who would let himself be cut in pieces for your poems and for yourself. You are his pride, his mystery, his vice. He isolates himself in this undivided love and this connivance with your poetry—difficult to discover, to understand and to defend. . . ' Letter from Paul Valéry to Stéphane Mallarmé.

murmur, *La suggestion, voilà le rêve!* No one could have been better qualified to defend the Symbolist kingdom and render it habitable for a generation that had never known its early glories.

Le Festin d'Esope had indeed continued the Symbolist tradition in its own way, while representing a new spirit and a new generation. But its editorial board had been all very young men of no reputation, and its circulation had been restricted, to say the least. It was essential, from the Symbolist point of view, to found an important, influential organ with which to counter-attack. Paul Fort, who had never allowed such mundane considerations as money or the lack of it to stand in the way of his projects, decided to found it. He began by choosing the editorial board. He had always been more respectful towards his elders than Apollinaire or Salmon, so the pillars of his still non-existent review were to be some of the survivors of the heroic days of the rue de Rome. They included Vielé-Griffin, Marcel Schwob, Henri de Régnier, Verhaeren, Maeterlinck, and Stuart Merrill. W. B. Yeats was to represent English Symbolism. The younger generation was present in the person of André Gide, only thirty-six years old, but famous ever since *Les Nourritures Terrestres* had revealed his precocious genius; and the youngest of all were Salmon and Nicolas Deniker, of the *Festin d'Esope*.

The name of the review, *Vers et Prose*, was definitely Mallarméan. It had been chosen after a great deal of quarrelling on the terrace of the *Closerie*, where Moréas' sarcasms had condemned each successive proposal to death as soon as it was made. Salmon, who was good at personal relationships, had been appointed secretary and assistant editor. The treasury consisted of two hundred francs, borrowed from Paul Fort's mother, which Salmon converted, on the editor's instructions, into two thousand ten-centime stamps. Then the two of them settled down to write two thousand letters to possible subscribers.

The results were encouraging and soon Salmon was hurrying delightedly from Maurice Barrès to Pierre Loüys, from Vielé-Griffin to Marcel Schwob, from Émile Verhaeren to Henri de Régnier, to beg for contributions, while Paul Fort plunged into the composition of his first editorial. It was to mark a turning-point, almost a moment of destiny, and was composed in a suitably portentous style.

'*Vers et Prose*', it proclaimed, 'has undertaken to reunite the heroic group of poets and writers of prose who have renewed the matter and manner of French literature, thus awakening a taste for that high art and lyricism which had long fallen into abeyance.

'Certain young writers will take their place beside them, thus affirming that their work is imperishable. These young writers have been chosen from among those who continue the tradition of the elders by whom they were first initiated, yet without abdicating their originality.

'Occasionally, specially chosen anthological pages which have never been published in volume form, will be added to unpublished works.

'In this way, we shall continue the glorious movement that originated in the early days of Symbolism; in this way, the most significant and noble literature will find its expression; and this will be the sole aim of *Vers et Prose*.'

Anyone who takes the trouble to look through the early numbers of *Vers et Prose* will find the names of almost every writer of importance in contemporary French literature: Claudel, Jammes, Duhamel, Paul Valéry—who had deserted literature for mathematics and broke the silence of years in *Vers et Prose*—all young men at that time, whose talent was discovered or recognised by Paul Fort or by Salmon, his assistant. There were a great many foreign contributors, as if in defiance of the nationalistic spirit of so many other reviews; English Symbolists like Symons and Dowson (whose famous *Cynara* was printed in the second number), and others including Oscar Wilde, William Morris, R. L. Stevenson, with 'Fiona Macleod' providing the Celtic twilight which seems to have had a curious appeal for the French fin-de-siècle and its aftermath. There were Huysmans, Barrès, Moréas, the last two names by no means representative of Symbolism. The editorial board, in fact, was singularly open-minded, both to the classicism of men like Moréas (which they considered as 'rooted in Symbolism') and the experiments of their juniors. After all, they had been obliged to swallow what, for many of them, had been the bitter pills of *Igitur* and the *Coup de Dés* and nothing the young generation could do was likely to surprise them. On the other hand, they were tiresome about questions of prestige and André

Salmon needed all his famous tact to prevent clashes between Henri de Régnier and Vielé-Griffin, each of whom felt that he should be acknowledged as the spiritual heir of the Master.*

Apollinaire, naturally, soon found a home in the review and managed to impose some of the most experimental of his early work. The first of his poems to be published by Paul Fort was *L'Émigrant de Landor Road,* which recalls his fruitless visit to London, the streets he had grown to love there and Annie's departure, which in the poem becomes that of the poet himself for the 'lyric prairies' of America. It shows distinct traces of the encounter with Picasso. The rows of red brick suburban houses, the 'waves of brick' of the *Chanson du Mal-Aimé,* have become colours, evolving in the direction of objectivity and abstraction. A verse like:

> Intercalées dans l'an c'étaient les journées veuves
> Les vendredis sanglants et lents d'enterrements
> De blancs et de tout noirs vaincus des cieux qui pleuvent
> Quand la femme du diable a battu son amant . . . †

with its juxtaposed touches of red, white and black, corresponds to the same evolution that Apollinaire had noted in the painting of Picasso as he emerged from the Blue Period.

In those days, painters were curious of literature and writers curious of painting. Very soon, Picasso and Braque were joining Apollinaire and Salmon each Tuesday in the horse-drawn omnibus that carried them over the Pont-Neuf and up the Boulevard Saint-Michel. At the *Closerie des Lilas,* Paul Fort was an indefatigable master of ceremonies, passing from group to group, reciting his own verses or other people's, reconciling different tendencies, calming the violence of Jarry, the susceptibility of Vielé-Griffin. Sometimes there would be a gala Tuesday in honour of some

---

* It is hard to see how Francis Vielé-Griffin, who appears now as a very minor Symbolist, could have persuaded himself and quite a lot of his friends that he was France's leading poet. Henri de Régnier has stood the test of time rather better.

† Widowed days inserted in the year
  Slow, bleeding Fridays for funerals
  Some white and some deep black, those vanquished by rainy skies
  When the devil's wife has been beating her lover . . .

outstanding personality—Francis Jammes, Émile Verhaeren, Laurent Tailhade, Paul Claudel. Sometimes Paul Fort would organise a 'picnic' and transport the whole band to suburbs that were still almost the countryside—to Barrès in Neuilly, on the edge of the still rustic Bois de Boulogne, to Verhaeren in Saint-Cloud, to Pierre Loüys in the Hameau de Boulainvilliers, or simply to Marcel Schwob's flat in the Ile Saint-Louis where the host's Chinese servant helped to produce the impression of a break with everyday environment. On ordinary Tuesdays, when there was no special programme and the company dispersed at 2 a.m., driven from the terrace by a sleepy *patron*, he would choose a few intimate friends (Apollinaire was invariably one of them) to 'noctambulise' through Paris until dawn.

And thus *Vers et Prose* had come to represent everything that was most vital in the young literature of that first decade of the new century. The *Closerie des Lilas* remained, as it had been for so many years, the focal point of French art and letters. Yet just at the time when Montmartre was losing its charm for so many who had loved it in their early youth, the famous café was changing too.

First, Marcel Schwob died at the age of thirty-seven, soon after the birth of the review, to the first numbers of which he had given his last articles. It was an irreplaceable loss. Schwob, with his twisted, bitter personality, his amazing erudition, his sarcasms, his fantasy and the audacity of all his judgements, had been an influence more powerful than anyone had understood until he disappeared. Two others among the great men of those early numbers were already failing visibly. Moréas, still elegant and insolent, was too proud to admit the losing struggle with poverty and illness, but it was becoming evident in his ravaged features. His ruined nerves made it impossible for him to stay long in the same place. He would arrive at the *Closerie* terrace, superb with his monocle and indigo moustaches, more like a fine cavalry officer than a poet. But before ten minutes had passed, he would decree, 'This café is sinister!' and hurry away—to the Halles, to far-off streets in the quarter of Saint-Denis, raging from one café to another, all through the night. His indomitable spirit kept him alive till 1910, when, in complete destitution, he died with great dignity.

As for poor Alfred Jarry, he had made occasional appearances during the first year. His arrival was heralded by a pungent smell of ether, which he inhaled, or drank, in such quantities that Rachilde said he seemed to be moving in an almost visible cloud of the drug. He lived in a ramshackle hut in the country and made these rare excursions to Paris when the boredom became too much for him. He refused to see a doctor, in spite of the urging of his friends. To Rachilde—the only person who had any influence over him—he explained: 'You understand, Ma-adame, it would be too much in their interest to dissect a person of Our calibre. It would give them a chance to learn something new.' Yet the end was obviously drawing near and presently his friends heard that he had been taken to hospital. From thence, they received majestically optimistic notes. 'We are getting better and better', and learned with surprise that this arch-cynic had asked for a priest and received Extreme Unction. Then there was a lapse into insanity and Jarry died, raving, in the summer of 1907. Two of the great teachers who had formed, by their mere presence and example, so many of the young generation of poets, had disappeared.

Apollinaire's article on Jarry, which appeared a couple of years after his death, in a series on 'picturesque contemporaries' was an act of homage that summed up the significance of *Père Ubu* for his generation:

'Alfred Jarry was to a rare extent a 'man of letters'. His least actions, his childish pranks, were *literary*. For he justified himself through literature and through it alone. Someone once said in my presence that Jarry was the last of the great burlesque characters. That is an error. In that case most of the fifteenth-century authors and a great many from the sixteenth, would have to be considered as merely burlesque. The word cannot be applied to the finest products of humanist culture. Indeed there is no word that can really describe that particular state of mirth in which lyricism becomes satiric; in which satire, applied to reality, goes so far beyond its object, that it destroys the object itself. Then it rises so high that it goes almost beyond the reach of poetry, while vulgarity, emanating from good taste itself, is transformed by some unimaginable phenona into a en necessity. These orgies of intelligence, which meexclude aslltiment, were only possible during the Renaissance and Jarry, miraculously, was the last of these sublime debauchees.'

*   *   *

Jarry's death, and the illness which forced Moréas to retire more and more into his solitude, corresponded with one of the most exciting periods of intellectual and artistic activity Paris has even known. Diaghilev's Russian Ballet visited the city for the first time in 1909. It was new art, a new mode of expression, a revelation that, strangely enough, passed almost unnoticed in a Montmartre preoccupied with more severe problems. There was the discovery of negro art; Cubism was blasting traditional conceptions of painting and sculpture; the possibilities of 'naïve' painting were suddenly revealed by the 'Douanier' Rousseau. A spirit of iconoclasm, a desire to destroy the old and discover the new, had seized the world of arts and letters. Rimbaud, who had been a monstrous exception in the Paris of 1872, would have been a commonplace in that of 1909.

It was in February 1909 that the bombshell of Marinetti's first 'Futurist Manifesto' exploded in the usually conventional columns of *Figaro*. It must have alarmed many a cultured breakfast table and been a terrible shock to readers who prided themselves on being 'modern' because they had learned to appreciate Impressionist painting and Symbolist poetry.

'We wish to extol the love of danger, the custom of energy and daring', proclaimed Marinetti from Florence.

'The essential elements of our poetry will be courage, audacity and revolt.

'Until now, literature has idealised pensive immobility, ecstasy and sleep; our desire is to exalt aggressive movement, feverish insomnia, the double march, the double somersault, the slap in the face and the blow of the fist.

'We declare that the splendour of the world has been endowed with a new beauty; the beauty of speed. A racing motor-car, decorated with pipes like serpents whose breath is an explosion . . . a roaring motor-car which seems to hurl itself into the mouth of the cannon, is a thing of greater beauty than the Victory of Samothrace.

'There is no longer any beauty apart from strife; any master-piece that is not aggressive in character. Poetry must be a violent attack against unknown forces, summoning them to submit to Man. . . .

'We desire to destroy all the museums, the libraries, combat moralism, feminism and all opportunist and utilitarian base-ness.*

Marinetti, of course, went further than anyone of any account in France was prepared to follow him—and indeed much further than he was prepared to go himself in practice. He did, however, give to the general feeling of effervescence and desire for novelty an expression which, just because it was such a violent exaggera-tion, throws a revealing light on the spirit of those exciting, changeful years. A good many writers and artists in fact were beginning to detect a faint, nostalgic haze around the *Closerie des Lilas* and *Vers et Prose,* to see them as reflecting traditions of the past, certain standards of Order and Beauty that would not, they were beginning to suspect, be those of the new century.

Apollinaire himself was ironical about Marinetti, yet he could no more hold aloof from him than he could from any of the mani-festations and signs of his time. It was now, when the centre of the stage had been deserted by Jarry and Moréas, that he began to represent, in the eyes of his contemporaries, the new spirit in art and literature. It was at this moment of almost abnormally in-tense intellectual activity that he really began to fill the role for which he felt himself to have been born—that of a 'rocket-signal' for his times. It was now that he began to reveal himself as a sort of 'maker of myths', an interpreter at first, and later a creator, of the 'modern spirit'.

Now, at that particular moment, this 'modern spirit' was being worked out and given expression in painting rather than writing. So it was natural that Apollinaire should have been absorbed above all in the new world that had been opened up for him by his discovery of the visual arts and his friendship with Picasso. It

* Other points in this first 'Futurist Manifesto' included 'the glorification of war . . . militarism, patriotism . . . contempt for women . . . .' So it is not surprising that Marinetti became one of Mussolini's earliest disciples and the Futurist movement the artistic expression of Fascism.

was through painting and sculpture that he was beginning to work towards a coherent vision of the future. The greater part of his writings during the period 1906–09 was concerned with the early stages of the Cubist movement and with painters directly or indirectly connected with it. His new friends were either painters themselves, amateurs like Gertrude and Leo Stein, men like Maurice Raynal, preoccupied with the philosophy of art, or dealers who specialised in the work of the rising generation. This preoccupation with painting had a direct effect on the evolution of his personal life, and the effects were, in their turn, to become the cause of a new evolution of his life as a poet.

One day he was in Vollard's shop in the rue Lafitte when Picasso introduced him to a tall, thin young girl who was peering at the pictures in a short-sighted way through a lorgnette. She had long, thin arms and legs, curly black hair and slanting eyes in a curiously triangular face. The first contact was difficult. Apollinaire, who was so self-assured in other matters, was extraordinarily timid where women were concerned. He had never learned to take them for granted, or even to consider them as merely human. Nice, harmless little Annie Playden, with her Sunday-school for the children of Honnef and her suburban prejudices, had seemed to him the personification of the Lorelei, or the Belle Dame sans Merci—fatal and perverse. He, who was notoriously thrifty (his enemies called it mean) was ready to spend every *sou* he possessed in order to impress some poor little prostitute who represented in his imagination a brilliant *cocotte* in the style of La Belle Otéro or Émilienne d'Alençon. When some more virtuous young woman attracted him, he would follow her humbly, sometimes for weeks on end, without daring to speak to her, then, once the ice was broken, spoil his own cause by a clumsy and even brutal ardour.

The young woman in Vollard's shop, however, was in a different category from either of these types. Her name was Marie Laurencin and she was a student at an art school where she was learning to paint on porcelain. She lived with her mother and Apollinaire soon discovered that she, like himself, was the illegitimate child of a mysterious and never-named father. Madame Laurencin, however, was quite unlike Madame de Kostrowitsky. She lived as a recluse, earning her living by embroidering designs

8

made by her daughter, whom she watched anxiously and guarded as far as possible from the temptations of the world. Their house was very neat and very silent and André Salmon, who visited them later, said that the relationship between the two women reminded him of that of a young nun with an older one. It was a long time before Marie dared to bring Apollinaire and his friends into this cloister-like calm.

But Marie Laurencin had another side to her nature. She was something of a 'New Woman', as they were saying at about that time in England. She was conscious of her own personality and had no intention of modifying it in order to conform to the standard pattern of the *jeune fille*. She was independent, an artist, and yet not in the least bohemian in the style of the girls who came to the *Closerie* or the *Caveau*. Altogether, she was a revelation to Apollinaire and destroyed a good many of his favourite ideas about women.

'She is gay, she is kind, she is witty, and so talented!' he explained to a friend. 'She is like a little sun. She is myself, in the form of a woman. She has all the delicious effrontery of the true Parisian. . . .'

Everything she said or did seemed to him adorable. Shortly after their first meeting, she and her mother moved to Auteuil, and he immediately left Montmartre and took an apartment in the rue Gros, in order to be near them. Her visits threw him into ecstasies:

'Just imagine, when she came to visit me in the rue Gros, she skipped through the whole length of the garden. And when she left, she skipped down the stairs—I live on the second floor. A real feat of acrobatics. When she reached the gate, she turned the skipping rope three times, very quickly, which is what little girls call, "the vinegar turn", and means, "Goodbye! See you soon! See you to-morrow!"'

The state of being in love corresponded, for Apollinaire, with a state of lyric creativeness. During the last few years, Apollinaire had developed chiefly as an intellectual and a critic, but with the appearance of Marie in his life he became a poet again. A whole series of exquisite lyrics bear witness to this new love: *Le Pont*

Mirabeau, which is perhaps the best known of his shorter poems, since it is automatically included in almost every anthology of French modern verse; *Marie, Cors de Chasse, Mon Destin* and so many others which reflect the complex charm of Mademoiselle Laurencin.

Linda Molina, little Maria Dubois of Stavelot, even the lively, intelligent Annie, had been quite ordinary girls whom Apollinaire had recreated in his imagination until he really believed they were fascinating sirens. Marie Laurencin was of a different calibre and and far more dangerous. He was not being entirely fanciful when he wrote of her as being his own female equivalent. She had something of his own gift of assimilation, his own intuitiveness, and his own spontaneous charm and gaiety. Perhaps, too, she had something of his own sense of personal publicity and swiftness in taking advantage of favourable circumstances. He introduced her to painters and writers, brought her to the *Closerie,* for the weekly reunions of *Vers et Prose,* than to the *Bateau Lavoir.* On Wednesdays, when he was 'at home', first in the rue Henner, then in the rue Gros, she acted as hostess for him. Soon she was reigning like a queen over the court of his friends. Salmon, Paul Fort, Moréas, admired her wit and originality; the Steins adopted her enthusiastically; even Max Jacob forgot his dislike for women in her presence. Only Picasso remained impervious to her charm. She irritated him beyond endurance and he habitually referred to her as 'that horrible woman who imitates animal noises'.

Gradually Marie began to bring her new friends to her home, where her mother accepted them with resignation, though the very sight of a Cubist painting filled her with misgivings. The blue drawing-room in Auteuil soon became a regular meeting-place for the dispersed ex-citizens of Montmartre. Marie presided, accompanied by her cat, who looked rather like her mistress and who, she explained, posed for all the women's faces in her pictures. She could often be persuaded to sing old ballads from Normandy or the Savoy region, or songs that were currently popular in dance-halls and *guinguettes.* She had a sweet, slightly husky voice and often accompanied herself on the harmonium. Sometimes the entertainment was varied by a séance of fortune-telling or table-turning, at which several of her new friends were adepts. Her mother would often preside, silently embroidering while Marie played her role as daughter of the house, demurely serving cakes and coffee. It took Madame Laurencin a long time to get used to these invaders of her peace and she revenged herself quietly by embroidering a scene in which Apollinaire figured and stitching his face in black, so that he appeared on her firescreen as a negro.

Marie, on the contrary, was perfectly at home in the Cubist atmosphere and in a very short time she had progressed from rather laborious portraits of herself and her friends and was beginning to paint in the new style. Although it is difficult to understand how she could have been considered, even through the eyes of love, as a Cubist painter, she had begun to stylise her figures and to develop a personality of her own. Apollinaire was determined that she should have a triumphant career and had appointed himself her impresario. He criticised, bullied and flattered, detected each original tendency and forced her to develop it. One painting in her new manner was a group portrait, figuring Apollinaire and herself, Picasso, Fernande Olivier and Fernand Fleuret, all with slanting eyes and a faintly Japanese look that echoed, though from afar, the cult for oriental sculpture. Gertrude Stein bought the picture and Marie stepped into the first rank of young, avant-garde painters, and was taken seriously by the art dealers. Apollinaire lost no opportunity of bringing her to the attention of the public:

'I cannot find words', he wrote in the *Revue des Arts et des Lettres,* 'to describe the typically French grace of Mademoiselle Marie Laurencin. She is conscious of the profound difference between men and women; a difference in their origin and in their ideals. Mademoiselle Marie Laurencin's personality vibrates with joy. She evolves freely in her own domain, which is that of Purity. . . .'

The lover is more in evidence here than the critic and Apollinaire had no excuse but his own passion for including Marie Laurencin in his volume of studies of Cubist painters. 'Her painting is analogous with dancing', he wrote then. The observation is in the true Apollinairian critical style and perfectly justified. Marie Laurencin's painting is delicate, graceful and rhythmic, conceived all in arabesques, but it has no relation to Cubism.

There can be no doubt that Apollinaire revealed Marie Laurencin to herself and that she was, to some extent, his own creation. In *Le Poète Assassiné*, lightly disguised as Tristouse Ballerinette, she exclaims:

> 'Nowadays, people find me so adorable that other women imitate me. What miracles are brought forth by the love of a poet! The miracle is accomplished now. I am beautiful and famous. . . .'

In other words, Apollinaire claimed to have been solely responsible for his mistress' metamorphosis. Marie was not entirely convinced. She was exceedingly independent, at least when she was out of her mother's house, and not inclined to be subservient to any man. As for Apollinaire, once the initial period of timid admiration had passed, he was a natural tyrant in his dealings with women. At the same time he believed, in theory, in the emancipation of women and rather liked to pose as their champion. He had discovered the writings of the Marquis de Sade in the 'condemned' section of the *Bibliothèque Nationale* and saw in Juliette a vision of liberated womankind:

'Justine figures the old type of woman, enslaved, wretched and less than human; Juliette, on the contrary, represents the new woman he [Sade] confusedly foresaw, a being of whom we have hardly an idea, who will rise above humanity, who will be winged and will renew the universe . . .' he wrote in his preface to the Collected Works, and behind this vision of 'freed' womankind, one divines Marie Laurencin . . . Marie, whom, in practice, he treated with all the *désinvolture* of the Superior Male, reserving the right to independence exclusively for himself and allowing none to her. The 'Kostro' of Neu-Glück had not really changed and he was soon showing the same jealousy and brutality that had terrified poor Annie Playden. Marie, it is true, fought back, but she needed Apollinaire as much as he needed her, and their stormy love continued for a good many years.

Apollinaire's discovery of Sade was important, because it placed a writer who had been considered until then merely as a pornographer* in a new perspective—that of 'the most truly free

---

* Sainte-Beuve was one of the very few critics to recognise that Sade was more than a mere pornographer and had made a real contribution to the history of philosophy.

man who has ever lived'. But it was also part of the great web he was gradually weaving, with himself like a spider at its centre, which we recognise ever more clearly as the years go by to be the pattern of the twentieth century. The long preface to the Collected Works contains some revealing phrases, such as:

> 'Numerous writers, philosophers, economists, naturalists and sociologists, from Lamarck to Spencer, are on common ground with the Marquis de Sade and many of his ideas that appalled and disconcerted his contemporaries are still entirely new. . . . It seems that the time has come for these ideas that have ripened in the squalid atmosphere of hidden sections of our libraries to be brought into the light. This man, who counted for nothing in the nineteenth century, may perhaps dominate the twentieth. . . .'

The prophecy was not as far-fetched as it seems at first sight. Apollinaire had probably never heard of Freud, who was still in the early stages of his researches into the psycho-sexual causes of human behaviour. Yet the subconscious mind, as explored by Freud, corresponds alarmingly with Sade's criminals. The four accomplices of the *Hundred and Twenty Days of Sodom*, especially, can quite well be considered, in the light of Freud's revelations, as the *impossible* underground tendencies of the human spirit, personified and translated into the realm of the Possible. The Sadian world is the world of the unleashed subconscious, the world of absolute chaos and absurdity.

> 'Sade', explained Jean Paulhan some forty years later, when a publisher was being prosecuted on account of a new edition of *Justine* and *Juliette*, 'came at a time when a rather slack sort of philosophy took it for granted that Man was naturally good and that if he was allowed to be true to his real nature, everything would be well. From that point Sade was led, by contrast, to show that Man was naturally evil, and to demonstrate in detail, by every means available, this natural evil which he was the first to reveal as based in his sexuality. . . .'

Sade's work, in fact, is based on an exploration of man that led him further into the remote and dark parts of the mind than anyone had been before. To-day, this refusal to admit bounds or barriers to the exploration of man's nature has become one of the main trends of contemporary literature, and indeed the ruling motive of the major writers of the century. And the concentration camps have proved that this exploration is not gratuitous, that the Sadian criminal not only exists, lurking in the subconscious jungle of the mind, but that he can emerge under certain conditions into the sphere of the Possible. Once this is recognised, it is only logical to admit the importance of Sade and the acuity of Apollinaire's judgement.

Apollinaire's long, important preface to the Collected Works of the Marquis de Sade was published in 1909. He had been working on the subject on and off during the previous year, but it had not at that moment been an absorbing preoccupation. Apollinaire's taste for obscenity was in the Gallic, Rabelaisian tradition, part of a vast curiosity about life in general. There was nothing morbid about it and Sade's disgust at life was entirely alien to his own nature. At the same time that he was discovering Sade—and siding so definitely with free, wicked Juliette, against good, cringing Justine—he was discovering and launching a personality as different as could well be imagined.

Henri Rousseau, in 1908, was a little, timid, bearded man of sixty-four, employed in one of the Parisian toll-offices. He was very poor and lived alone in a neat small room on the Left Bank. He had no family but had been engaged for a number of years to a capricious 'fiancée', aged fifty-nine, who considered him too old for her and could never make up her mind to marry him. He supplemented his tiny income by giving drawing lessons to the neighbours' children. The parents were probably rather proud to think that this patient professor had been exhibiting for the last twenty-two years at the *Salon des Indépendants*. No one, it is true, had ever paid much attention to his paintings, except to laugh at them. They were generally huge canvases representing tropical jungles, peopled with figures and animals, drawn with the naive carefulness of a child's inventions. He explained these paintings by saying he had once been a soldier and had accompanied the ill-fated Emperor Maximilien on his Mexican campaign. The story seemed rather incredible, but old Monsieur Rousseau was so transparently honest that it was impossible to disbelieve him.

It was Jarry who finally 'discovered' the Douanier. The two

men were both Bretons from Laval and Bretons never forget
their origins. Jarry, who knew that Montmartre would always
welcome anything new and amusing, introduced him to Wilhelm
Uhde, a German painter who was the first of several of his compatriots to open galleries in Paris and give exhibitions of modern
art. Rousseau's paintings, as a matter of fact, could hardly have
been described as 'modern' at that time, since they owed nothing
to the Impressionists (or to any other school, since Rousseau was
remarkably ignorant of any art but his own) and had nothing in
common with the Cubists.

Apollinaire, who was to launch Rousseau with considerable
fracas in the art world, did not appreciate him immediately. One
glimpse of Picasso's Blue Period Paintings had been enough
to convince him that a terrible power, at once destructive and
creative, was at work. With Rousseau, his first reaction had been
almost hostile. Only a year earlier he had commented with
unusual asperity on his exhibit at the *Salon*:

> 'Monsieur Rousseau's exhibit is both touching and pleasing.
> This self-taught artist has natural qualities that cannot be
> denied, and it seems that Gauguin admired his blacks. On the
> other hand, the Douanier lacks general culture. His ingenuity
> is unconvincing. It comprises too many elements that are
> chancy and even ridiculous. He knows neither what he wants
> nor where he is going. . . . And how irritating is Rousseau's
> tranquillity! He knows no disquietude. He is pleased with
> everything he does, though without conceit. Rousseau should
> have been a mere artisan.'

Once the two men had met, Apollinaire changed his mind.
Perhaps it was the very contrast between the Douanier's personality
and his own that delighted him. The simplicity, the complete
lack of 'disquietude' that had annoyed him in the pictures, enchanted him in the man. Rousseau was so simple and trusting
that, as André Salmon put it, 'he confided in anyone and everyone, trusting them with his joys and sorrows, his fiancée's letters
and the keys of his cupboards'. He was incapable of seeing evil,
or even imagining that it existed. Above all, he was incapable of
imagining that anyone could make fun of him or pretend to an
admiration they did not feel so as to mock at him afterwards

among themselves. Later on, a good many people did behave in this way, but Apollinaire and his friends were perfectly genuine in their amused affection and the respect they came to feel for his painting.

Apollinaire's personal feelings often guided his artistic judgement, but instead of leading him astray as personal feelings generally do in such matters, they were often like a lantern that led him along the right path. Once he had come to love and understand Rousseau, the painter's 'ingenuity' appeared to him as a quality rather than a defect and his 'tranquillity' ceased to be irritating. The attitude of Apollinaire, Picasso and his friends to an art that contrasted so sharply with their own intellectualism, was a mixture of surprise, pity and admiration. André Salmon, who has painted a touching picture of the Douanier in his Memoirs, tells us that:

'It was not for his lack of dexterity or his ignorance of drawing that we loved Henri Rousseau: nor did we cherish him for his immense naïveté, or for what seemed to André Derain and Maurice Raynal his fundamental idiocy. We loved the man for his purity, the courage with which he faced a life that was so cruel to him, for a sort of angelic quality; and the artist for his astonishing sense of grandeur, for his magnificent ambition of achieving huge compositions at a time when—with the exception of Picasso and, in a less profound way, Matisse—so few artists composed, though not because they would not have liked to do so. . . .'

It was the personal contact with Rousseau that revealed to Apollinaire a certain grandeur and simplicity which his own intellectuality had at first prevented him from recognising in the pictures. Once he really understood Rousseau, he saw in him the raw material of Myth and could not rest till he had given it shape. While he was still constructing, through Cubism, the myth of the artist-intellectual, completely lucid and conscious of what he was doing and why he was doing it, he was creating at the same time the counter-myth of the unconscious artist. No doubt it satisfied his taste for ambiguity. Rousseau had nothing in common with any school or movement and knew nothing of those metaphysical doubts which have given rise to most of the permutations of post-Renaissance art. He was simply himself, happy to be himself, and pleased like a child to see his rich imagination taking form on a canvas. Here was a purely spontaneous, individual form of art, a necessary reaction against the cerebral art that is more obviously characteristic of the twentieth century.

Apollinaire understood the *necessity* of Rousseau's kind of painting and set about launching the Rousseau-myth with the same careful organisation and sense of publicity he had brought to the launching of Cubism. It was to be given a really explosive start with a banquet in the old man's honour. This was to be held in Picasso's studio, with painters, critics, admirers and friends assembling to do him homage. It was done on a grandiose scale: the façade of the *Bateau Lavoir* was decorated with a huge streamer bearing the words: 'Homage to Rousseau'; a wonderful meal was ordered from a neighbouring food-shop; the poets had written poems for the occasion or composed songs to be sung by anyone who could claim a reasonably good voice. It was planned with a view to making history—or at least the history of Montmartre—and it succeeded.

The story of the banquet has been told so often that it has become almost as well-known as Rousseau's pictures. The strange thing is, though, that everyone tells it differently. According to some, it was a drunken orgy; to others, the 'orgy' (which took place after Rousseau's departure) was contrived in order to scandalise the American puritanism of the Steins; for some, it was a genuine demonstration of friendship and admiration for Rousseau; others are still convinced that the whole thing was an elaborate practical joke. Acid discussions still break out among elderly survivors as to whether André Salmon did, or did not, eat the yellow trimming on Alice B. Toklas' hat; the conditions in which the food for the banquet finally appeared on the table are a subject of bitter dispute. The only point on which everyone agrees is that the occasion was a landmark in the lives of the guests. As Maurice Raynal's account was the first to be published, perhaps it will be best to rely on his memory and let him tell the oft-told story in his own words:

'The feast was held in Picasso's studio. This was a veritable hangar, with immense beams that were too imposing to be true.

The walls had been cleared of their usual decorations and on them were hung only a few fine negro masks and a map of Europe, the bare necessities, in fact, with the large portrait of Yadwrigha, the Polish schoolteacher* in the place of honour. The room had been decorated with garlands of Chinese lanterns. The table was set on trestles and laid with all sorts of things for the meal.

'At eight o'clock, everything was ready, except for the dinner.

'The guests were expected to be fairly numerous. They included three connoisseurs and collectors, come from New York, Hamburg and San Francisco more or less specially for the occasion; painters like Mademoiselle Marie Laurencin, Jacques Vaillant, Georges Braque, A. Agero, etc. . . . then writers and poets like Guillaume Apollinaire, Max Jacob, Maurice Cremnitz, André Salmon, René Dalize, myself and a number of charming ladies, who were pretty and not dressed up as artists.

'By six o'clock in the evening, a certain effervescence already reigned in the assembly, which had met at Fauvet's Bar for a preliminary *apéritif*. Everyone was very gay. The talk was witty and lively, the women were laughing. . . .

'The time came to make for the banqueting-hall.

'At last the guests began to climb the rue Ravignan. Only one was forgotten—a Dane who showed no sign of finishing a speech he had commenced in the bar. There was a tumultuous arrival in Picasso's studio. The two neighbouring studios had been requisitioned, one to serve as a cloakroom for the ladies, the other for the men. Above the hubbub, the seats at table were indicated according to strict etiquette and while the room was seething with noisy protests, three discreet knocks sounded on the door. Immediately, the noise ceased and complete silence reigned.

'The door opened. It was the Douanier, wearing his soft felt hat, his stick in his left hand and his violin in his right.

'At the apparition of the Douanier, a wave of sentimentality

* This Yadwrigha had been the object of one of Rousseau's many tumultuous and unsuccessful loves. Although no one had ever seen her, she became part of the Rousseau myth for his friends.

swept over the company. The picture he presented was certainly one of his most touching compositions. He gazed around him, visibly enchanted by the Chinese lanterns, his face wreathed in smiles.

'Meanwhile a series of events which have never been fully understood caused the dinner, which the amphitryon had never-theless ordered from a well-known restaurant, to exaggerate the general mood of fantasy to the point of not coming at all.

'We waited for an hour, for two hours—all in vain. It was only after two hours and twenty minutes had passed that our host, suddenly striking himself on the forehead, recalled that he had made a mistake in the day for which he had given his order. The dinner, in fact, arrived two days later.

'When Rousseau saw that we were all getting ready to hurry out and search for provisions, he was seized with a fine fit of gaiety, which remained with him throughout the whole even-ing. An improvised meal was organised. The foragers returned, loaded with drink rather than with food, since in such cases one is always afraid of going thirsty. However, as our host had a reserve of about fifty excellent bottles, there was no risk in this case. Joy reigned from the moment when the first tins of sardines were opened, so that the speeches and songs started at once. Maurice Cremnitz rose, asked for permission to sing—a permission which was energetically refused—and broke out with a song in honour of Rousseau, set to an English tune. The chorus ran:

> This is the painting of Rousseau
> Who tames Nature
> With his magic brush!

The Douanier then produced his violin—a sort of child's violin —and played a work of his own composition, entitled 'Bells'. Other songs followed and soon someone suggested dancing. The Douanier played one of his own waltzes. Soon there was no holding him. One of the lanterns was dripping burning wax in regular drops on his head, so he changed his place and sang through the whole of his repertory.

'Guillaume Apollinaire had been catching up with two months' arrears of correspondence on a corner of the table. Now he improvised a humorous—but not mocking—poem, which he recited, still hot from his pen, when Rousseau had finished singing.

Tu te souviens, Rousseau, du paysage astèque
Des forêts où pourrissaient la mangue et l'ananas
Des singes répandant tout le sang des pastèques
Et du blond empereur qu'on fusilla là-bas . . . *

'Suddenly, there was a knock on the door. It was the barman Fauvet come to warn us, with all possible tact, that one of our lady guests had been found sitting on the pavement in front of his establishment. This lady had gone out to get some air, and an error of judgement and a fall had set her rolling right down the rue Ravignan to the bar. All the ladies looked at each other; one of them looked in the glass to make sure it was not herself; then we passed the matter over, without attaching importance to it. At that moment, there was a scuffle in the passage over a deplorable mistake committed by one of the guests against the door of the men's cloakroom. It was becoming more and more difficult to sort out the coats. The women were dancing to the sound of the Douanier's violin, supported by an accordion and a harmonium. Heads were whirling, dawn was breaking, the bottles were empty and some of the guests had already slipped away.

'Under such conditions, it was not easy to be sure how the celebrations finished.

'We did hear, however, that the Dane turned up for dinner two days later. Apparently he had been lost during the interval in the alley-ways.

'It was he who got the best dinner, for that day, at the agreed moment, the restaurant sent up the food for the banquet.'

Whether the details are exact or not, it is certain that the guest of honour thoroughly enjoyed himself. He was anxious to prove his gratitude to his new friends and set to work on a portrait of Apollinaire and Marie Laurencin. It demanded a great many sittings, generally preceded by little notes to remind the notoriously unpunctual poet of his engagement:

* Do you remember, Rousseau, the Aztec landscapes—
  The forests where mangoes and pineapples lay rotting
  The apes spilling all the blood of water-melons
  And the blond emperor they shot out there . . .
Raynal quotes the whole poem.

'Dear friend,

Don't forget to come to-morrow with your charming little wife, at about half-past one, as we decided. Don't forget to bring the flowers I want to use as models for the pinks in the picture. If you see Picasso and the other gentlemen, please give them my best wishes, including Madame, and thank you for your kind reception. . . .'

The portrait advanced slowly, since Rousseau was the most conscientious of painters and felt he owed it to his benefactors to produce an exact likeness. In order to achieve this, he would carefully measure each feature with a school compass, then reduce it to the required proportions. Marie Laurencin was too thin for his taste, so he painted over her body a long, pleated dress, designed to give her the bulk denied by nature. As he painted, he sang to his models to keep them in a good humour. The portrait was finished at last, entitled 'The Muse Inspiring the Poet' and exhibited at the *Salon des Indépendants* in 1909. The critics made fun of it, cruelly in several cases, but Rousseau remained serene and convinced of its beauty. As for Apollinaire, at least one of his friends has testified that he considered it most unflattering and was only prevented by the pleading of Marie Laurencin from relegating it to the cellar. Perhaps this is why he did so little to defend his protégé at the time. Or perhaps he was too absorbed with Cubism and the evolution of his own affairs, literary and sentimental. Rousseau died the following year and it was not till 1914, when he once more had a review of his own, that Apollinaire publicly proclaimed his faith in the genius of the Douanier and even sacrificed vanity to friendship by insisting that the portrait was exactly like him.

'Few artists have been more laughed at during their lives,' he wrote then, 'and few men have faced with more serenity such mockery and scurrilous attacks as he met with. This courteous old man always preserved the same tranquil temper and his happy nature enabled him to see in these very mockeries the interest that even the most ill-disposed were obliged to take in his work. This serenity, of course, was a form of pride. The Douanier was conscious of his own strength. Once or twice, he let fall the opinion that he was the greatest painter of his times.

And perhaps, on several points, he was not far wrong. Although he had no artistic training in his youth, it seems that later, when he wanted to paint, he studied the masters with passionate interest and was almost alone among modern painters in understanding their secrets. . . .

'Douanier was absolutely sincere in his painting, and that is rare to-day. There is no trace of mannerism, procedure or system in his paintings. This accounts for the variety of his work. He was as sure of his imagination as of his skill. The gracefulness and richness of his decorative compositions result from this certainty. . . .

'Rousseau was an incomparable portrait painter. I twice had the honour of being painted by him in his sunny little studio in the rue Perrel. I have often seen him at work and I know what care he gave to every detail, what talent he had for preserving the primitive and definitive conception of each picture right up to the moment when it was finished, and I know also that he left nothing to chance. . . .'

Rousseau died alone, abandoned by his capricious fiancée, in the middle of the summer holidays, when all his friends were away from Paris. When they returned, they did what they could for him and Apollinaire wrote the epitaph that was engraved on his tombstone by the sculptor Brancusi:

Gentil Rousseau tu nous entends
Nous te saluons
Delaunay sa femme Monsieur Quéval et moi
Laisse passer nos bagages en franchise à la porte du ciel
Nous t'apporterons des pinceaux des couleurs des toiles
Afin que tes loisirs sacrés dans la lumière réelle
Tu les consacres à peindre comme tu tiras mon portrait
La face des étoiles.*

* Dear Rousseau, can you hear us
  We greet you
  Delaunay, his wife, Monsieur Quéval and myself
  Let our luggage pass through the doors of heaven without paying duty
  We will bring you brushes, paints, canvases,
  So that during your sacred leisure in the true light
    You may paint
  The face of the stars, just as you painted my portrait.

VIII

'A coming young man'

By this time, Apollinaire had established his reputation as an art critic, but as a poet he was known only to a restricted élite. *L'Enchanteur Pourrissant* was published in a limited edition in 1909, enriched with a curious poem entitled *Onirocritique,* which the Surrealists have since claimed as a pre-surrealist work. However, it did little to enlarge the inner circle, composed chiefly of brother poets, to whom he was known. His work, moreover, had appeared almost exclusively in little reviews published by his friends. Even *Vers et Prose* had not yet attained a really wide public. The only 'intellectual' review that could really bring fame to a young writer at that period was the old-established *Mercure de France,* directed by Alfred Vallette and his wife, the novelist 'Rachilde'. Apollinaire was in touch with it as a protégé of Marcel Schwob and Remy de Gourmont but had never been invited to contribute. The Vallettes had an assistant, a strange, solitary, bad-tempered man named Paul Léautaud, who lived alone in a neglected villa in the suburbs among a tribe of undomesticated cats. He was thirty-five at this time, poor and eccentric and of little consequence outside the immediate circle of the *Mercure,* and no one guessed that he was keeping the brilliant, cruel diary, with its terrible portraits of his contemporaries, that was to bring him fame many years later. A bitter man, a cynic incapable of love except for dogs, cats and other animals, he had little in common with Apollinaire, who was full of love for things, places and people, and whose irony, though it was a key part of his nature, was quite untouched by cynicism. Moreover, he was engaged at the time in compiling a new edition of his vast anthology of modern French poetry, and made no secret of the fact that he had little taste for Mallarmé in particular and poetic obscurity in general. It did not seem likely at first sight that he would be the man to introduce Apollinaire first to the *Mercure* and then to the world of publishers.

The two men met for the first time at one of the famous 'Tuesdays' of the *Mercure*, when Alfred Vallette and Rachilde entertained the world of letters. Léautaud has recounted their meeting: 'The first time I attended one of these Tuesdays when Apollinaire was also present, he planted himself in front of me, standing sideways. He held a finger to his chin and said, "Look, I have exactly the same profile as Julius Caesar!" One must admit it was a curious way to make acquaintance.'

Léautaud was always delighted by bizarre behaviour, so this curious method of introducing himself served Apollinaire well. The two men began to talk and were soon enthralled by each other's conversation. After a time, Léautaud enquired why his new friend had never contributed to the *Mercure*. Apollinaire replied that he had sent a manuscript months earlier and had never even received an acknowledgement. Léautaud took him to his office, turned out his drawers on the spot and soon discovered a wad of papers. It was the manuscript of *La Chanson du Mal-Aimé*. 'When I read *La Chanson du Mal-Aimé*—which was not the text published in his volume, since he spoilt it afterwards—for the first time, I was transported', Léautaud recalled later. 'In this poem there is something bohemian, a strangeness . . . realism . . . and a great deal of ambiguity. . . . It was something new. . . . It held mystery, something strange and disquieting. . . .'[1]

The poem appeared the following month, with a new verse, added as prefix, in homage to a new love:

> Et je chantais cette romance
> En 1903 sans savoir
> Que mon amour à la semblance
> Du beau Phénix s'il meurt un soir
> Le matin voit sa renaissance.*

It was the consecration every young writer hoped for and Apollinaire's feet were at last on the road to success. The *Chanson* was noticed and admired, especially by Elimir Bourges, who had a great influence at that time in literary circles. Bourges shared the

---

* And I chanted this ballad in 1903, never guessing that my love, like the fine Phoenix, would die in the evening, only to resuscitate next morning.

9

younger man's taste for things bizarre, erudite and ambiguous. It was he who persuaded the publisher Stock to accept a collection of short stories which was published under the title *L'Hérésiarque et Cie*. It contained the tales written in Germany—*Le Passant de Prague, La Rose de Hildesheim,* and that which gave the volume its title—which had been published by the Revue Blanche and had marked his début as a writer and the others had been written gradually during the intervening ten years. Apollinaire set great store by them and later, when he was in love with Madeleine Pagès during the war, wrote to her that the only two of his works in which he was really interested were *Alcools* and *L'Hérésiarque et Cie*.

> 'I am very fond of it,' he wrote then, 'and am weak enough to think that I have great talent as a story-teller. . . I like best *Simon-Mage,* which is difficult for most readers. I believe it is the first time anyone has written in a way that is so precise and even scientific, yet at the same time so supernatural, about the angels, which play their true role in this story—the role for which they were invented. You will also notice that *L'Hérésiarque* dates from before the religious struggles in France and before the heretical period which followed immediately after them. . . .'

Apollinaire as a story-teller had remained essentially baroque, and the later stories, like *Simon-Mage* or those recounting the adventures of the 'Baron d'Ormesan' show the same eccentric erudition, the same mingling of the macabre and the comic, the same preoccupation with the supernatural, that had distinguished the fantasies of the twenty-year-old Guillaume de Kostrowitsky. He was probably right in his own estimation of the book as one of his two masterpieces. His talent—in its creative aspect, at least, was essentially ironical and since irony, unlike satire, depends for its effect on terseness, the short story is its ideal vehicle. *L'Hérésiarque* places him among the greatest of French short story writers, but when he tried to exploit that success by writing a novel, the result was weak to say the least of it.[2]

With the appearance of *L'Hérésiarque et Cie* in 1910, Apollinaire suddenly ceased to be merely a young man of promise and entered the ranks of established writers. The book, in fact, came near to winning the *Prix Goncourt*, at a time when the award carried more prestige, though less material rewards, than it does to-day. The other candidates for the prize that year were Colette, Marguerite Audoux (whose touching story of *Marie-Claire* was one of the first authentically 'populist' novels), Louis Pergaud and several lesser-known writers. Finally Pergaud's *De Goupil à Margot* carried the day, but the mere fact that Apollinaire had obtained several votes earned him a wider reputation than he had known before.

He was thirty years old now—an age at which men pause and take stock of their lives. From this point at which he had arrived, it was perhaps not unpleasant to gaze back at the 'ill-spent' days of his youth, which he seemed to have left so definitely behind him. The sordid poverty, the unemployment or heterogeneous jobs at which he had scraped a bare living, the stormy love-affairs, the bohemian life in Montmartre which looked more romantic in retrospect that it had ever been in reality—all that lay in the past.

His feet seemed to be planted firmly on the road to success and he must have taken stock of the situation with a certain satisfaction.

The days of poverty were over. He was not rich, but he was earning enough money to live in reasonable comfort, and earning it in a way he enjoyed. His articles on the Cubist painters had won him a solid reputation as a critic and André Salmon often ceded to him his own art column in *L'Intransigeant,* which carried reasonable pay and the possibility of reaching a wide audience; he was contributing to the most influential literary reviews in Paris; the Goncourt vote had resulted in good sales for *L'Hérésiarque* and the *Mercure* was prepared to publish a volume of collected verse. His name provoked curiosity and interest, if not among the general public, at least in that section of it which was interested in art and literature. His opinions carried weight. He was a personality. His influence, which had been occult until then, was beginning to be recognised.

His personal life, too, was happier than it had ever been. He seemed to be creating for himself at last the stability of which, even at the most bohemian periods of his existence, he had always dreamed.

> Je souhaite dans ma maison
> Une femme ayant sa raison
> Un chat passant parmi les livres,

Des amis en toute saison,
Sans lesquels je ne peux pas vivre.*

he wrote at about this time. It was a reasonable dream, the dream of a man at home in the world, well-balanced and at peace with himself.

The friends were there, so were the woman, the books and even the cat, whose name was Pipe. Some of the friends were old and many new; some were trustworthy and others he would have done better to avoid. Apollinaire held a weekly 'at home', in the fashion of the day, and received them each Thursday in his apartment in the rue Gros, among the Cubist paintings, the African masks, the library of rare and curious books and the portrait of Ubu, sculpted by Jarry out of a chestnut, which hung from a nail in the wall and acted, he believed, as a talisman. Picasso and Salmon often visited him there, though they complained that he was less available nowadays ('Guillaume has disappeared since his book was published by Stock and wades in far-off orgies', wrote Salmon—always picturesque rather than exact—to a friend). Mollet continued to play his role of erratic secretary. René Dalize would arrive from distant ports, elegant in his naval uniform, with an opium pipe negligently protruding from his pocket. Louis de Gonzague Frick, who had been in a slightly higher class at the *Collège Saint-Charles*, also remained a faithful friend. He added a note of severe elegance to these carefree reunions, arriving dressed in his invariable tail-coat, top-hat and monocle, speaking in a voice of studied affectation and sprinkling his conversation, even on the most ordinary subjects, with Greek and Latin words, and rare expressions. His slightest actions were ceremonious. It was at this period that he would present himself each morning at Apollinaire's door, top-hatted and monocled, carrying the apple which the poet was supposed to eat for his breakfast for the sake of his health. The fruit was presented with a deep bow and a carefully-turned phrase referring to its medicinal virtues, or to the state of the weather. Occasionally, the apple would be accompanied by a poem, composed during the night. Then, with another bow, he would silently and discreetly retire.

* I desire in my house
A woman of sound mind
A cat strolling among the books,
At all seasons those friends,
Without whom I cannot live. (*Le Bestiaire*)

Sometimes there was André Billy—the enthralled disciple who had discovered through Apollinaire and Salmon a new conception of poetry. They had lost sight of him since the days of the rue Saint-Jacques and the *Festin d'Esope*, and in the interval he had developed great ambitions and become a literary critic, whose judgements already carried weight. 'A twentieth-century Rastignac', Paul Léautaud wrote acidly in his diary. Certainly his tendency to blind admiration had disappeared with extreme youth and nowadays he was often critical of the direction Apollinaire's work was taking. He nevertheless became one of his closest friends and from that time on did all he could to bring him to the attention of the public.

Naturally, there were new friends, for Apollinaire accumulated them rather like a snowball gathering as it rolls. Among them were two couples who were to play an important part in his life and prove themselves, in a time of crisis, far more faithful than some of his oldest companions. One of them was formed by Robert Delaunay and his Russian wife, Sonia. Delaunay was still in his early twenties but he was already beginning to reveal himself as one of the most remarkable theorists of contemporary art, as well as a highly gifted painter. Like Apollinaire he believed that the history of painting had reached a decisive point and that 'throughout the whole world we find a complete transformation in man's vision, and above all, in his methods of representation'. On the Thursdays when the Delaunays came to the rue Gros, the conversation was sure to turn sooner or later to the burning question: What about the Eiffel Tower? It was a problem that obsessed Delaunay at this time and that soon became almost as important for Apollinaire and one or two others. How could it be painted? Treated realistically, its vast proportions seemed to dwindle; it became mediocre, unimportant. When he applied to it the old laws of Italian perspective, it appeared on the canvas narrow, elongated, almost fragile. Its personality seemed to change according to the angle from which it was viewed. From a distance it dominated Paris, stiff and perpendicular; as one came nearer, it seemed to lean gracefully towards one. When one stood on the first platform and looked upwards, it seemed to twist and spiral up into the sky; and seen from the very top, it squatted cumbersomely down over the four great supports that spread beneath it. Nor could it be isolated from its surroundings. It was part of Paris, and without Paris it was no longer really itself. The first aeroplanes—objects of endless curiosity to Parisians—would often circle around it, and they too were part of the Tower, as were the lovers who seemed to be so irresistibly attracted to its summit, and the crowds of tourists who gaped around its base.

How could one possibly translate such multiplicity on a single canvas? The question was discussed endlessly in the rue Gros, or in Delaunay's own studio where the Tower mocked them from innumerable canvases—truncated, dizzily inclined, viewed from above, viewed from below, surrounded by houses, splendidly alone—and never truly itself. It was a problem that had been absorbing Apollinaire for a long time, although in a different form. *Villes de France et d'Europe et du monde—Venez toutes couler dans ma gorge profonde.* . . . How to compress the universe into a single poem, the Eiffel Tower (multiple as the universe) on to a single canvas? Delaunay's experiments fascinated him and at the same time he found them rather disquieting. Cubism seemed to be getting out of hand. The plastic problems Picasso and Braque had begun to solve three years earlier were revealing themselves as more and more complicated. For the moment Apollinaire, who was anxious to please everyone, contented himself with watching, curiously and cautiously, to see what would come of these experiments and whether the Tower would ever yield up its secrets.

The second couple with whom he was at once on terms of intimate friendship was formed by Serge Jastrebzoff, who called himself Edouard Férat, and his sister, Baroness Hélène d'Oettingen. They were Russian aristocrats who had come to Paris with Diaghilev. Férat designed costumes and scenery for the Russian ballet that had been a revelation to Paris a couple of years earlier and had adopted this new name for the sake of simplicity. They were brilliant and unpredictable and brought to these gatherings the prestige of beauty and wealth. They were as generous with their friendship as with their money and, like Apollinaire himself, always ready to stay up all night. Strangely enough, though, the ballet provoked little interest in this circle. Cubism was entering into its second phase—the phase of purity and austerity—with Picasso on one hand and Delaunay on the other tending more and more towards abstraction. The feast of colours and the sensuous music that Diaghilev had imported from a semi-oriental land were a little out of key, and the idea that any of the Cubist painters might design a stage décor seemed almost blasphemous. The two Jastrebzoff's themselves were soon at the heart of the Cubist movement, but it was a long time before they could succeed in drawing any of their new friends into contact with Diaghilev. Their role was rather to be that of patrons—and the species was already becoming rare. It was through them, through the roubles that flowed to Paris from the great estate near Moscow, and through their steady confidence in him, that Apollinaire was to come near to fulfilling his ambition of imposing his ideas on a circle much wider than that of his personal friends.

Max Jacob was always a rather disturbing element in the rue Gros. No one quite knew what to make of him or how to place him. He was the only one of the original band of friends who still lived in the *Bateau Lavoir,* and no one, except perhaps Picasso, knew the whole truth about this ambiguous existence. Max found a peculiar delectation in humility and would never admit that he was a poet of any importance. Yet he already had a sort of celebrity—a restricted celebrity, but it was enough to rouse Apollinaire to one of the rather naive and childish fits of jealousy that the successes of his friends sometimes provoked in him. 'Modern poetry skips all explanation', Max would say, and his poems were at once simple and complicated, as if they were a direct reflection of his sardonic, vacillating personality. Quite a number of very young writers were fascinated by this mingling of irony and lyricism, baroque clowning and equally baroque mysticism. They already considered themselves as his disciples, but it was not easy to be the disciple of a man who carried the art of paradox to such bewildering lengths. Max welcomed them, just as he welcomed the fine ladies who found a new thrill in rolling up the steep streets of ill-famed Montmartre to have their horoscopes drawn up in the mouldering studio of the rue Ravignan; and just as he welcomed some of the least recommendable citizens of his quarter. In the same nonchalant way he was dispersing his talents in novels, essays, poetry, painting, music, conversation, and excelling in all of them.

But it was not to discuss his social success, nor the rather equivocal *Saint-Matorel,* on the recital of whose 'mystical and burlesque adventures' he was sporadically engaged, that he would make the long journey from Montmartre. At this period he was generally in a state of exaltation after some new and invariably picturesque religious experience. Grace had descended on him, inexorable as a thunderbolt, in September 1909, when he had been vouchsafed a vision of Christ, radiating from the wall of his room. We have the story in his own words:

'I had returned from the *Bibliothèque Nationale,* I was hunting for my slippers and when I lifted my head, there was someone on the wall. There was someone! There was someone on the crimson wallpaper. My chair fell to the ground, a flash of lightning had left me naked. Oh, immortal moment! Oh, truth! Truth, tears of truth! Joy of truth! Unforgettable truth! The heavenly body was there on the wall of my poor room. Why, oh Lord? Oh, forgive me! He was there in a landscape I had painted myself, but it was He! What beauty, elegance and gentleness! His shoulders, his movements! He wore a robe of yellow silk, with blue embroidery. . . .'

Max had hurried to a priest and asked for baptism, but there was something about him—his way of talking, his whole manner of being—that prevented people from taking him seriously. The priest had laughed at him and though the fathers of Notre-Dame de Sion, specialists in the conversion of Jews, were more comprehensive, they were in no hurry to receive him. So Max, in despair, prayed in all the churches of Paris (generally in a loud, imploring voice, to the scandal of the congregation), read the Gospels and occasionally had visions which threw him on his knees in cinemas and other unsuitable places.

Most of his friends were inclined to ascribe these visions to Max's addiction to ether.* Occultism was fashionable in intellectual circles and a good many members of the group found that a whiff of opium or hashish helped them to get in touch with

* None of his friends at this epoch took Max Jacob's religious experiences very seriously. 'Our Christian poet', Apollinaire sometimes called him, ironically. It was his own fault, no doubt. On the surface his religion was composed of exhibition, exaggeration, drama and spectacular lapses. Even in later life, when he had retired to Saint-Benôit-sur-Loire and lived in semi-monastic retreat, the comic element never quite disappeared from his peculiar brand of piety. It was this incorrigible clowning that prevented even his intimates from understanding how deep was his sincerity. His death

the Unknown. Apollinaire himself had learned both from Dalize
and Max Jacob that 'the black blood of poppies' could enlarge
deliciously the frontiers of experience. He enjoyed the cosy con-
viviality of long, dreamy evenings when time ceased to exist, but
he never became an addict and dropped the habit as easily as he
acquired it.

Fortune-tellers, sorcerers, practicians of the black arts, thrived
in Paris at the time and some of them, like the Sar Péladan
and Stanislas de Guita, had one foot in the world of literature and
the other in that of occultism. Apollinaire's circle, with its strong
taste for everything bizarre, was in touch with many of these
sorcerers and Apollinaire has named some of them in the poem
entitled *Sur les Prophéties*. Madame Salamour who 'learned to read
the cards in the South Sea Islands' and had been present at a
cannibal feast which she would describe to those who had gained
her confidence; a cartomancian named Marguerite; a certain
Madame Deroy, whose predictions were infallible; a diviner who
read the future in men's shadows. Unnamed—perhaps because

---

revealed a Max Jacob without the mask he had worn all his life. He had been
deported by the Germans in 1943 to the Jewish camp in Drancy, where it
had never even occurred to him to explain who he was or to claim any special
treatment. He had been suffering from bronchial pneumonia at the time of
his arrest and conditions in the camp soon brought him to a critical state. He
was removed to the infirmary, where he died. The doctor who treated him
there has given a singularly moving recital of his death: 'Max Jacob showed
an admirable humility and resignation. He desired to die; his time had come.
He said: "I am with God." He hardly spoke; he asked for nothing; he did
not suffer. He prayed. To me he expressed only one desire: to receive a
Catholic burial. With what tact, what discretion, he expressed this plea, so as
not to hurt the feelings of us Jews. He murmured: "You see, I have given my
life to this passion." We promised and we managed to keep the promise. It
was all over within twenty-four hours; he faded away, literally, with an
extraordinary modesty and submission. Not the least revolt, or reproach and
no death agony. He was already far beyond all struggles. He seemed happy.
His friends tried in vain to encourage him to live, to give him hope that he
would be freed. He replied gently: "I am with God." The Germans, knowing
he was dying, signed an order for his liberation at that moment. But Max no
longer awaited his freedom from them, but from Him who looses all terrestrial
chains. At what hour did he die? In the morning, just when the lamps go out.
It was much greater than resignation. It was an absolute adherence to
departure, and with unimaginable simplicity and grandeur.' (Reported by
Madame Janette Deletang-Tardif in *Poésie*, no. 44.)

nearly everyone was a little afraid of him—was Joséphin Péladan, generally known as the 'Sar' Péladan, animator of the Rosicrucians in France, Cabbalist, Catholic and redoubtable magician. He had been momentarily interested in Cubism; Apollinaire as well as Picasso and Max Jacob had frequented him in their Montmartre days and had perhaps heard him utter the terrible menace that impressed even the most sceptical: 'I have only to recite a certain formula and the ground would open beneath you and swallow you up. . . .'

The painters and writers who frequented these professionals often practised a little amateur magic of their own. Never since the days of Victor Hugo can men of letters have spent so much time telling each other's fortunes. The Norwegian painter, Dierck, was skilful with the divining rod; Fernand Fleuret could read the cards and interpret tea leaves and coffee grounds left in cups; Apollinaire rather fancied himself as a magician, but had to admit that his predictions were seldom fulfilled. Max Jacob, on the other hand, had recently taken up chiromancy and was uncannily successful at it. His conscience tormented him terribly since his conversion, and it was not always easy to persuade him to display his talent, but when he did so, the results were sometimes disquieting.

Louise Faure-Favier, who was a colleague on the *Mercure* and had become a close friend of Apollinaire and Marie Laurencin, recalls one of these séances . . . Max bending his bald head, peering through his pince-nez at one hand after another, prophesying: to René Dalize, that he would die before he could reveal his talents; to Marie, that she would be unhappy in love and live her married life in a foreign country (an almost impossible idea for one who loved only France and, in France, only Paris); to Louise Faure-Favier, that she would rise to great heights and preside over a dinner at which there would be cabinet ministers among the guests; to Apollinaire, a fame he would not live to enjoy. . . . Here the séance was interrupted since Apollinaire, who was both touchy and superstitious, flew into a rage, slapped poor Max's face and rushed out of the room, slamming the door. Nobody else took it seriously, but every word of the predictions came true.*

* René Dalize was killed in the 1914–18 war; Marie Laurencin's marriage exiled her to Spain; Louise Faure-Favier became a journalist specialising in aviation and was the first woman to fly in the new high-flying aeroplanes.

Broken mirror spilt salt or fallen bread
May these faceless gods spare me always
Actually I do not believe but I watch and listen
    And note
That I read quite well in the lines of the hand
For I do not believe but I watch and whenever
    possible I listen . . .

wrote Apollinaire in *Prophéties*. The 'actually I do not believe' has
a note of defiance. He had never forgotten his mother's superstitious practices, and his memories of the Roman sorcerers were
tinged with a sort of awe as well as with humour. If he was
sporadically obsessed with religion, it was above all with certain
ritual practices that appealed to his imagination because they
could be related to magical operations, and with minor personages
associated with magic—Simon the Magician, Saint Apollonius of
Thyanus, and so on. For him, religion and superstition were
inextricably mingled. For instance, on a visit to Serge Férat, he
had admired a charming little ikon on the wall. Férat—always
generous and a *grand seigneur* on the Russian scale—immediately
offered it to him, but Apollinaire refused on the ground that the
gift of a religious object brings bad luck. A few days later, the
ikon had disappeared and when Hélène d'Oettingen next visited
Apollinaire's rooms, she found it hanging on the wall. 'A thing
like that can only be stolen', Apollinaire whispered to her, and
broke into the deep, trilling laugh, half stifled behind his plump
and shapely hand, that remains in the memory of all who knew
him.

Not only he, but the whole group of friends, must have been
singularly robust, both physically and psychologically, for they
seem to have thrived on a diet of drugs and amateur magic that
few people would find wholesome.* However, although Apollinaire's rising reputation led him to frequent a vast circle of
writers, there existed among them what might be called an opposition group, that thoroughly disapproved of all these goings-on.
Among them was a clan of young men who called themselves,
collectively, *L'Abbaye* and represented exactly opposite tendencies.

* Those of Apollinaire's friends who survived the Great War have lived,
with a few exceptions, to a singularly robust and vivacious old age. Only
poor Fernand Fleuret succumbed to an abuse of these peculiar pleasures.

Their names were Jules Romains, Georges Duhamel, Charles Vildrac. They considered themselves the guardians of the French tradition of Cartesian clarity and logic. They had determined, with the assurance of the very young, to put an end to 'hermetic literature'. Jules Romains (who was creating at the time the poetic movement he baptised *Unanimisme*) has recalled their common ambition of creating 'the sort of poetry that would speak once more directly to men as it used to do'. First of all, he decided, such poetry must touch the average reader by using a language he could understand without difficulty. Then it must speak of the things which interested him, to which he could respond, the things within his own experience. . . .'

There were, in fact, plenty of points in common between the ex-contributors to the *Festin d'Esope* and these aggressive new-comers. All desired to see the décor of their lives, as men of the twentieth century, accepted as the legitimate matter of poetry. All of them felt that a certain sort of Symbolism belonged to the past. So it was quite natural that Louis de Gonzague Frick, who knew the members of *L'Abbaye* well, should have declared to them solemnly one day: 'It is of the greatest importance that you should meet Guillaume Apollinaire.'

So the contact had been made, first with Apollinaire, then with Max Jacob. They were all young and ready to enjoy themselves in any company provided it was gay and amusing; Apollinaire and Max were two of the wittiest men in Paris; Apollinaire at least never disagreed openly with anyone. There was a superficial friendship, but the friction soon began to be felt, especially with Duhamel, who detested anything that smelt of Symbolism, 'finicky artistry' and words that did not mean exactly what they said. As for Apollinaire, he refused to accept doctrines that could only limit the possibilities of art and confine it within the boundaries of what, to the average man, is immediately comprehensible. He had always hated, too, the idea of 'schools' in art and had always fought against the idea that there existed a Cubist School rather than a number of people, working each in his own way but seeing the world in roughly the same perspective. The exclusiveness of the young 'Unanimists' annoyed him and when Jules Romains's drama *L'Armée dans la Ville* appeared, he gave it what was perhaps the only really hostile review he wrote in his

life. It was not forgotten and Duhamel, at least, revenged himself
when his chance arose.

'Apollinaire's death', wrote Romains long afterwards, 'only
accentuated the division between us. In spite of the horrible
disillusionment of the war we never renounced the idea of constructing for modern man—for the man of the street, the man of
the masses and the great cities—a spiritual home that would be
both harmonious and habitable. We refused to despair of the
twentieth century, which had been born just as we awoke to the
life of the intellect. But on the other side, the Symbolist seces-
sion was recommencing. Oh, it had new characteristics! It was
armed with new grievances and also with a new magic. . . .
The offensive of anti-reason, the offensive of blind forces . . .
was being prepared along the whole front of our ancient
civilisation.'

Under the façade of comradeship, the two tendencies that had
divided French art and literature since the turn of the century were
preparing to measure their forces. It was not, of course, really a
question of literary styles, but of two fundamentally hostile
conceptions of what modern man is, and what he wants. One of
them accepted the 'average man' as he is, glorified him in his
'average' state and offered him the spiritual nourishment he was
ready to absorb; the other proposed to open up the world of
suggestion and mystery and invite into it anyone who was ready
to make the effort, to accept a dialogue with the poet and to
complete in his own, personal way the murmured words that
reached his ear.

Apollinaire refused to admit that aesthetic differences could
affect personal relationships, or to realise that an aesthetic position
is always of an organic nature and springs from the deepest
roots of individual temperament. 'Friends at all seasons' and
liberty to work as he pleased were all he asked. If he met adversaries, he counted on his personal charm to disarm them. For the
time being, he succeeded in doing so. All sorts of natures, all
sorts of tendencies, were grouping around him. And that in itself
was enough to make him happy.

The 'woman of sound mind', who completed the idyllic picture
he had composed for himself, was, of course, Marie Laurencin.

She presided over his weekly 'at homes' and acted in general as mistress of his house, though he would never trust her with the cooking. When friends stayed to dinner, he would disappear into the kitchen, concocting strange dishes from recipes of many lands, which were sometimes a success—and sometimes not. Meanwhile, Marie would make conversation, or sing, or rush back and forth to search for missing ingredients. Their friends all expected that she and Apollinaire would marry. In spite of the quarrels, the scenes of jealousy and the clashes that arose from Apollinaire's despotism and Marie's independent nature, they seemed to need each other and, in many ways, suited each other perfectly. Apollinaire later denied that he ever thought of marrying her, but it seems that the matter was often discussed and had even reached the stage of family interferences.

Madame Laurencin had recovered from her first mistrust of Guillaume and his friends and would probably have accepted the match, but Madame de Kostrowitsky remained resolutely and superbly hostile. She could never forget that she was a Polish aristocrat and she expected her sons to make brilliant matches with rich and well-born young ladies. It never seemed to occur to her that anything in their antecedents might cause these hypothetical heiresses, or at least their parents, to hesitate. Mademoiselle Laurencin was not at all the sort of daughter-in-law she had imagined, even for her elder son, whom she held in low esteem and expected to come to a bad end. Her opinion still counted for Guillaume and he probably preferred to put off his decision as long as possible rather than come into open conflict with her.

Yet marriage would have been the normal outcome of Apollinaire's psychological development at this point. It would have come as a sort of culmination of a mental equilibrium attained after a long struggle and in face of great difficulties. He had always been skilful in hiding the traces of wounds received during the years at the Collège Stanislas and during the rest of his chaotic adolescence, but they had always been present and accounted for much that passed for eccentricity and vanity. Now they were healing at last. For the first time in his life, he could feel himself to be integrated—no longer a foreigner, the bastard son of unavowable parents, or a penniless stranger in a hostile city. Tradition meant a great deal to him, as it so often does to rootless people and now at last he could see himself as part of the French literary tradition, linked to the past and actively helping to create the future. He even confided to some of his friends the curious ambition of entering, at a more mature age, the solemn *Académie française*. They found the idea irresistibly funny and Picasso amused himself by sketching an Apollinaire-Academician, wearing the triangular hat, with the academic sword at his side. Yet the fact remained that he was already part of Paris, that everyone who was of any consequence in its intellectual avant-garde knew him, and everyone who hoped to become of consequence wanted to know him; that he had friends in every camp and that his advice and patronage was sought by anyone wanting to launch anything new in art or literature. Even the friends who mocked his ambitions would have admitted that he was well on his way to becoming an official figure. It would be enough to continue as he was doing, to publish a book every two or three years, to contribute to leading journals, to show respect for his elders and at the same time to impress his juniors by his audacity . . . it was the traditional path to the Academy and his feet appeared to be firmly set on it.

Or so it seemed during the full, happy year that followed the publication of *L'Hérésiarque*. No one could have suspected that Fate held a trick in store—the nastiest she could play—that was to throw him back into all the doubts and insecurity of his adolescence.

IX

The Turning Point

Tu es à Paris chez le juge d'instruction
Comme un criminel on te met en état d'arrestation.*

Marcel Schwob once said that, 'bad characters are much more interesting than honest men, since they are original. Virtue is the same everywhere; only vices leave their mark on the personality.' Apollinaire agreed with him. He had always chosen his friends for their originality rather than their reliability and, like most of 'Picasso's gang', had found profit and enjoyment in the underworld of Montmartre. By 1911, he was beginning to settle down into a relatively bourgeois way of life, but the taste for strange companions remained.

Among these, he specially enjoyed the company of a young Belgian named Géry Pieret, whom he had first met on the staff of that semi-fraudulent 'Shareholders' Guide' where he had made his debut in journalism. Pieret was slick and amusing—full of inventions and wonderful stories. His lack of scruples only made him more entertaining in Apollinaire's eyes, since it contrasted with his own innately conformist morality. Pieret's intrusions into his life were sporadic but always welcome since he provided useful literary material and was indeed the original of the 'Baron d'Ormesan' of *L'Hérésiarque,* inventor of a new art: '*Amphonia* . . . founded on Aristotle's peripateticism.' In plainer words, he acted from time to time as guide to tourists who listened, open-mouthed and wide-eyed, as he led them through Paris inventing, in a variety of languages, the names and histories of sites and monuments. Among other activities he counted painting, poetry and a little light-hearted swindling and Apollinaire sometimes employed

* Apollinaire: *Zone.*

132

Guillaume Apollinaire and his Friends by Marie Laurencin

Robert and Sonia Delaunay

him as secretary to deal with correspondence that had got hopelessly out of hand.

It was Pieret who involved him in what the Press christened 'The Affair of the Statuettes', but the consequences were due to plain bad luck. Pieret was rather a connoisseur of antiquities and spent a good deal of time at the Louvre. He had noticed how poorly the place was guarded and one day, partly as a protest and partly because they had taken his fancy, he picked up two Phoenician statuettes, tucked them into his overcoat, engaged the guardian in conversation for a few minutes, without attracting any attention to his unusual bulk, and left the museum. Then he hurried round to Neuilly to show his loot to Apollinaire. A few years earlier, the joke would probably have seemed as good to his friend as it did to himself, but Apollinaire had decided to become respectable and exploded into one of his famous outbursts of rage. However, the statuettes remained temporarily in his rooms and Pieret, rather crestfallen at his reception, took the train for Marseilles the same evening.

Now it happened, unfortunately for all concerned, that a few days later—on August 22, 1911, to be exact—the famous *Mona Lisa* was stolen from the Louvre. The loss roused a tremendous clamour in the Press and there was a nation-wide outcry against the administration of the museum. Apollinaire realised at once how dangerous the presence of the statuettes in his rooms might become for him, and how easily they might be connected with the missing picture. Somehow he had to get rid of them, but they were not the sort of objects that are easy to dispose of.

In this moment of crisis, he seems to have lost his head completely. At first he had thought of throwing the two little figures in the Seine, then Picasso, consulted in secret, suggested a plan that seemed to him amusing. The statuettes would be slipped into the front window of the newspaper *Paris-Journal*, in order to prove how easy it was to steal from the Louvre. Unfortunately, the proof had already been made and an enterprising journalist who had made an inventory of its whole contents, chose that moment to reveal that one hundred and twenty-three pictures and objects were missing. The police took the appearance of the statuettes among the news photographs of *Paris-Journal* less as a joke than a clue. They had little difficulty in tracing them back to Apollinaire

10

and on September 7th, he was arrested for receiving and for probable complicity in the theft of the *Mona Lisa*.

The series of poems entitled *A la Santé** and a few posthumously published verses, tell the whole story of Apollinaire's experience of prison life. They are very simple and direct. There is no longer any trace of the man-of-letters, but only a bewildered frightened prisoner telling of his misery—just as Villon and Verlaine had told of theirs, when vice or imprudence had led them into the same plight. . . .

There were the horribly humiliating rites of arrival . . .

> Avant d'entrer dans ma cellule
> Il a fallu me mettre nu
> Et quelle voix sinistre ulule
> Guillaume qu'es-tu devenu. . . .†

Then there was the feeling of loss of identity on becoming a number instead of a name; the impression that he was a link in a chain formed by the criminals who had inhabited his cell through the years and had left their names and qualities engraved on its walls and furniture. One of them—a certain Dédé of Ménilmontant —had scratched his name on the bedstead, just below the pillow, and added the comment, 'for murder', and each night this name seemed to accompany Dédé's successor as he fell into an exhausted sleep.

Then there were the interminable hours of the day that nothing could fill:

> Dans une fosse comme un ours
> Chaque matin je me promène
> Tournons tournons tournons toujours
> Le ciel est bleu comme une chaîne
> Dans une fosse comme un ours
> Chaque matin je me promène . . .‡

* *Alcools.*

† Before entering my cell
  They made me strip naked
  What sinister voice ululates
  Guillaume, what has happened to you? . . .

‡ In a pit like a bear
  I take my walk each morning
  Round & round & round for ever
  The sky is blue as a chain
  In a pit like a bear
  I take my walk each morning . . .

During those days when everything human seemed to have failed him, Apollinaire clung—like Villon and Verlaine before him—to the consolation of divine love and pity. The 'innocent little child' of Monaco, who had never been quite stifled by experience or acquired scepticism, suddenly appeared again, as if all that had happened during the intervening years had been wiped out:

> Que deviendrai-je ô Dieu qui connais ma douleur
> > Toi qui me l'a donnée
> Prends en pitié mes yeux sans larmes ma pâleur
> > Le bruit de ma chaise enchaînée
>
> Et tous ces pauvres cœurs battant dans la prison
> > L'Amour qui m'accompagne
> Prends en pitié surtout ma débile raison
> > Et le désespoir qui la gagne . . .*

Perhaps it all seems like an over-dramatisation of a situation which, after all, did not carry much serious risk. Apollinaire knew that there was no real evidence against him and that influential friends had intervened as soon as his arrest was known. His old schoolfellow, Ange Toussaint Luca and another capable lawyer applied at once for his provisional release and Pieret himself, after prudently passing the frontier, wrote to the examining magistrate to explain his own role in the affair and exculpate his friend. Six days later, he was free again and celebrating his release at a banquet organised by his friends. Typically, he arrived when the meal was almost over, having called in at *Paris-Journal* on the way to write a last-minute article on 'My Life in Prison'.

Apparently the whole thing was over, although it was to be more than a year before an official acquittal was obtained. It was certainly some time before even his closest friends understood how deeply he had been marked by this experience. Actually, it meant

---

* What will become of me, O God who knowest my misery
> Thou who hast sent it me
Take pity of my tearless eyes my pallor
> The noise of my chained chair

And all these poor hearts beating in prison
> The love that has followed me here
Take pity above all on my fragile reason
> And the despair that gains on it . . .

far more to him than it would have done to any of them. Most of them had been inclined to look on the whole affair as a joke, and when he appeared, stout and hilarious as ever, at the banquet, it looked as though he agreed with them. They had forgotten—or perhaps they had never known—how deeply he had been marked by the insecurity of his early life and few of them realised that the rather naive ambitions which they considered as a mild form of megalomania, were really symptoms of an almost neurotic desire for social integration. The shock and humiliation of his arrest had jolted him out of the hardly-won security in which he had never quite managed to believe. It had thrown him back among the outcasts, among those who have no family, no country of their own, and no rights in the country in which they live.

'My dear Toussaint,' he wrote to his boyhood friend in December, three months after his liberation, 'I did not answer you earlier because your letter got lost in the mess on my writing table, which I am tidying up now and which was the result of my move.

'So I hadn't got your address and now I have found it, I am writing to you at once. From now on I shall write to you regularly, in the hope that these epistolary relations between two such old friends as us, will do us both good.

'I still haven't recovered from my affair. I still await the solution with anxiety. *L'Œuvre* has attacked me, through Gouhier, as a foreigner and author of the anthologies of Aretino, Sade, etc. This terrifies me, though I hope I shall not be prosecuted for it. Don't speak of this letter to anyone. Indiscretions can be committed so quickly and with the best intentions.

'Try to find out how and in what conditions I can become naturalised. What would happen to me if I were expelled from France? These doubts make it impossible to find enough peace of mind to work. I ask only for peace and obscurity and I am the object of constant persecutions. . . .'

It was certainly the little suite of prison poems, which his friends had never seen, rather than the boisterous article in *Paris-Journal*, that revealed the truth. Apollinaire really felt at this period that a single stroke of bad luck had been enough to deprive him, vulnerable as he was by circumstances, of his name, his reputation, his freedom and his very clothes. Instead of being one of the intellectual centres of his adopted city, he suddenly discovered that he was only living there on sufferance.

In prison, Apollinaire had felt himself in rather a vague way to be doomed and ill-fated, but after his release it became gradually evident that he had real grounds for misgivings. He had, in fact, a great many enemies, who were all the more dangerous because he had never suspected their existence. He himself had probably never hated anyone in his life. He was tolerant and easy-going and much more inclined to pity than to blame. Never, for instance, had he imagined that a difference of opinion on the subject of art or poetry could rouse personal animosity. Others were not so generous and a good many people who disliked the artistic trends he had come to represent, seized this opportunity to launch personal attacks which, by discrediting the man, might discredit at the same time the 'foreign' intrusion into French art and letters.

The nationalist, xenophobic spirit that had flared up in France at the time of the Dreyfus case had never really died down and was at one of its periodic peaks of aggressiveness at this moment. There were anti-semitic manifestations, anti-republican demonstrations, meetings of protest against the 'internationalist spirit'. French writers have always enjoyed meddling with politics and a certain number of poets and novelists had made themselves the champions of the movement. Léon Daudet was their chief, bringing with him the prestige of his father's name and his own rather brutal and overwhelming personality. There was the poet and critic, Arthur Cravan, with his review *Maintenant,* in which he insulted everyone and slung the epithet 'Jew' at anyone who, displeased him. Why Cravan, who was an adventurer of Irish origin and claimed to be the son of Oscar Wilde, should have made himself the champion of French nationalism, is not easy to understand. Nor did anyone trouble to understand. Nationalism was in the fashion, so was Ubuism, and Cravan modelled himself on Jarry, gave eccentric lectures and had an immense success. These were the extremists, but there were many writers and painters who, without going as far in their hatred of *métèques* as Daudet and his disciples, shared most of their ideas. Reviews like *Les Guêpes*— with which several of Apollinaire's personal friends, notably Romains and Duhamel, were connected—were spreading the nationalistic doctrines of Barrès and Charles Maurras and campaigning against internationalism in art and literature. An editorial by Henri Clouard, published in 1909, gives an idea of the climate of the nationalist-internationalist polemic:

> 'We stand for the genius of France against the foreign invasion. Nothing can be strong that is not determinate, and thus limited. The barriers which enclose us enable us to mount higher and the elevation of our flower will be measurable by the depth of our roots. It is thus in our own interest to march towards the same horizons that our fathers knew and we shall be careful to safeguard those qualities without which we should be nothing. Thus, our review will denounce the Foreigner. Tearing away the cloak of so-called Reason, we shall reveal the perfidious body of sentimental prejudices born among hostile nations. We refuse to admit that, under the illusory banner of 'Free Art', Scandinavians, Russians, Hungarian Jews, Portuguese and all the barbarians of Cosmopolis, should continue with impunity to disorganise our intellectual habits and undermine our methods.'

From the point of view of poets whose ideal sprang from the classicism of Anatole France and who claimed Barrès as their living master, there was indeed cause for alarm. Things had moved quickly since the days—not so far off—when Symbolism had appeared vaguely exotic. Within the last five or six years Paris had seen an astonishing increase in the roles played by non-Frenchmen in literature and especially in painting. The first decade of the century had been marked by a revolution that had gone almost unnoticed in its early stages and which, by the time it was recognised as a revolution, had become an accomplished fact. During that period, in effect, the French school of painting had unobtrusively ceased to exist and had been replaced by a 'Paris School'* that was not French at all, but Latin, with a touch of Slav, German and Anglo-Saxon.

So Nationalist intellectuals—still hot with memories of Dreyfus and Boulanger—discovered that everything they most hated had crystallised into the form of this 'Paris School' which, at the period, was synonymous with Cubism, while Cubism itself was

---

* The term *Ecole de Paris* was not actually used till a good many years later.

inseparable from the names of Spanish emigrés like Picasso and Juan Gris or from the half-Spaniard, Picabia. Closely connected with it—indistinguishably indeed for the outsider—were Italians like Severini and the inevitable Marinetti who, with a great fortune behind him, was campaigning noisily for Futurism. Among lesser names there were Germans, Poles, Americans ... and everywhere, linked with every innovation, at the heart of Cubism itself, was Guillaume Apollinaire, with his uncertain origin and cloudy past. His arrest was a great opportunity for the Nationalists to make out a case against *métèque* intellectuals.

As soon as the affair became public, a section of the right-wing Press moved into action and demanded Apollinaire's expulsion as an undesirable alien. Everything possible was done to discredit him. The police had been busy interrogating his concierge and neighbours and had acquired a number of picturesque details. Most of these were erroneous or distorted and were founded more on the adventures of the amorous Hospodar of *Les Onze Mille Verges*, than on banal reality. However, they constituted a very uncomfortable dossier for a man in Apollinaire's position.* Journalists like Urbain Gouhier, of *L'Œuvre*, described him succinctly as 'a pornographic writer' who was corrupting French literature. Léon Daudet, who had been one of the chief supporters of *L'Hérésiarque* the previous year, denied that he had ever voted for the book. The huge circle of friends who had surrounded him, flattered his vanity and intrigued to have their names mentioned in his articles, took fright and melted away. Even Picasso, one of the most intimate of all, betrayed him: when the examining magistrate questioned him on his relationship with Apollinaire, he denied having more than a superficial acquaintance with him.

Others were more faithful. André Salmon, André Billy, René Dalize were among those who defended him in the Press and consoled him in private. Not all of them, perhaps, were entirely convinced of his innocence and for a long time a slightly sinister aura clung to him. Even the vision of an observer as generally perspicacious as Léautaud seems to have been blurred by the fog of scandal, for he noted in his diary at about this time:

* The contents of this dossier were later recognised to be largely unfounded on fact and were destroyed by order of the Chief of Police.

'I certainly feel great sympathy for Apollinaire. He pleases me both as a man and a writer. . . . But what a strange personality! One feels him to be full of hidden things. Where does he come from, what has he done, what does he think, what are his acts, his habits, his sentiments? I say to myself, laughingly, that I prefer not to know. B. says he is weak and can be led into anything. . . .[1]

Friendship and love had always been of immense importance in Apollinaire's life. Now his friends—those 'friends without whom I cannot live', had deserted him or misunderstood him, and at the same time he was rejected by the woman he loved.

From time to time, during the previous three years, the question of marriage had been discussed between Apollinaire and Marie Laurencin and even between their families.* Now it was Madame Laurencin who changed her mind and refused to consider her daughter's marriage with a 'jail-bird'. Or at least, that was the explanation Marie Laurencin gave some years later to a friend. The truth seems to be that she made no difficulties in falling in with her mother's point of view. When Guillaume had been an influential critic and a rising talent, she had put up with a good deal of the same jealousy and brutality that had frightened away Annie Playden. Now that he had become compromising rather than useful, she seems to have found that the disadvantages of the liaison outweighed the advantages.

Things came to a head one day when Serge Férat and some other friends were lunching in Apollinaire's rooms in the rue Gros. Marie was supposed to help with the cooking of some specially complicated dish and Guillaume, busy in the kitchen, was becoming more and more nervous at her absence. At last Férat volunteered to go round to her house and see what had happened. He found Marie peacefully sewing. To his rather nervous enquiry, she replied directly and to the point: *Dis-lui M. . . .!* Apollinaire replied: 'Tell her the same from me!' but Férat noticed that he had turned terribly pale.

* A few years later Apollinaire wrote to his fiancée, Madeleine Pagès, that he had never considered marrying Marie Laurencin and that it was she who had desired the match. Louise Faure-Favier, who was an intimate friend of both, and several other friends, feel that he arranged the story in such a way as to satisfy both his new love and his own self-esteem.

There had been so many scenes and disputes, so many ruptures and reconciliations, that their friends refused for a long time to take this new quarrel seriously. However, Marie had finally decided to break off the relationship and not all Apollinaire's own pleading, nor the friends he sent to plead for him, could make her change her mind. He could no more understand his dismissal than he had understood the flight of Annie Playden. And just as Annie, after her departure for America, became the symbol of treachery and false love, so Marie, his 'little sun', became the pitiless Tristouse Ballerinette of *Le Poète Assassiné*. . . .

'In the clearing appeared a dark and slender young girl. Her face was sombre and starred with eyes that moved like brightly-plumaged birds. She wore her hair loose, but short. It left her neck bare and was as thick and black as a forest by night, and by the skipping rope she held in her hand, Croniamental recognised Tristouse Ballerinette. . . .'

Croniamental, the poet is persecuted by the scientific philistine, Horace Tograth and finally lynched by an enraged crowd. Tristouse, the woman he had rendered 'beautiful and glorious' by his love, gives him the *coup de grâce*, gleefully poking out his eyes with her umbrella.

Marie Laurencin's name appears, too, in the rough draft of *Zone*, coupled with that of the irresponsible Géry Pieret, in one of those short passages of personal revelation which Apollinaire used to compose in moments of great stress, and then delete from the final copy:

> J'ai vécu à Auteuil près de trois mois
> Entre les deux larrons comme Jésus mourut en croix
> Et l'un, le criminel, ce fut le bon larron
> Il sera malheureux et mourra en prison
> L'autre, le mauvais larron, c'était une femme
> Elle m'a pris ma vie, ce fut un vol infâme . . .*

---

* For nearly three months I lived in Auteuil
  Between the two thieves, like Jesus dying on the cross
  And one, the criminal, was the good thief
  He will be wretched and will die in prison
  And the other, the wicked thief, was a woman
  She stole my life, that was an infamous theft . . .

The break, coming so soon after the shock of his arrest, threw Apollinaire into a state of prostration that alarmed his friends. Auteuil, with its memories and the proximity to Marie's own home, had become unbearable for him, so Serge Férat and Hélène d'Oettingen installed him in their house in the Boulevard Berthier and left him in the care of their mutual friend, Marc Brésil. It was like looking after an invalid, and a difficult one at that.

'On Saturday morning', wrote Brésil to the Baronne d'Oettingen, giving an account of his mission, 'I found him still as plaintive, as downcast, as prostrate as he was during the first days after the rupture. Above all, don't speak to him about this; pretend to believe in his energy, in his lucid, inflexible will-power. He is never so weak as when one pities his weakness. . . . I pretend to laugh at the idea that I could be of any use to him and he smiles, and hïs sense of irony helps him to rally. He agrees then that I must indeed be very young to imagine that he is so soft-hearted, and he makes an effort to prove that this is not true. It is quite simple, as you see, but his energy hardly lasts beyond the time it takes to affirm it. . . . We shall certainly get a result in the end, but we must give this crisis time to work itself out. Paul Reboux has asked him for two stories for *Le Journal*. So far, I have not managed to make him write them and it is hard to blame him when one sees him miserable and prostrate, so kind in a desperately sad way, and so tired . . . tired of everything.

'He must be made to feel himself supported by friendship. The sham friends—I hardly dare to call them double-faced—he has met with here and there, seem to have made it hard for him to believe in friendship. . . .'

The crisis did indeed pass, though much more slowly than most people imagined. It left its mark on his personality and thus, inevitably, on his work. It is easy to recognise the change that followed immediately after the dividing line of the prison poems, and which roughly separates the volume he was to publish under the title *Alcools*, from the later poems in *Calligrammes*.

X

'We are all prophets'

*A la fin tu es las de ce monde ancien.**

The scandal of the 'Affair of the Statuettes' delayed the publication of Apollinaire's collected poems until May 1913, but nearly
the whole contents of *Alcools* had been written before the events
of September 1911. The influence of Symbolism is always evident,
in spite of certain experiments in style and the 'psychological
discontinuity' which was his really original contribution to French
poetry, and there is never any feeling of a definite break-away
from French poetic tradition.

Apollinaire, in fact, had always insisted on his attachment to
that tradition. Perhaps he clung to it all the more obstinately
because the very idea of tradition had always meant so much to
him and held for him a specially personal meaning. To belong to
French literature, while introducing into it his own cosmopolitan
experience of life, had meant belonging to France, striking roots
in a soil he could feel to be his own. He had certainly been sincere
when he had insisted, in his lecture on 'The New Phalanx', 'None
of the young poets I admire holds aloof from the French poetic
tradition', and when, in the same year, he had written to Toussaint
Luca, 'I am seeking only for a lyricism that will be at once new
and humanistic.'

Yet in that same year 1908 he had been crusading for Cubism,
defending *Les Demoiselles d'Avignon*. There was a contradiction
here, and a significant one.

Up to the disastrous Autumn of 1911, one can recognise a sharp
distinction in Apollinaire's attitude towards poetry and towards
painting. Apollinaire, the poet, was a traditionalist, while

* Apollinaire: *Zone*.

143

Apollinaire, the art critic, had been ready to applaud and sponsor the most audacious innovations. Painting and poetry were for him two entirely separate arts, and he had even written, in 1907, in an article on Matisse, that: 'There is no connection between painting and literature and I have been careful not to create any confusion in this matter. The aim of Matisse is plastic expression, just as the aim of the poet is lyric expression.' In fact, he was ready to associate himself with the most ruthless breaks with tradition, so long as they were made by others.

Now, after the incident of the *Mona Lisa* and the separation from Marie Laurencin, the rebellious, iconoclastic side of his nature, which had been, so to speak, dammed off in the tributary river of painting, seems to have flooded over and invaded the whole of himself. From this time on, he began to make daring experiments with poetic form and to practise exactly the confusion between painting and poetry he had condemned a few years earlier. *L'Emigrant de Landor Road* had contained a transitory reflection of his preoccupation with Cubism, but *Lundi rue Christine* went much further. A Cubist painter would have decomposed and rearranged the spectacle of this banal café in the neighbourhood of Montparnasse, in such a way as to reveal a vision of its 'reality', based on the Cubist belief that 'the objects which strike us most immediately are not always those richest in plastic truth.'[1] Adopting this technique he had hitherto left to Picasso, Braque and other painter friends, Apollinaire chose those elements of his surroundings which seemed to him richest in poetic truth— fragments of conversation, objects, sounds—without presenting them in a conventionally recognisable pattern and the result was the first Cubist poem.

The cinema undoubtedly had a share of responsibility in this voluntary confusion of two arts. Apollinaire had always been fascinated by this new medium and had realised its importance from the first, flickering strips of successive images that had still recalled the magic lantern shows of his childhood. The rows of excited spectators on their benches, encouraging the persecuted heroine, hissing the villain, applauding wildly at each narrow escape of the hero; the operator frantically turning the handle of his projector; the startling phrases flashed on the screen, had always excited his imagination to the utmost and seemed to him to reveal 'the dramatic truth inherent in life'. During these last years, moreover, the cinema had been developing with tremendous speed. There had been great technical improvements; producers had become vastly ambitious. Great historical or biblical epics like *The Last Days of Pompeii* or *Quo Vadis* were in fashion. Victor Hugo's *Les Misérables* and Eugène Sue's *Les Mystères de Paris* had been adapted for the screen; an association called *Le Film d'Art* had conceived the idea of asking well-known writers and musicians to collaborate in its productions; in a lighter style there was the apparently endless series of the exploits of 'Fantomas', the contemporary Superman, half-criminal, half-hero, for ever at war with 'Inspector Juve' whom he regularly foiled in the disguise of a monarch, astronomer, orchestra-conductor, bull-fighter, oculist and so on. New cinemas, new companies, were springing up all over Europe and America, and audiences were growing so fast that builders and producers could hardly keep pace with them.

Apollinaire and his friends saw infinite possibilities in these new films and were as entranced by them as they had been a few years earlier by the clowns of Medrano's circus. Night after night found them installed in the seats of one or other of the city's already numerous cinemas and each film—even the most apparently frivolous—gave rise to interminable discussions. 'Close-ups', 'fade-outs', the swift succession of images, each revealing a new aspect of the subject, seemed to them essentially 'modern', above all essentially 'Cubist'. This art, they felt, was as close to the people as the old epic recitations had been in the days of the Troubadours. 'The operator projecting his film is playing the part of the *jongleur* of old', said Apollinaire.

André Salmon and Max Jacob were cinema-addicts as ardent as himself and like himself they were trying to accustom people to the idea that a poem may be conceived simultaneously, like a scene out of real life, or a scene from a film, flashed on a screen. Such a poem would partake at once of poetry, music and painting. It would give a 'simultaneous' vision of life, and the poet would thus be a painter in his own way. The idea pleased Apollinaire greatly and he was soon composing 'lyrical ideograms' designed to be printed in contrasting types, with the words arranged in pictural forms. He was exceedingly proud of these complicated and ingenious little compositions and planned to publish them under the title, *Et moi aussi je suis peintre*.*

The word *Simultanéité* was in fact becoming more and more significant in Cubist circles. It was constantly to be heard in the Delaunay's studio, where Apollinaire had been a frequent visitor since 1911.² Robert Delaunay's attempts to paint the 'total reality' of the Eiffel Tower had led him to make a whole series of almost scientific experiments with colour and out of these he had at last evolved a style of painting which, he claimed, represented 'a new aesthetic system, representative of our epoch'. Naturally, this system was christened *Simultanéisme*.

A new aesthetic system! Nothing could have been more tempting to Apollinaire at that moment. He already had a lucid vision of the ineluctable approach of Abstraction and understood it to be the logical outcome of the state of mind, the manner of viewing life and the world which he himself had done so much to create. It was in Delaunay's studio in the rue des Grands Augustins that Abstraction was taking shape, and the atmosphere there was so exciting that, in the heat of arguments when he insisted that Delaunay was really a Cubist, although a heretical one, he often forgot he was suffering from a broken heart. The most dynamic elements in painting and literature used to foregather here and exchange ideas that were already far in advance of those which had been born in Picasso's studio in the *Bateau Lavoir*. It was there he met Francis Picabia, who was still a poet as well as a painter, and who was already insisting—as if the coming event of Dada was already throwing its shadow before—that *all* combinations of words, without exception, were permissible in poetry and that the more meaningless and irritating they seemed to be, the greater was their true poetic value. Apollinaire had been impressed from the first by his intellectual exuberance, his racing cars, the enormous lies in which he himself half-believed, his Spanish generosity and his contempt for every kind of dogmatism—even the kind that labelled itself 'modern'. He coupled Picabia's name with that of Delaunay and Marcel Duchamp in an article on Cub-

---

* *And I too am a painter.* Apollinaire was so excited over his ideograms that he apparently forgot that Mallarmé, long before him, had experimented with types and spacing and had created not only 'visual' poems but a poem-symphony that approximated poetry with music.

ism, as having 'broken with the conceptionalist formula in order to practise an art which no longer submits to any kind of law', and tending towards 'an entirely new art which will have the same relationship to painting, as it has been understood till now, as music has to literature'.

Blaise Cendrars had the same stimulating effect on him as Picabia but caused him a good deal of anxiety. He was a Swiss, who had sometimes been brought to the rue Gros by Delaunay—a bony, pale-faced boy whom Salmon had described unkindly as resembling 'a cold cooked potato, endowed with speech and thus enabled to transform railway time-tables and guide-books into heart-rending poems'. A perpetual thirst for adventure had driven him to Russia, then to the United States, and he had only recently arrived back in Paris, terribly sure of himself and totally lacking in respect for his elders. He was as determined as Picabia to toss aside all the traditional forms and find a way of expressing a purely 'interior' poetry. He too had frequented the cinema and had taken its lessons to heart.

Now Apollinaire, like Salmon and Max Jacob, had been accustomed to think of himself as the avant-garde of contemporary young poets and it had not occurred to them that a new generation, even younger and more modern, was creeping up behind them. Salmon was nonchalant; Max Jacob was too much preoccupied with his religious experiences, with aspirations to sainthood and the fascinations of Evil, to worry about his own position in the literary world. Apollinaire, on the other hand, was highly sensitive on this point and Cendrars had been a thorn in his flesh from the first. Delaunay had once accused him of 'trying to express old ideas with new techniques', but Cendrars went much further.

'You, a modern poet!' he would exclaim. 'We'll see about that! One can't be really modern till one has blown everything to pieces!' This judgement, coming from a younger man, was terribly wounding.

One evening, Cendrars read aloud to the Delaunays, some friends and Apollinaire a poem which he had printed at his own expense in America and had called *Pâques à New York*. After the first few lines, a deep hush fell on the studio. Something important was happening.

Une foule enfiévrée par les sueurs de l'or
Se bouscule et s'engouffre dans de longs corridors.

Trouble, dans le fouillis empanaché des toits,
Le soleil, c'est votre Face souillée par les crachats . . .

read Cendrars and verse by verse the great city took shape, becoming at the same time the epic of Modern Man.

These men and women, whose ears were attuned by long practice to catch every authentic echo of the new world that was being born around them, realised its significance at once. Apollinaire had been listening in silence, with closed eyes, and Sonia Delaunay noticed that he had turned very pale. When Cendrars had finished reading, he congratulated him and asked for the manuscript, which he read attentively several times. He seemed sad and discouraged and said at last, 'It's astonishing! Beside this, the book I am preparing seems worth nothing.' The dissatisfaction he had been feeling with everything that attached him to his own past crystallised at this moment. The break with Symbolism was achieved at last.

And so it came about that when *Alcools* appeared a month or so later, the volume opened with a long poem, written almost at the last moment and entitled *Zone* . . . the famous *Zone* that has given rise to so many literary quarrels, that owes so much to Cendrars and yet, strangely, is perhaps the most personal of all Apollinaire's works. It stands out like an act of defiance, a comment on all the early work, the poem of a final choice, of refusal of the past and acceptance of everything that may lie in the future. In it, he rejects all his old loves, all those cities that had intoxicated him in his youth, declares *à la fin tu es las de ce monde ancien* and opts, in place of the hellenistic culture that had dominated Europe since the Renaissance, for

. . . une jolie rue dont j'ai oublié le nom
Neuve et propre du soleil elle était le clairon
Les directeurs les ouvriers et les belles sténo-dactylographes
Du lundi matin au samedi soir quatre fois par jour y passent
Le matin par rtois fois la sirène y gémit
Une cloche rageuse y aboie vers midi

Robert Delaunay: *The Eiffel Tower*

Blaise Cendrars in 1920

Les inscriptions des enseignes et des murailles
Les plaques les avis à la façon des perroquets criaillent . . .*

Then, once the choice has been made, everything is transformed. The particular becomes the general, everything is per-
sonalised; the sunlit street, the workmen, the secretaries, the
posters and all the rest, merge into a single fantastic vision of the
century:

Pupille Christ de l'œil
Vingtième pupille des siècles il sait y faire
Et changé en oiseau ce siècle comme Jésus monte dans l'air
Les diables dans les abîmes lèvent la tête pour le regarder
Ils disent qu'il imite Simon Mage en Judée
Ils crient s'il sait voler qu'on l'appelle voleur
Les anges voltigent autour du joli voltigeur
Icare Enoch Elie Apollonius de Thyane
Flottent autour du premier aéroplane . . .†

Art has created Order out of the everyday sights of the street
entre la rue Aumont-Théville et l'avenue des Ternes, so that they no
longer appear as isolated phenomena of daily life, but as an integral part of creation. The present is no longer the sequel to the
past, as it had been in the days when he and André Salmon had
discovered beauty in the apparatus of modern life that poetry had
neglected or despised. From now on it was to be the springboard
from which he could project himself into the future, explore

* A charming street whose name I forget—It was clean and new as the sun's
trumpet—The directors, the workmen and the pretty shorthand-typists—
From Monday morning to Saturday evening pass there four times a day—In
the morning a siren wails there three times—An angry bell barks out
at midday—The inscriptions on signboards and walls—The name-plates
the notices scream like parrots. . . .

† Pupil Christ of the eye
Twentieth pupil of the centuries he can do it alone
And changed into a bird this century mounts like Jesus to his throne
The devils in the pit raise their heads to peer
They say he is imitating Simon Magus of Judea
They shout if he can fly let us call him the fly one
The angels fly round the flying-trapeze man
Icarus Enoch Elias Apollonius of Thyane
Hover around this first aeroplane . . .
                              [trans. by W. S. Strachan.]

11

untraced paths and exercise that 'art of prediction' for which he felt himself to have a special vocation.

It was in this frame of mind that Apollinaire prepared *Alcools* for press and, in a last-minute revolt that shook the staid offices of the *Mercure* to their foundations, suppressed all traces of punctuation from the final proofs. The result satisfied him and made little real difference since, after a luncheon in Louise Faure-Favier's apartment in the Ile Saint-Louis, René Dalize and then Madame Faure-Favier herself read several poems aloud without even noticing the change. It was a triumph for Apollinaire's contention that 'punctuation is not indispensable to poetry. A poem is sufficient in itself and should not need stops and commas and even less exclamation marks and rows of dots in order to be understood. Rhythm and cadence suffice for that if it is the work of a true poet.'

The volume attracted a good deal of attention, partly because of all the publicity attached to Apollinaire's person. On the whole it was favourably received, but even such staunch supporters as André Billy were scandalised by the absence of punctuation and complained of it as a dangerous innovation. Most of the critics compared him with Villon and suggested that he would do better to avoid 'certain extravagances'. Henriette Charenson, who specialised in feminine reactions, declared that *La Chanson du Mal-Aimé* was not likely to move the heart of any woman. Few seemed to notice the significance of *Zone*.

Besides the friendly critics, there were some vigilant enemies who seized this opportunity for attack. Georges Duhamel had not forgotten some ironic comments made by Apollinaire on the 'Unanimist' group and this sort of poetry represented everything he and his friends most disliked. Now he moved up to attack with arms that had little to do with literary merit.

'Nothing', he wrote, 'could remind one more of an old junk shop than these collected poems published by Monsieur Apollinaire under the simple but mysterious title: *Alcools*. I call it an old junk shop because a mass of heterogeneous objects has found a place there and, though some of them are of value, none of them has been made by the dealer himself. That is just the characteristic of this sort of industry: it resells, but it does not produce. Sometimes there are strange objects for sale; on its grimy shelves one may discover a rare stone hanging from a nail. All this comes from afar, but the stone is pleasant to look at. The rest is a collection of faked paintings, patched exotic garments, bicycle accessories and articles of intimate hygiene. A truculent and bewildering variety takes the place of art in this assemblage. One barely catches a glimpse, through the holes of some moth-eaten chasuble, of the innocent and ironic eye of the dealer, who is part Levantine Jew, part South American, part Polish gentleman and part *facchino*. . . . One thing Guillaume Apollinaire possesses that is really his own is a many-coloured cosmopolitanism which one may detest, but which one must admit to be savoury. . . .'

The attack touched Apollinaire at his most sensitive spot. 'Polish gentleman' might have passed, although he was always annoyed by any reference to his Slav ancestry, but 'Levantine Jew' was more than he could bear. Max Jacob was dispatched, monocled and top-hatted, to provoke the author of the insult to a duel. In the end, the affair was settled peacefully, as was another attack on the same lines by Arthur Cravan which also provoked a challenge. But they had shown Apollinaire that he would never escape from the stigma of being a 'foreigner' wherever he went. Even Cendrars's generous letter, that ended, 'You are my master; you are the master of all of us', could not console him. Nor could the praise of André Gide, who had just published *La Porte Étroite,* which Apollinaire judged as the finest novel of its decade.

At this point, in fact, he wanted one thing, and one thing only— to escape from the past, from the outcast, the prisoner, the un-happy lover, into the future, his own elected domain, where he felt himself truly to belong. A poem written during this period and adopted later as one of his 'rocket-signals' by the younger generation, begins, '*Allons plus vite, nom de Dieu, allons plus vite,*' and exactly expresses his state of mind. The time was ripe for the overthrowing of old things, at whatever cost.

Marinetti was the perfect companion for such a mood. Apol-linaire had made some ironic comments on the first *Futurist Mani-festo* and been careful not to compromise himself too far with his old friend's noisy campaign. At this point, however, Futurism

seemed exactly the vehicle he needed to express his exasperation with the past. In June 1913, 'The Futurist Anti-tradition'
appeared under his signature. It opens with a list under the concise
heading 'Destruction', which includes such temporary *bêtes noires*
as grammar, punctuation, typographic harmony, 'sublime' art
(yet 'sublime' had long been one of his own favourite adjectives),
plot in the short story, line and verse in poetry, boredom in
general, and other objects of hatred and contempt. Then follow
two more lists, one dedicated to the famous and insulting *mot de
Cambronne* (set to music) and the other consisting of writers and
artists to whom he offers the 'Rose' of his favour. The first list
includes Venice, Versailles, Pompeii, Bruges, Oxford, Benares,
Florence, Montmartre and other traditional homes of art; 'critics',
'good taste', 'academism', and the names of Montaigne, Wagner,
Beethoven, Shakespeare, Goethe, Baudelaire and a number of
other literary idols. The second is headed by the names of Marinetti and Picasso.

A few years later, when this particular state of mind had passed,
Apollinaire used to show some embarrassment when reminded of
this iconoclastic outburst and give various explanations to prove
that he had not meant what he said. However there was nothing
in the pamphlet to suggest reservation of meaning. Yet neither the
experiments in 'Cubist' poetry, nor the desire for the destruction
of old standards of beauty, were gratuitously revolutionary.
Disillusion and disappointment had brought on a rather showy
volcanic eruption, but it corresponded to a change in the man
himself, in his vision of the world and above all in his conception
of the poet's mission. This was the time of a poetry that was
conceived as an instrument for discovery, in which everything
was sacrificed to the cause of invention—

> Perdre
> Mais perdre vraiment
> Pour laisser place à la trouvaille. . . .*

The time had come to renounce the nostalgia for the past that is
part of the very texture of the human spirit and to look only
towards the future; to refuse all the ancient civilisations in order

* To cast away—Truly to cast away—So as to leave room for discovery.
(*Toujours*)

to build up that new, still unguessed-at civilisation that was to be the work of poets and artists.

One of the things, in fact, that divided Apollinaire so sharply from the poets of a previous generation, was that he possessed what we should call nowadays a social conscience. It had been smothered for a long time under his desire to write about himself and his experiences, and had been rendered unrecognisable by his taste for irony and paradox, but it was actually quite as strong in him as in his antagonists Romains or Duhamel, who were so sternly set on doing good to the masses. He believed essentially in the social function of the artist, but his idea of that function was far removed from the 'social realism' that was soon to come into fashion. He had always distrusted politics. 'I consider politics to be hateful, lying, sterile and harmful', he had written to Karl Boes in 1902, and had never changed his mind. For him the artist had a mission as a revealer of hidden things and his social duty was simply to use the powerful instruments at his disposal in order to reveal mankind to itself.

The instrument, in his case, was the Word. Like every true poet, he was conscious of the occult potentialities of words and felt for them something of the primitive fear and wonder that had surrounded them in those forgotten times when they had been magical sounds charged with powers of incantation rather than the trivial coinage of daily conversation. No doubt he remembered Mallarmé, whose influence is so constantly apparent in his work, though—with an habitual ingratitude—he seldom if ever acknowledged it:

'I claim', the Father of Symbolism had written, 'that there exists a secret parity between certain ancient procedures and the sorcery that poetry will always remain. . . . To evoke the unnamed object, in an intentional shadow, by allusive, but always indirect words that are themselves tantamount to silence, is an effort resembling that of creation. The verse thus becomes incantation!'

Like the Symbolists, Apollinaire believed it was the function of the artist to restore words to their first estate, to cleanse them of the incrustations of centuries and renew their ancient and terrible brilliance.

Mallarmé had started the revolution for the liberation of words and Jarry, Paul Fort, Salmon, Max Jacob and he himself had carried it on in the spirit of the twentieth century. They had experimented with metre, refused to recognise the cast-iron principle of alternating male and female rhymes and established for ever the liberty for succeeding generations to use purely oral rhymes instead of subordinating them to arbitrary rules of spelling. Then, as the rebellious heirs of Symbolism, they had shown that the whole of life is the raw material for poetry. With its new rhymes and new images, French poetry had lost the stately airs of the bourgeoisie; it was no longer confined to drawing-rooms and polite society, but it had become once more poetry in the sense that Villon had understood the word, four and a half centuries earlier, making use of the outright language of the people. The frontiers had been broken down and it was in this atmosphere of joyful freedom, which he himself had done so much to create, that Apollinaire's lyricism had come to full flower.

Alcools had been the manifestation of that stage in his life. Now, with the passing of years and the burden of experience upon him, he began to feel more and more strongly that experiments in style were not sufficient. Once its occult power had been restored to the Word, he felt—and here he was far indeed from the aristocratic and purely aesthetic Symbolist tradition—it might be used to create, not only a new poetry, but a new world. So after the turning point of *Zone* his work began to deal with a universe that already existed in men's hearts, but which was to be made manifest by poetry. There lies the true theme of the haunting *Musicien de Saint-Merry* which has roused such long echoes among the Surrealist poets:

> Je ne chante pas ce monde ni les autres astres
> Je chante toutes les possibilités de moi-même hors
> de ce monde et des astres . . .*

And it is the theme, too, of *Les Collines*, written just after the outbreak of war:

> Voici le temps de la magie
> Il s'en revient attendez-vous

* I do not sing of this world nor of the other planets—I sing of all the possibilities within myself outside this world and the planets . . .

A des milliards de prodiges
Qui n'ont fait naître aucune fable
Nul les ayant imaginés

Profondeurs de la conscience
On vous explorera demain
Et qui sait quels êtres vivants
Seront tirés de ces abîmes
Avec des univers entiers . . .*

Apollinaire starts this long poem by describing the combat of two aeroplanes over the city, and soon one of them comes to represent for him his youth, the other, the future. With the defeat of the symbol of his youth, he sees a revelation of himself as dedicated to the future, which it is his mission, as a poet, to reveal to mankind:

Où donc est tombée ma jeunesse
Tu vois que flambe l'avenir
Sache que je parle aujourd'hui
Pour annoncer au monde entier
Qu'enfin est né l'art de prédire

Certains hommes sont des collines
Qui s'élèvent d'entre les hommes
Et voient au loin tout l'avenir
Mieux que s'il était le présent
Plus net que s'il était passé†

* Here comes the season of magic—It approaches you may expect to see—Millions of prodigious happenings—Which have given birth to no fable—Since no one has ever imagined them.

Depths of man's consciousness—You will soon be explored—And who can tell what living beings—Will be drawn from those depths—Together with whole universes.

† Where has my youth fallen
    You see the future aflame
    Know that I speak to-day
    To announce to the whole world
    That the art of prophecy is born at last.

  Certain men are like hills
  That rise above other men
  And see the whole future lying afar
  Better than if it were the present
  More clearly than if it were past.

Victor Hugo, Rimbaud, Gérard de Nerval and many others had combined before him the function of seer with that of poet. Perhaps Apollinaire took himself less seriously than they had done. The mood of the twentieth century was ironic rather than ecstatic. Its seers were no longer the majestic prophet that Hugo had contemplated in himself, nor the luciferian being of terrible purity that Rimbaud had struggled to attain through the 'systematic derangement of all the senses'. The Apollinairian seer —the seer of the twentieth century—was a figure in whom tragedy was never far from the burlesque. He was Croniamental, the hero of *Le Poète Assassiné*, lucid, comic and doomed. He was the man who had 'drunk the whole universe', and, having drunk his fill, could rise above time and space, so that past, present and future became one:

> 'His [Croniamental's] eyes devoured everything they saw and when the lids closed like rapid jaws, they swallowed the universe which renewed itself unceasingly through the opera-tion of him who wandered over it, imagining every detail of the huge worlds on which he fed. The clamour and thunder of Paris broke out afar, then all round the young man. He paused, out of breath, like a burglar who has been chased too far and is ready to give himself up. This clamour showed that his enemies were on his track. His mouth and eyes grew cunning and now he walked slowly, taking refuge in his memory. Thus he went on his way, while all the forces of his destiny and his conscience set Time aside, so that the truth of all that is and was and was to be, should become apparent. . . .'

Croniamental felt it his duty to combat Horace Tograth, the German-Australian scientist who was conducting a world-wide crusade against poetry. His comic and picaresque travels through Europe in search of Tristouse Ballerinette, his betrayal by Picasso, lightly disguised as *l'Oiseau du Bénin*, the encounters with monks, rabbis, artists and peasants, the mingling of farce and tragedy, are all an image of Apollinaire's own life, and beneath all the irony lies the true theme of the story: the poet has a duty to mankind, the duty to show men how to become fully conscious of the world and themselves, to give to every man eyes to see beyond the limitations of the past and the present. In the letter-poem *Pro-phéties*,3 he explains:

We are all prophets my dear André Billy
But people have been made to believe for so long
That they have no future that they are definitively ignorant
    And idiots from the time of their birth
That they take it all for granted and no one even thinks
Of asking himself if he knows the future or not
There is nothing religious about that
Nor about superstitions and prophesies
Nor in what is called occultism
There is above all a certain way of observing nature
And interpreting nature
Which is perfectly legitimate.

For Apollinaire-Croniamental, it was the poet's function to prepare the world for that 'season of magic', when poetry and prophecy would no longer be the exception, but a commonplace. The poet of *Alcools* had been a pure poet, that of *Calligrammes* was to be a poet-prophet. The first was the descendant of Symbolism; the second, the ancestor of Surrealism.

XI

Montparnasse: 'Capital of Cubism'

Montmartre had lived gloriously, then outlived its own legend and been deserted by the last of the true *Montmartrois*, abandoned to enterprising architects and to sham bohemians. Then there had been a period of dispersion, when there was no real 'artists' quarter', and men who had been accustomed to meet several times a day, in cafés, in the streets or in shops, had to make long omnibus journeys to each other's homes. Then Picasso moved from Clichy to Montrouge, and from thence to Montparnasse, followed by a number of his friends, and almost at once the quarter became, in Apollinaire's words, a new 'refuge of fine and free simplicity' for artists.

It was during the year 1912–13, while Apollinaire and Delaunay were creating 'Orphism' and 'Simultaneity' that the few square yards of the *Carrefour de Montparnasse,* where the boulevard of that name transects the Boulevard de Raspail, became, and was to remain for a quarter of a century, the nerve centre of international art and letters. On the one side was the *Café du Dôme,* whose regular clients were mostly Americans or rich Germans—dealers or amateurs—who met there to discuss the new French painters and decide which of them should be given their chance in the galleries of Berlin or Munich.* Opposite, there was the *Rotonde,* at first the rendezvous of every Slav who dabbled in the arts, but which soon became a second home for the ex-*Montmartrois.*

Picasso, first of the 'Montparnos', had taken a studio in the rue Schoelcher, where he led a surprisingly bourgeois and orderly existence under the eye of his new wife. He was still in the most

* The *Dôme* was so popular with German painters, and was so identified for them with the heart of modern art, that a group of young painters used to exhibit in Berlin under the title *The Dômists.*

austere period of his production, banishing as far as possible from his canvases the colour he loved, in order to concentrate on pure form. In the *Rotonde* he would meet his old friends and relax a little while from his harassing obsession. There he would often come across Vlaminck, who was his enemy now and who lived in the rue Denfert Rochereau, where he gave parties that scandalised the severely proper Matisse, in his disused convent nearby. Derain came there too, and Francis Carco, who had emerged at last from the retreat during which he had written his novel of the Montmartre underworld: *Jésus-la-Caille*. There was Suzanne Valadon, with her son Utrillo; there was Fernand Léger, a massive young man from Normandy, whose studio was like a mechanic's shop, full of dynamos, wheels and ball-bearings. In Léger's canvases Man and Machine became practically identified one with the other; he was already on the way to becoming the interpreter of the Machine Age—a 'Tubist', as one critic described him—and claimed that he alone really invented, as the Chaldeans, the Romans, the Goths had done, instead of copying like all their successors.

Ambroise Vollard sometimes appeared, but he was obviously ill at ease. He had fought bravely for the Impressionists in his youth, but things had moved too fast for him and he neither liked nor understood the spirit of Montparnasse. He would sit there, dreaming with half-closed eyes, wake up to bargain for the picture that had attracted him to this benighted quarter, then hurry back with it under his arm to the rue Lafitte.

There was Modigliani too, whom no one had taken seriously in Montmartre, except as an arbiter of elegance. Now he was recognised as one of the leading characters of Montparnasse—one of those who, like Apollinaire and Picasso, were pointed out to newcomers as part of the local sights. He had discovered his own style now and though some of his contemporaries had their doubts about those ovoid faces, those blank eyes he managed to fill with resigned, childlike suffering, none of them could resist the spell of his personality, of his violence and gentleness, his courage in face of illness and poverty and his uncompromising determination to paint in his own way without any concession to Cubism or any other fashion. 'Over-long necks and a great deal of wit, a touch of true, earnest madness', Max Jacob would say of him, and Montparnasse accepted him as he was, forgiving, or even applauding the scandals he caused in the quarter.

It was Modigliani who had discovered 'Rosalie', the Italian ex-model, who kept a tiny restaurant in the rue Campagne Première where she fed all the dogs and cats of the quarter and served delicious Roman dishes that reminded him and Apollinaire of the feasts of their childhood. 'Rosalie's' soon became one of the places where initiated *Montparnos* came to dine—generally on credit. Her rival was Baty's, which had the advantage of more space and an incomparable wine cellar, but where the *patron* could never hope to equal her cooking. Further up the Boulevard Raspail was the little *Café des Vigourelles*, frequented by the rowdy youth of the quarter on evenings when the *Bal Bullier* was closed. There Dunoyer de Segonzac, Luc-Albert Moreau, Derain, Férat and René Dalize used to foregather with Apollinaire. The *patron* was flattered to number so many artists among his clientèle and had been heard to declare solemnly, 'Gentlemen, although I only keep a café, I too am a lover of the arts. On the Sundays when I do not go to the cinema, I visit the Louvre.'

In the narrow rue de la Grande Chaumière was the famous *atelier* that attracted noisy crowds of art students, and all along the street the shop windows were bright with artists' materials and unsaleable canvases, left in exchange for brushes or tubes of paint. The angle of the road, where it intersected the Boulevard Montparnasse, had lately become a human market where models offered themselves for sale. Each Monday, they swarmed in from every quarter of Paris and its distant suburbs—nobly bearded old men, huge Neapolitan matrons, dark-eyed Spanish beauties, negroes, fragile adolescents, all hoping to catch the eye of some painter on the look-out for their particular type. This weekly gathering was a great annoyance to the shopkeepers, who complained, first that the motley and often unwashed crowd disgraced the quarter and discouraged respectable clients, and, secondly, that it hid their window displays and thus lost them business. One of those who complained most and most often summoned the police to chase the crowd away, was a certain M. Hazard, who had been even quicker than the models to smell out a possible profit in the new, international aspect of Montparnasse. His large grocery stores were stocked to provide Americans with their grapefruits, Russians with salmon-eggs to remind them of caviar, Hungarians with paprika-flavoured sausages, Germans with sauerkraut. M. Hazard was the symbol of Montparnassian cosmopolitanism.

Except on Mondays, the quarter still had an almost provincial calm. The boulevards were still lined with the great chestnut trees that survived till after the Second World War, and so little traffic came to these quiet outskirts of Paris that there was generally at least one knot of artists arguing in the middle of the street. One could tell the tendencies of the painters by their clothes. The more conventional artists, who were still painting 'from life', without distortion, wore the traditional bohemian dress, with wide hats, flowing capes and hair of unorthodox length. The Cubists, and in general those whom Apollinaire called the 'men of the future', prided themselves on dressing like the bourgeois and were inclined to wear sports suits in what they believed to be the English style. Picasso, who had discarded the electric blue boiler suit of his Montmartre days, was especially addicted to this sort of dress and completed it by a check cap, instead of the usual bowler.

Apollinaire, though he was to be seen almost every evening in the *Rotonde*, did not actually live in Montparnasse. He had taken a flat up under the eaves of a high building in the Boulevard Saint-Germain, a little apart, yet near enough to become a sort of peripheric centre for the *Montparnos*. It was a sort of pent-house, reached by a narrow staircase, almost a ladder, that contrasted surprisingly with the majestic flights of stairs between the lower floors. The apartment was small and overcrowded with the heavy Breton furniture—symbol and menace of the maternal wrath—which had necessarily found a place. Shelves and tables were covered with objects of all kinds, masks, fetishes and the miscellaneous bric-à-brac in which Apollinaire delighted. Among them were a few carefully chosen horrors, such as a bronze ink-stand representing the Basilica of the Sacré-Cœur, which he had collected as a sort of act of defiance against the prejudices and conventions of cultured society. The passage was entirely lined with shelves full of the yellow, paper-back books which, as he used to say, looked like slabs of yellow butter. The walls of the rooms were rather low and entirely covered with pictures crowded so closely together that their frames touched on every side. Most of them were souvenirs of the Cubist campaign; there were several Picassos of the Blue Period, two fine Derains, two Chiricos, paintings by the Russian 'Rayonnist', Larionov. The cat Pipe had accompanied him from Auteuil and stalked majestically among the piles of books on the floor—not the sort of books which serious-minded visitors expected to find (Apollinaire claimed that he had read only a few of the great French classics) but cookery books, Italian novels, minor Symbolist poets, seventeenth-century memoirs and such contributions to a heteroclite and apparently useless erudition as the 'Psychology of Scavengers' bought for a high price, because of its rarity, from a bookstall somewhere on the quays of the Seine.

A peculiarity of the new apartment was that the front door opened directly on to the top step. People were often alarmed to see an eye peering down at them as they waited there. Apollinaire had bored a peephole to enable him, in principle, to eliminate undesirable visitors. In practice, he could seldom bring himself to refuse anyone who wanted to see him. The friends who had prudently disappeared at the time of his arrest were drifting back. Incapable of nursing a grudge, he welcomed them, made excuses for them and forgot, or pretended to forget, the past.

His celebrity was growing steadily now, confirmed by the publication of *Alcools* and of the *Méditations Esthétiques*, with its studies of the Cubist painters. He was tremendously busy, caught up in the incessant intellectual activity of Paris, explaining and proselytising for Cubism, Simultaneity, Orphism, Dramatism, Futurism . . . all the forms through which the artists of the day were groping for a way to express the complex and multiple truth of the world in which they lived. He was constantly in touch now with painters and writers in Germany and Italy and when one of them visited Paris, he would naturally hurry to the flat in the Boulevard Saint-Germain. Here, he would feel himself, as in the studios of Picasso and Delaunay, to have reached one of the sources of the new art.

More and more foreigners were arriving in Montparnasse in this year of 1913. Many of them were very young. They had been schoolboys when Picasso and Apollinaire were elaborating Cubism in the *Bateau Lavoir*, and when Vlaminck and Derain were probing the secrets of red-daubed statuettes from Dahomey. They had followed the evolution of the *Ecole de Paris* from their distant homelands and it seemed natural to them, whether they painted as Cubists or not, to regard the world from the Cubist angle of vision. They had arrived in France, irresistibly attracted by the prestige of Paris and quite prepared to live on *café-crêmes* and expedients in return for a spiritual freedom they could never have tasted in Warsaw or Budapest.

Soon these young foreigners were outnumbering the Frenchmen in Montparnasse. There was Kisling, the Pole, whose personality was as aggressive as his painting and who once fought a sabre duel, in front of the *Rotonde*, with a compatriot who had offended him. There was the sculptor Zadkine, who had arrived from his native Russia via Scotland, where an austere father had placed him in an even more austere boarding school. He would recount his escape, with his harsh Russian accent, telling how he had arrived penniless in London and found sporadic employment with an old woodworker, eating on days when there was work to do and fasting on others. One day, his employer had said to him, 'If you want regular work, you must show what you can do. A rose, for instance.' And he presented him with a block of wood. Zadkine worked at night for many weeks and when he had finished, every petal was as transparent as that of a real flower. So he had left the woodworker and taken it to the professor of sculpture at the Central School of Art who accepted him as a student. There, as he modelled copies of the Discobolus, he had heard rumours of a very different kind of art in Paris, and so he had arrived in Montparnasse.

Marc Chagall, too, had come from Russia, bringing with him a ceaseless nostalgia for his native Vitebsk, with its goats and cows and miracle-working rabbis. He was too naive, and perhaps too much of an Oriental, to appreciate the painters of Montparnasse, within their intellectual approach to art and habit of analysing their own work. He preferred to sit alone on the terrace of the *Dôme* dreaming of fine red cows and gazelle-eyed Jewish virgins floating in the sky above the roof-tops and chestnut trees, while he sipped the glass of coffee which, with a piece of bread bought on credit from a sympathetic baker in the rue de la Grande Chaumière, formed his usual daily diet.

Then there was Foujita, fresh from Japan, initiating himself, with the aid of a number of the quarter's prettiest women, into the customs of the West; and Diego de Riviera, who was experimenting with Cubism before returning to become the official genius of his native Mexico; and the Americans, Bruce and Frost, disciples of Delaunay and who were to introduce abstract art into the United States; and the Russian Soutine, the Bulgarian Pascin, and many others, all young, bewildered or aggressive according to their natures, and generally under-nourished. Visitors from more conservative quarters of the city came to stare and generally went away muttering about anarchists and *métèques*. 'This band of foreign invaders', wrote an angry chronicler, 'represents nothing, not even their own countries. . . .'

The establishment of this international conclave on the Left Bank resulted in a close liaison with most of the world capitals. There was constant coming and going between Paris and London, Berlin, New York, all the capitals of Central and Eastern Europe. The contact with Germany was the strongest of all, since Berlin and Munich, alone of the European cities, had seen an evolution in art that was almost comparable to that in Paris. For several years already there had been a frenzy of activity among the young German painters. They had suddenly discovered Van Gogh, Gauguin, Matisse, and above all Cézanne, 'the supreme master'. In 1905, *Die Brücke* had been founded in reaction against the hideous 'modern style' (an international term at that time, pronounced in various ways according to the nationality of the speaker) which had swept over Germany at the end of the century. It had exhibited paintings by foreigners like Van Dongen, Chagall and Munch, as well as experimental work by the young German artists.

Then, in 1911, Kandinsky had founded the *Neue Künstler-vereinigung* and soon after, the *Blaue Reiter* which specialised at first in the work of the Expressionist painters, who were seeking, like the Cubists in Paris, for a way to express the 'new reality'. Kandinsky had been convinced from the first that the new movements in France and Germany were tending in the same direction, both representing definite attempts, though carried out in sharply contrasting manners, to break down or transcend the laws of time and space. The *Blaue Reiter* exhibited the early work of

Rouault, Derain and Picasso, and Kandinsky sent a copy of his book *Ueber das Geistige in der Kunst* to Delaunay. The impact of this work on Delaunay, and through him on Apollinaire, was at least partly responsible for the development of 'Simultaneity', the abolition of Subject and the first experiments in 'pure painting' or abstract art.

By 1912, Delaunay had been in contact with Klee, Macke and Marc, and had begun to have a good deal of influence over the young German painters. It was in that year, notably, that Paul Klee had spent a few days in Paris and had discovered Cubism and Orphism. His reaction to Cubism seems to have been hostile, because of what he described as its 'immobilism' and a tendency to 'destroy in the name of construction'. A visit to Delaunay's studio, however, was a revelation for him. There he saw for the first time pictures which he described on returning to Berlin as 'sufficient in themselves, borrowing nothing from nature, having an entirely abstract existence in the world of Form . . . a kind of living, plastic creation that is almost as different from a design on a carpet as a fugue by Bach would be.' It was through *Orphisme* (the term finally invented by Apollinaire to describe both De-launay's painting and his own poetry) that Klee really discovered the technique he was to use from that time on in his life-long struggle to attain through Form 'the Infinity which envelops the visible and the invisible'.

When Klee returned to Berlin, he had become more convinced than ever of his 'prophetic mission' as a painter. Delaunay himself, who was sceptical by nature and almost entirely preoccupied by technical problems, must have been astonished to learn that his theory of prismatic colouring had become an excuse for meta-physics. The young German had, in fact, been so timid and dis-creet that a few years later neither he nor Sonia retained any recollection of his visit to their studio.

The principal go-between for French and German painting was H. Walden, who had founded in Berlin the journal *Der Sturm* and the gallery of the same name. This gnome-like little man, with his hair flowing to his shoulders and his jerky, hopping gait, had a consuming passion for art. Most of his life was spent in travelling incessantly throughout Europe in search of new painters. He had an infallible eye for talent and had discovered Delaunay as early as

1910, at a time when the Expressionist Movement was at its height and *Der Sturm* was publishing lithographs by Kandinsky, Pascin, Chagall and Kokoschka, who were all considered at that time as Expressionists. He had discovered the Italian Futurists too—although this needed less perspicacity, since they were carrying out aggressive publicity campaigns in most of the European capitals—and he had published their 'Manifesto' and a number of Futurist poems. Marinetti had even given a lecture in his gallery and had had such a success that Futurism had spread like measles over the Berlin of 1912, with its avid desire for novelty in any form.

In the same year, Walden published in *Der Sturm* an important article in which Apollinaire traced the ancestry of Cubism and explained the new directions in which it was moving. It stands out like a landmark at this moment when Cubism had reached its apotheosis:

'Cubism', he wrote, 'should be understood as an art consisting of research into a new form of composition with formal elements, which it discovers not in visual reality but in conceptional reality.

'This tendency leads inevitably to a poetic style of painting which cannot be judged by any ordinary standards since it is only in the case of simple Cubism that the painter is still obliged to make use of the geometrical surfaces necessary for the complete figuration of an object. . . . If, however, he takes the trouble to understand the true role of that object, then he will stand aloof from its mere appearance, so that only its veritable and objective reality remains. It is impossible to deny that painting of this kind is justifiable.

'Anyone can understand that a chair will still have four legs, a seat and a back, from whatever angle one looks at it, and that if one of these elements is taken away, it will lose an essential element of its reality.

'The primitives painted a town, not as it would appear to a person standing in the foreground, but as it was in reality, that is, with its doors, its towers and its streets. Many of the innovations we find in this art to-day confirm its human and poetic character. . . .

'It has seemed to Delaunay that if an elementary colour really determines its complementary colour, then when the contrary occurs, and the complementary colour is not determined, this elementary colour will break up in the atmosphere and provoke, simultaneously, all the colours of the solar spectrum.

'This tendency can be described as Orphism. I believe it is more promising than (other tendencies in Cubism) and it is natural that its receptivity should have attracted many young German painters.

'This dramatic movement in art and poetry is growing constantly in France. It is represented by the work of Fernand Léger . . . by certain canvases of Mlle Laurencin, by recent works by Picabia . . . by the work of Marcel Duchamp who is attempting to symbolise the movement of life itself, etc.

'A number of extremely interesting German painters like Kandinsky, Marc, Meidler, Macke, Jan Censky, Munter, Otto Freundlich, etc., belong instinctively to this movement.

'The Italian Futurists, products of Fauvism and Cubism, also appertain to this Orphism, as do all those who are in revolt against the conventional forms of perspective and psychology. . . .

'It is a movement in the direction of pure painting, since it carries us up towards the greatest heights without the aid of any convention whatever, whether literary, artistic or scientific.

'This is where inspiration begins.

'We are aiming in the direction of plastic lyricism.

'Parallel with painting, there is growing up in France a literary movement which also aims at a concrete and direct lyricism which the Naturalist writers were incapable of attaining.

'This creative tendency is spreading everywhere.

'Painting is no longer an art of reproduction, but one of creation.

'These two movements, Cubism and Orphism, lead us into the regions of absolute poetry and pure light. . . .'

The article had been followed, in January 1913, by an exhibition entirely consecrated to Delaunay. He and Apollinaire had been

Walden's guests in Berlin for the occasion and on the opening day Apollinaire gave a lecture on modern painting. The trip was not, apparently, very successful. Apollinaire was probably still too preoccupied with his broken heart to enjoy himself. He complained that all German women were spotty, while Delaunay—a true Frenchman who disliked foreign customs—could not bear the feather beds. On their way home, they had visited Macke in his studio in Bonn and exchanged ideas on the future of 'pure painting', but on the whole, they had been glad to find themselves back in Paris.

The stimulating intellectual atmosphere there calmed Apollinaire's exacerbated nerves. He had been plunged at once into the excitement of the publication of his *Méditations Esthétiques* and of *Alcools,* into the fascinating task of applying Cubist theories to poetry. It was the period of opium-smoking with Picabia and Dalize, of the Futurist Manifesto, of the challenges to Cravan and Duhamel; the period of poems which sometimes went beyond what Pierre Reverdy was to describe as 'that mysterious boundary which the mind must be capable of attaining but beyond which it must not pass', and on the far side of which lies the chaos of intellectual sterility; and which sometimes sends ringing out one of those unique cries of hope and despair that justify everything, and give a meaning to everything.

Such were the diverse manifestations of spiritual distress. Behind them lay the pangs of disappointed love and the neurosis of security.

XII

'The little motor-car'

It was Louise Faure-Favier who suggested a holiday in Normandy. She, who was the friend of Marie Laurencin as well as of Apollinaire, and who understood him better, perhaps, than any of his male friends, knew exactly the state of mind he was in at the time and guessed that it could prove dangerous in the long run. The trip was to be an evasion, a discarding of all the tension and worries of Paris, and at the same time it was to be a final attempt to bring about a reconciliation between the two ex-lovers. André Billy decided to join them and the party was finally completed by René Dalize, accompanied by a certain Vera.

Louise and Marie were the first arrivals and awaited their friends in Villequier, by the Seine, where Apollinaire and Billy joined them two days later. They had come on foot from Rouen and Apollinaire had developed an appetite so formidable that he could pay little attention to the two charming girls—one in pink, one in blue, with wide straw hats hanging like flower-baskets over their arms—who met them at the ferry. It was not till dessert was served that he was able to pay them a few compliments, and by that time the innkeeper was seriously alarmed by the amount of food that had disappeared.

Once they had calmed their host's fears that he would be out of pocket by the end of their stay, the six Parisians settled down to enjoy a few days of idyllic happiness. Some river pilots were staying in the hotel and Apollinaire added to his store of recondite information by questioning them about the secrets of the Seine, its tides, the manœuvres which enabled them to accost the ships in the midst of its treacherous currents. There were long excursions, on foot or by hired waggons—to Caudebec, to the lovely Benedictine Abbey of Saint-Wandrille, to the Forest of Brotonne, with its herds of wild deer. For these city-dwellers, the lush Norman countryside was a new and exciting experience. Only Marie Laurencin was a little reticent and complained to her friend Louise that there was too much air, that the eggs were too fresh and the milk smelt of cows. 'In Paris', she concluded, 'at least the eggs have a taste and the milk hasn't.'

Billy and Apollinaire, both tireless walkers, visited the ruins of Jumièges and amused themselves by evoking the shades of Flaubert and Bouilhet. But there was none of the Flaubertian cynicism to mar this radiant holiday.

'Apollinaire and I', André Billy recalls, 'mocked at no one but ourselves. There was no bitterness in us, no intellectual revolt, no conceit, none of the artist's contempt for the bourgeois, but on the contrary a subtle and ingenuous harmony with the world, a fraternal and joyful communion with the universe. It was an intoxication—for that is the only way of describing the feeling—that I had never discovered except in company of Apollinaire.'

Apollinaire had, indeed, this 'intoxicating' effect on many people, and many of them, like Billy, never saw beyond or beneath this capacity for giving out happiness. Actually, there was a good deal of tension and anxiety to spoil the charm of Normandy for him and the holiday ended in disappointment, for Marie Laurencin refused to change her mind. 'He is too bad-tempered', she explained briefly to Louise Faure-Favier, and when Apollinaire returned to Paris all his hopes of reconciliation had disappeared.

Serge Férat and his sister saw the truth at once. They were more intuitive than Billy, or even than the sensitive and devoted Louise Faure-Favier. Perhaps it was because they were Slavs that they could understand the Slav aspect of a nature in many other ways so typically Latin. They knew that gaiety and despair are not always contradictory and they saw in certain eccentricities of behaviour the signs of melancholy rather than exuberance. They decided that something must be done to divert their friend's attention and thus hit on the idea of buying *Les Soirées de Paris*.

There had been a good deal of discussion about this rather shaky little publication during the walks in Normandy. It had been founded a couple of years earlier by Billy, René Dalize, André Tudesq and Apollinaire himself and had been a cause of dissension from the first. Apollinaire had published in it a number of the poems that were to appear in *Alcools*, and a certain amount of art criticism, but none of his fellow-editors had been convinced of the importance of Cubism, nor, indeed, of the value of Apollinaire's latest poetic experiments. In the number of December 1912 he had managed to publish *Zone* and the article entitled *Réalité, Peinture Pure*, inspired by the painting of Delaunay and published in German in the same month in *Der Sturm*. Perhaps he had slipped them in during a moment of inattention on the part of his co-editors. At any rate, there had been violent protests, almost a quarrel with Dalize, and from that date on, his contributions had become rare and relatively orthodox.

He was, in fact, finding it more and more difficult to publish his own work. His 'ideograms'—those exasperating or seductive little pictures of a bird, a pipe, a bouquet of flowers, composed of words that yielded their secrets as one turned and twisted the printed page—were not likely to appeal even to such an eclectic review as *Vers et Prose* and were ruthlessly turned down by *Les Soirées de Paris*. It occurred, therefore, to Férat and Hélène d'Oettingen that if Apollinaire could have full control over the latter review, he would be able to express himself freely at last, and at the same time find a new interest to distract his mind from his own troubles. As *Les Soirées de Paris* had never managed to attract more than forty subscribers and was in a singularly precarious financial condition, Billy would normally have been glad to get rid of it. In this case, however, he was suspicious of his friends' intentions. He had no wish to see his review used for spreading what he considered as pernicious doctrines, and suspected that if Apollinaire and the Férats got control of it that was exactly what would happen. Finally, Apollinaire manœuvred all the protagonists out of Paris, which he believed to be unlucky for this sort of negotiation, and brought them to La Baule, on the Breton coast, where Serge and Hélène had rented a villa. Billy's obstinacy looked like holding out even in the sea air, but in the afternoon Apollinaire whispered to his friends that they should stay in the drawing-room while he cornered his victim in the kitchen. The two were absent for a long time, but at last Apollinaire appeared, radiant with success, and announced, 'It's done!' Férat was confirmed in his opinion that his friend was a master diplomat and, indeed, Apollinaire was extraordinarily skilful at handling people and persuading them to do whatever he wanted.

The first number under the new editorship appeared in November 1913. It contained five reproductions of Cubist still-lives by Picasso, a 'Cubist' poem by Max Jacob and Apollinaire's own account of the *Salon d'Automne*, in which he praised and explained the exhibits of the Cubist painters. The forty subscribers immediately withdrew their forty subscriptions and the booksellers had to be heavily bribed with *apéritifs* before they would consent to put copies on sale.

The second number contained Apollinaire's own 'orphic' poem, *Lundi rue Christine*, then his 'idéogrammes' began to appear. There were reproductions from paintings of uncompromising Cubists like Metzinger, Gleizes, Francis Picabia; there was the famous number consecrated to the memory of the Douanier Rousseau; there were contributions by Apollinaire's foreign friends, and specially by Italians like Soffini, Severini, Chirico, who were trying to persuade their compatriots to admire something newer than the Dome Cathedral or the Palace of the Signori.

Apollinaire had been unlucky so far with his own reviews, but *Les Soirées de Paris* was soon being widely read and attracting first-class contributors. For the first time, he had both his platform and his audience. The editorship of an important review restored his confidence, just as Férat and his sister had hoped. He was a more important personality in the capital now than he had been before the affair of the statuettes. The editorial office in the Boulevard Raspail became, almost immediately, a centre for the aspiring talent of Montparnasse. All the young painters of the *Rotonde* and the *Dôme* came there—for was not *Les Soirées de Paris* the almost official organ of Cubism?—and so did the writers who had known each other in Montmartre and others who had just arrived in Paris to make their literary fortunes. Among the latter, there were two who, young as they were, already showed vigorous personalities and the promise of real talent: Jean Cocteau, with his wasp waist and high toupee of hair, who straddled the world of bohemia and that of high society and who was to introduce Montparnasse into the *salons* of his fashionable patronesses; and Pierre

Reverdy, fresh from Narbonne, in the South, who was living in one of the deserted studios of the *Bateau Lavoir* and working in a printer's shop for the privilege of printing his own poems on his employer's press. It was a new generation, all too ready to take the discoveries of their elders for granted and to go farther and faster than they had done. Apollinaire sometimes wondered uneasily whether they, like Zadkine and Léger, thought him old-fashioned.

As for Marie Laurencin, this absorbing new interest was proving as good a cure as Férat and his sister had hoped. Love was gradually fading into a tender friendship, and perhaps Apollinaire was already beginning to suspect that there would be other loves for him and that the 'fine phoenix' had not yet finished his successive resuscitations. When Marie told him in June that she was about to marry a German painter, a 'Dômist' named Otto von Waetgen, he was more surprised than broken-hearted.

Apollinaire has described the climate of that early summer of 1914, when no one—or at least none of the habitués of the *Dôme*, the *Rotonde*, the *Bal Bullier*, or Rosalie's little restaurant in the rue Campagne Première—imagined that a chapter of the world's history was drawing to its close:

'It was not without a certain tender gravity, but it was above all light-hearted. . . . The year 1914 opened in a whirl of gaiety. The period was dominated, like that of Gavarni, by Carnival. It was the fashion to dance, there was dancing everywhere. Feminine fashions lent themselves so well to fancy dress that women disguised their hair with brilliant and delicate colours, reminiscent of those luminous fountains that astonished me when, as a child, I visited the Exhibition of 1889. . . . Naturally, the balls at the Opera House were revived. At the first of them, each of the women received a locked box, while each man was presented with a key and the mission to discover the appropriate keyhole. This ribald pleasantry seemed an excellent augury for the future. And perhaps one day, when the war has been forgotten, together with the tango, the *maxime* and the *furlana*, it will be said of this pacific year of 1914 'Much will be forgiven it because it danced so much.'[1]

It was in this climate of careless pleasure that he prepared the July–August number of the *Soirées de Paris*. It was a number largely consecrated to 'Fantomas,' the film hero whose exploits had become for them at once a joke and a myth. Apollinaire and Dalize, says André Billy, were capable of discussing him, apparently quite seriously, for hours on end. When Max Jacob proposed founding a 'Society of the Friends of Fantomas', Apollinaire declared himself a life member and opened the columns of his review to the study of this important subject. So Max, serious as ever in his buffoonery, had produced a poem in honour of his hero, followed by a weighty essay, composed of a 'critical section' and a 'philosophical and moral section'. This 'Fantomas Special Number' also contained reproductions of paintings by Vlaminck and Léger; poems by Georges Rouaut, who was still hesitating, like many artists at that period, between painting and poetry; a section on the poets of the Anglo-American School of 'Imagists' who had grouped themselves around Ezra Pound—Aldington, H.D.,* Fletcher, William Carlos Williams, James Joyce and Ford Madox Hueffer; and a proposition by Léopold Sturzwage for an entirely new art, to be known as 'Colour-Rhythm', whose one disadvantage was that it would necessitate the projection of one to two thousand images on a screen in order to obtain a 'rhythm' lasting three minutes; and Apollinaire's own 'ideogrammes' and his account of the month's exhibitions.

Once the review had been sent off to the printers, its editor was free to think about the long summer holidays that stretched before him. He was short of money, as usual, and undecided how to spend his time, when *Comœdia* suggested that he should send a reportage from Deauville. He was to be accompanied by his friend André Rouveyre, who was to illustrate the articles.

The holidays started well, since the journey was made by motor-car. Apollinaire's passion for this mode of travel was as strong as it had been in 1901, when he had set out for the Rhineland in Madame de Milhau's de Dion-Bouton. Deauville was beginning to acquire the reputation of one of France's most fashionable seaside resorts, attracting the rich and famous figures of the day and frequented by a cosmopolitan society in which the English already figured in the majority. The season was at its height and the two friends prepared to amuse themselves. The first few days were delightful. They lay on the beach, walked,

* Hilda Doolittle, wife of Richard Aldington.

called on Tristan Bernard, who had a villa in the neighbourhood and received them, as Apollinaire noted complacently, with every consideration. While Rouveyre sketched the leading personalities in the Casino, Apollinaire corrected the proofs of his album of 'ideogrammes'—*Et moi aussi je suis peintre*—which was due to appear the following month. Rouveyre had brought with him three little toads, who took up a good deal of their time and attention, as they had to be constantly fed with live flies.

'Sometimes', Rouveyre recalled later, 'we went together to the Casino; suddenly I would realise [Apollinaire] was no longer there. I would find him at last, peacefully installed in the public library, writing, lost to the world. He had been there for the last hour, he would say, and add: 'Don't disturb me, I'll have finished in two minutes.' I knew what to expect: an hour or two later he would join me at lunch, when I was already half through the meal.

'These luncheons were excellent and he would sing the praises of each dish, explaining its history, its origins, the way it was prepared and the way different peoples accommodated it to their taste. It was the same with the wines and liqueurs; he knew all about them, about their subtleties, their most secret chemistry. In fact, he was a great magician of pleasure in everything that concerned the mind and the senses. It did one good just to see him.

'A whole troop of elderly people and cosmopolitan young women would crowd around him when the coffee and drinks were served, listening to him as he reigned in their midst, kindly, talkative and given to gently laying down the law. For our hotel was frequented by groups of foreigners who came for the whole summer, chiefly Polish, Czech, Hungarian, Russian or German girls. The proprietor was the daughter of a certain Professor Delbost, whom I had never heard of, although Guillaume apparently knew every detail of his life. . . .'

Presumably they read the newspapers and noticed that the international situation was alarming, but it had been taken for granted for so long that civilisation had reached a point where war was impossible that the news was not taken too seriously. All the same, it disturbed the serenely frivolous atmosphere, and on July 29, in a letter to Férat, Apollinaire mentioned, 'People are worried about war here. Nearly everyone is getting out. I don't believe in it.' Next day, he added, he intended to bathe and work at his monthly article for the *Mercure de France*. Two days later, they were spending the evening in the Casino, watching the tango that had recently been imported into France and had become the latest craze on the dance-floor, when news of a general mobilisation broke up the gathering. Although they still hoped this might be simply a move designed to intimidate the Kaiser, the two friends decided to return to Paris. They roused the chauffeur and started off at daybreak, leaving behind them a number of terrified German girls, who had awoken too late to the realities of the situation. The annual automobile races were due to be held in Deauville the following day and they were reassured by the numerous racing cars that passed them coming from Paris. But in Lisieux, when they stopped to mend a puncture in the light of a gas-lamp, the lamp immediately went out and Rouveyre asked nervously. 'Do you think it is an omen of war?'

Apollinaire recounted the departure from Deauville and their journey in a poem entitled *La petite Auto* which proves, not quite that he was the prophet he liked to imagine, but that he had a remarkably lucid view of the future:

> Je sentais en moi des êtres neufs pleins de dexterité
> Bâtir et aussi agencer un univers nouveau
> Un marchand d'une opulence inouïe et d'une taille prodigieuse
> Disposait un étalage extraordinaire
> Et des bergers gigantesques menaient
> De grands troupeaux muets qui broutaient des paroles
> Et contre lesquels aboyaient tous les chiens sur la route
> Et quand après avoir passé l'après-midi
> Par Fontainebleau
> Nous arrivâmes à Paris
> Au moment où l'on affichait la mobilisation
> Nous comprîmes mon camarade et moi
> Que la petite auto nous avait conduits dans une époque
> Nouvelle
> Et bien qu'étant déja tous deux des hommes murs
> Nous venions cependant de naître . . .*

* Within myself I sensed new beings full of dexterity
  Building up and organising a new universe

Paris was plastered with mobilisation posters and seething with patriotic emotion. When he and Rouveyre reached Montparnasse, they met a procession moving up the Boulevard in the direction of the Lion de Belfort, manifesting against the *métèques*. For the 'great dumb flocks that browse on words', the quarter had suddenly taken on a sinister aspect, as if it were peopled with enemy agents.

The mood of the *Montparnos* was, indeed, rather out of tune with that of the country in general and even with the rest of the literary Paris. For the editorial board of *Les Guêpes*, for the young writers who surrounded Maurras and Barrès, it might indeed seem that the Great Adventure had begun. But these intellectuals, nourished on pacifism and internationalism, saw things in a different perspective and most of them would have agreed with Léautaud, who was noting in his diary, 'War is the legalised return to the savage state.'

Yet the mob that screamed, 'Shoot the traitors!' in front of the *Rotonde* were mistaken. The *Montparnos* were not much given to patriotic ardour; they had few illusions about the war and their dreams were not of military glory, yet they did their duty and some of them did more. If one examines the military records of the habitués of Montparnasse, one discovers that those who were French citizens proved to be no worse soldiers than the rest of their compatriots and that some of them were even heroic; while many of the foreigners who could have returned peacefully to neutral homelands volunteered for the French Army.

Most of his friends took it for granted that Apollinaire, the stateless cosmopolitan, would disappear from the scene, and spend

---

A shopkeeper of untold wealth and prodigious size
Was arranging an extraordinary display-window
And gigantic shepherds were leading
Great dumb herds that browsed on words
And around whom all the dogs in the road were barking
And passing that afternoon by Fontainebleau
We arrived in Paris
At the moment when the mobilisation posters were going up
And my comrade and I understood then
That the little motor-car had brought us into a new Epoch
And though we were both mature men
We had just been born.

the war in some neutral country. It would have been easy for him to do so. The Delaunays, who had been spending their holidays in Funterrabia, decided to remain in Spain and pressed him to join them; friends in Switzerland invited him for the duration. To the general surprise he presented himself at the nearest recruiting office. The organisation there was still rather uncertain and no one knew what to do with a Russian citizen who had never had any kind of military training. His offer was politely refused and he reappeared as a civilian, furious and disappointed. Once more he had been rejected, once more he had to face the fact that he did not 'belong', either in France or anywhere else.

Meanwhile, Paris was becoming a deserted city. Most of his friends had been sucked up into the machine of war, had joined or were about to join their regiments. Picasso was in Avignon; Marie Laurencin, who had mocked at Max Jacob for predicting that she would live one day in a foreign land, had fled to Spain with her German husband. Montparnasse was deserted, and indeed almost a dangerous area, since popular rumour had decreed it was a nest of spies and the police were constantly descending on the cafés and arresting anyone brave enough to stop for a drink on one of the familiar terraces. The popular press had found an easy scapegoat in Cubism and frequently recalled the success it had had in Germany and the fact that the owners of the two Paris galleries that specialised in Cubist painting were Germans.* Soon it became fashionable to speak of *Kubismus* and to think of all the *Montparnos* as pro-German. In actual fact, most of them—including the foreigners—had joined up, or at least offered their services. 'Nearly all of them are here', wrote the *Bulletin des Écrivains* under the title 'The Cubists Face the Pointed Helmets', and quoted their correspondent, Albert Gleizes: 'I send you this card from Toul, the outpost of the Eastern Front. There is no question of Cubism or Simultaneity at present. When shall we discuss them again? And when shall we take them up once more? Soon, I hope, and with the glorious knowledge of having defeated the German felon.'

Marinetti had been arrested in Italy for publicly tearing up seven Austrian flags; Kisling had appeared at the *Rotonde* in an

---

* Frantz Jourdain, President of the *Salon d'Automne*, is said to have explained, on hearing that war had been declared: 'At least, this will mean the end of Cubism!'

extraordinary uniform composed of an Artillery cap, a Sapper's cape and the baggy trousers of the Colonial regiments; Blaise Cendrars had joined the Foreign Legion ... but the idea of *Kubismus* had caught the public fancy and was not to be eradicated by mere facts. Apollinaire, as its mouthpiece, found himself isolated and suspect. He, who disliked solitude and poverty above all things, now found himself faced with both of them. It was practically impossible for a writer to earn a living in war-time Paris. There could naturally be no question of producing another number of *Les Soirées de Paris; Vers et Prose* had ceased publication too, and so had all the reviews to which he generally contributed. Even the solid *Mercure de France,* where he had been publishing a monthly column for the last three years, temporarily failed him, so did *Comœdia,* where his illustrated report on Deauville slept all through the war years.* As for the daily papers, they had been reduced to a single page and were interested only in news about the war.

There was no help to be expected from his family either. Albert, who could usually be counted on in times of trouble, was in Mexico. Madame de Kostrowitsky, in her new villa at Le Chatou, lamented the closing of the clandestine gambling dens on which she counted for a precarious income. Apollinaire hesitated. The German troops were advancing steadily on the capital. It looked as though the enlistment which would have regularised his situation was impossible, yet it seemed to him equally impossible to leave his beloved France. Finally he compromised by accepting an invitation from friends in Nice. There he made a second attempt to enlist and this time he was successful.

'After leaving with Siegler for Nice', he wrote from Nîmes to Picabia in Paris, 'I could have gone to Spain with a friend who offered me the most sumptuous hospitality there. S. did all he could to persuade me to accept. They were annoyed at my refusal, not so much S. as the other.

'But it was impossible to leave France in circumstances that would have been dishonourable for a man and I was overjoyed when the Enlistment Board in Nice declared me fit. While I'm

* The article finally appeared in 1920, when Apollinaire was dead and Rouveyre desperately ill with tuberculosis contracted on war service.

waiting, I cavalcade about and shoot in the garrison till it's time to shoot in war.

'Only one thing is lacking—money. It would be kind of you, my dear Francis, if you could send me fifty francs a month for the few months before I leave for the Front. It will not last long and you know, my dear Francis, that I don't like to ask for money. I will give it back to you immediately after the war and you will be rendering me a real service. But write me a long letter even if you refuse this service I ask you.

'Here, it's bitterly cold. The food is as you can imagine. No coats, but we're very gay all the same. My mates in the barracks are all waggon drivers or coachmen, except for a gardener and a policeman from the section for the supervision of prostitutes in Marseilles. . . .

'We don't even think about the war. We're too busy for that.

'There are departures from time to time and those who go are fitted out from head to foot with new equipment. We get our news from the convalescents, sent back from the Front after being wounded.

'I am an aspirant-corporal and I very much want to get my pips. If you could put in a word in my favour to the Commander of the 38th Dépôt, Captain Arnaud, without it seeming to come from me, you would be doing me another big favour. You will have heard that Dupuy* was hit by two bits of shrapnel and is now back in the front line.

'If it were possible to get me—as a volunteer—promoted to sub-lieutenant, even up at the Front, I should be glad to go up there as soon as possible for nothing is worse than the boredom of a garrison town, specially when one hasn't a sou.

'Write me a long letter and tell your wife to write to me too. They've forced me to grow a moustache. My concierge in Paris has changed. The new one's a bitch. My cat Pipe is well, my charwoman has taken her and sends me news of her. All this is probably very uninteresting compared with the things that are happening in the North of France. But by some strange aberration we pay no attention to the war. . . .'

Picabia had no sympathy with his friend's 'enthusiasm for

* René Dalize.

uniforms' and declined to further his military ambitions. He was not the first, nor the last, to be scandalised by Apollinaire's joyful acceptance of war. Léautaud, among others, was gravely puzzled and wrote, 'Your letter was a great surprise to me. I should never have thought you had these tendencies, these sentiments. There were evidently things about you I never knew. Or else, something has changed you. . . . ?' A romantic delight in soldiering, a juvenile desire for military honours, were not in the Cubist style. There was something inexplicable here, a volte-face that disconcerted and sometimes irritated those who looked on the war as a necessary evil. Guillaume Apollinaire still existed, remained the poet, the enchanter, the 'magician of pleasure' his friends had known in Montmartre, in Neuilly and in Montparnasse; but he had a double now—Gunner de Kostrowitsky, the life and soul of the canteen, punctual and conscientious at drill and exercises, ambitious for rank and rather looking forward to an exchange of fire with the lines where the Francophile artists of *Der Sturm* and *Der Blaue Reiter,* disguised by their pointed helmets, would perhaps be arming against him.

XIII

The Good Soldier

*Ah Dieu! Que la guerre est jolie.**

Love and war were to prove the two great sources of Apollinaire's lyric inspiration. The two elements are less bizarrely mated than one might suppose. André Billy, when they had tramped together by the banks of the Seine, under the soft Normandy sun, had detected in his friend a fundamental harmony with the world, an absence of intellectual protest that was quite different from the attitude of the Romantic or even the Symbolist poets. The world and its ways seemed to him essentially good, so perhaps it was not unnatural that the two functions which had absorbed most of the male part of humanity's attention throughout so great a portion of the world's history, should have brought him at least as much joy as pain. 'O war, multiplication of love!' he once wrote, with surely spontaneous joy, on the battlefields of Champagne, and this connection, intimate to the point of identification, is everywhere apparent in the poems of the war years.

'The life of a soldier, for a man of his nature and character', writes André Rouveyre, 'became, as soon as he experienced it, an incontestable and powerful stimulus. He suffered from it, but it strengthened him immensely. Then, almost immediately, it brought about a renewal of his poetic genius. There we touch on the deep-lying reasons that caused him, in his finest poems of this period, to speak of the war as if it were a marvellous holiday. . . .'

It was natural for him to accept war as part of life and to make the best of it, and perhaps he accepted it all the more easily because

* Apollinaire: *L'adieu du Cavalier.*

of the difficult situation from which it released him. From the moment he had signed his enlistment papers in the recruiting office in Nice, he had been freed of the insecurity, the 'foreignness', that had weighed on him for so long in Paris. 'I joined the Army on January 28, 1915,* I am a French citizen', he announced to Louise Faure-Favier, and to Max Jacob: 'We are on our way to glory, and if we win through, we'll try for the Academy.' Some of his friends, and especially Picabia, felt that he was forcing the note and resented it, but it was natural enough in the circumstances.

So Apollinaire enjoyed himself hugely, although Nîmes was dreary in those months of early winter and he was suffering from his usual disease of impecuniosity. As a volunteer he had the right to train for the rank of corporal. The aspirant received a new sky-blue uniform, of which he was distinctly vain. 'I look rather well in my artillery outfit: spurs, leggings, riding-breeches, jacket, cap, belt and pistol holster', he wrote to Paul Léautaud, who was the last man on earth to understand how he could take pleasure in such things. He was entirely absorbed in his new life, identifying himself as completely with it as he had identified himself a few months earlier with literary life in Paris. To Louise Faure-Favier he explained:

'I am so used to the barracks now that I feel as if I had always been a soldier. In spite of the hard parts of the job, I am as gay as ever, just as all my comrades are.

'As far as I can discover, I shall be leaving for the Front in about one and a half months and we shall not be kept hanging about once we are capable of taking command.

'I never imagined this destiny for myself. Me, dexterously measuring angles! It's incredible, yet it's true. Dynamometers, goniometers, slide-rules, maps, hold no more secrets for me and from what the commander at the depot has told me, I shall be given a battery to command within a fortnight, a battery of 90's. You see I am no longer doing mere exercises, I take aim like a master gunner, at least as far as the 75's are concerned, for

* Apollinaire enlisted on December 4, 1914. The task of his various biographers has been complicated by his total disregard for time. One date evidently seemed to him as good as another, so it is sometimes almost impossible to work out the sequence of events.

I know less about the 90's and the 120's, although we have no munitions here for the 75's. But all this can't interest you, my dear friend, tell me about your life in Paris and whether you are frightened.

'I am not afraid myself, yet the first time I heard cannon fire it made a disagreeable impression on me. It was the 90's and it seems the 75's are even more unpleasant, but as cannon they're very nice to manage and it's a pity I shall not be going with them. I think we are only going to train with batteries of 90's and 120's here. The 120's make a very deep noise. Well, I shall have to go wherever I am sent.

'So life is still pleasant. The most boring things are saddling, grooming the horses and learning indoor service. . . . '

Riding was part of artillery duties in those days and had to be learnt, at the expense of sores and furuncles. He enjoyed riding school too, though he was the wrong shape for a horseman and had never sat on a saddle in his life, and one of his fellow-pupils recalls his shriek for help as his horse broke into a gallop for the first time: 'Stop me! My horse is limping!' Finally he came to ride quite well and became very attached to the fat, white mare who had caused him such alarm.

> Notre moral est excellent
> Et le beau temps est très galant
> On se fout des obus comme d'une tartine
> Et mon cheval Loulou hennit très gentiment
> D'une voix argentine
> C'est un bidet charmant
> Au revoir mon Rouveyre
> Guillaume Apollinaire,*

he wrote gaily just before his departure for the Front. He was keeping up a voluminous correspondence with friends all over

---

* Our morale is excellent
  And this fine weather is most gallant
  We don't give a damn for the shells
  And my horse Loulou neighs most sweetly
  With her silvery voice
  She's a charming nag
  Goodbye my Rouveyre—
    Guillaume Apollinaire.

France, exchanging poems, letters, letter-poems that rhymed because rhyme came spontaneously in moods of elation, with soldiers and civilians. The regimental postman delivered as many letters for Corporal Kostrowitsky as for the rest of the battalion put together. They came from Francis Carco, mobilised in Besançon, where he was writing *Les Innocents* and dreaming of Montmartre; from Louis de Gonzague Frick, who remained an imperturbable dandy under the most murderous conditions and was to become famous in military circles for reporting to his colonel, after a reconnoitring mission; '*Messieurs les Allemands* appear to be in retreat'; from André Billy, temporarily attached to the War Office and a great provider of rhymed news about mutual friends ('Yesterday I saw Salmon all dressed in blue—With yellow braid on his breeches—And on each of his buttons blackened by fire—Was a little hunting horn . . .'); from Rouveyre in his labour battalion; from Léautaud, obstinately remaining in Paris among the dogs, cats and monkeys he starved himself to feed; from his publishers; from editors of reviews that might one day appear again; from charming women only too anxious to adopt him and console his loneliness.

Apollinaire even enjoyed the promiscuity of Army life that is generally so painful for intellectuals. His old friend Fernand Fleuret has told how, in his desire to win sympathy wherever he went, he would habitually identify himself with his companion of the moment, 'penetrate his thoughts, guess his tastes, some-times even unconsciously copy his mannerisms', so that in the course of a single day, his friends might notice several different ways of speaking and different tones of voice. This faculty of adapting himself to his companions, whoever they might be, stood him in good stead in the rough-and-tumble of the barracks, among men so much younger than himself and with such different backgrounds. In the canteen his radiant good humour and re-markable capacity for absorbing a certain white wine sold by the local nuns ensured him a wide popularity. The lives of these peasants, their families, their loves, the work on their farms in Brittany or the Berry, really interested him. They found their way into poems scribbled at night—the Territorial, mixing himself an anchovy salad and talking about his sick wife; three gunners sleeping, arm in arm, perched on their cannon; a professional tenor who sometimes moved him to tears by singing grand opera after lights out. He discovered to his joy one or two men who had read his work, notably a twenty-year-old corporal, René Berthier, who was a fervent admirer and dreamed of following in his footsteps. A wounded man described to him in the canteen the beauty of shells flaring into the night. Other convalescents fascinated him with their talk of life in the trenches. War still seemed romantic and ardent, as it had been in the great conflicts of the past and would never be again.

Some of his comrades seemed to him almost children. They were boys of nineteen, still bewildered by the sudden wrenching from their homes. Apollinaire remembered the girls he had loved at their age—Maria, Linda, Annie—and pitied them because they would perhaps never know the delights of love:

> Un fantassin presque un enfant
> Bleu comme le jour qui s'écroule
> Beau comme mon cœur triomphant
> Disait en mettant sa cagoule
>
> Tandis que nous n'y sommes pas
> Que de filles deviennent belles
> Voici l'hiver et pas à pas
> Leur beauté s'éloignera d'elles
>
> O Lueurs soudaines des tirs
> Cette beauté que j'imagine
> Faute d'avoir des souvenirs
> Tire de vous son origine . . .*

Beauty of women, beauty of war . . . the one enhancing the other and completing it. Beneath the exaltation, the acute pleasure

* A foot-soldier almost a child
  Blue as the passing day
  Fine as my own triumphant heart
  Said as he donned his hood
  So many girls growing to beauty
  While we are far away
  Here comes winter and step by step
  Their beauty will slip from them
  O sudden bursts of gun-fire
  I who have no memories
  Can imagine beauty only
  As it flashes from you

in small things, one senses the complementary stimulation of love. In Nice, even before his enlistment, Apollinaire had met Louise de Coligny-Chatillon, who had a wide and eclectic experience of love in spite of her youth. Her family belonged to the ancient nobility of France—a fact which immensely impressed him; she had already been married and divorced and now she was profiting to the utmost from her new freedom. Apollinaire himself had re-discovered in Nice the sensuous charm of the South that had formed the background of his childhood. With Louise he wandered in the familiar Old City, 'with its odours of fruits and spices, mingled with the smells of living flesh, of sour pastry, of dried cod and of latrines',[1] which transported him back to the days of the Lycée and adolescent adventures with Ange Toussaint Luca. They smoked a little opium—since this was the fashionable vice—spent their evenings in the circle of Louise's brilliant, worldly friends. She was intelligent enough to guess that her admirer was a man who was already, or who would soon become, important; and astute enough to sense possible advantages in his obvious devotion. At the gay dinners in fashionable restaurants she was apt to mock at his lack of aristocratic polish, but when they wandered by the sea, through the Mediterranean nights that evoked such poignant memories, she would move his heart with confidences concerning a singularly unhappy childhood. The frantic greed with which she seized on life was surely a reaction from the severe convent boarding school, where she had passed her life from the age of four till her marriage at seventeen. Even at that time she must have been unstable, capricious and wholly lacking in self-control, but the oppressive school régime, interrupted by holidays spent for the most part under lock and key in her own room, had accentuated these defects instead of curing them.

Perhaps it was precisely these defects, and even her vices, that attracted Apollinaire. The lessons of experience had never ridded him of the primitive male instinct that saw in every woman a wild creature to be tamed. Louise was a challenge. 'I know now why I was so fascinated in Nice by that orange gleam that appeared at mid-day over the Place Masséna', he wrote to her from Nîmes, 'it was because I love liberty and rebellion above all things. But I love them because they are a challenge to me. . . .'

He might have written the same words to Marie, or even to

Annie. The Polish Hussar was always incorrigibly present in him when it came to his dealings with women, but behind the raping, plundering Hussar, there always lurked a sentimental and terribly vulnerable lover. Louise—*Le P'tit Lou*—was probably not the 'demon-child whose kisses bring madness', against whom he raged in romantic despair, but she proved to be more than a match for him.

In Nice she had flirted outrageously, provoked him, then cruelly wounded his pride and accorded him nothing. Perhaps the disappointment had something to do with his haste to enlist. At any rate, he wrote one of those sorrowful, forgiving letters that suit such occasions and departed to join his regiment in Nîmes.

When he left the barracks for his first excursion into town, 'Lou' was waiting at the gates. She had been piqued to find her devoted lover capable of showing such independence, and she had no intention of allowing herself to be abandoned. Apollinaire was in transports of joy. His new mistress opened up for him an erotic paradise such as he had never yet known. The joy of victory coloured the most banal details of a soldier's life. When she was absent he sent a spate of letters and poems; whenever he could free himself, she joined him for a few brief, rapturous hours in some hotel in Nîmes, Nice, Menton, Marseilles. . . .

Dans la chambre de la volupté
Où je t'irai trouver à Nîmes
Tandis que nous prendrons le thé
Pendant le peu d'heures intimes
Que m'embellira ta beauté

Nous ferons cent mille bêtises
Malgré la guerre et tous ses maux
Nous aurons de belles surprises
Les arbres en fleurs les Rameaux
Pâques les premières cerises

Nous lirons dans le même lit
Au livre de ton corps lui-même
—C'est un livre qu'au lit on lit—

Guillaume Apollinaire in 1914

The *Café du Dôme* in the Cubist days

Nous lirons le charmant poème
Des graces de ton corps joli . . .*

The would-be cynic believed he had tamed his panther and
made plans for the future. Lou was to live in Nîmes, to be constantly near him until the time came for him to leave for the front.
He discovered a little apartment in an old house with a garden,
spent more than he could afford in making it charming and waited
for Louise to take possession.

He had reckoned without her emotional instability. She was
probably incapable of loving anyone and she was obviously
forgetting him. Her letters were less and less frequent and it was
becoming less and less likely that she would ever move into the
two little rooms he had described to her in such minute detail,
with the hanging gas lamps, the bedside rug, the old cashmere
shawl he had bought to disguise the iron bedstead, and the view
on to the garden. From joyful, tender and erotic, the poems
become reproachful, then despairing; the letters are half-hearted
attempts to regain a freedom he did not really desire:

'I am not asking you to come to me (sacrifice accomplished).
No, don't come here, it's absolutely useless since you do not
love me and soon I shall have ceased to love you. But go away,
so that I may find peace and the courage to work. You have
annihilated me during these last two months. It's not your fault

* In the voluptuous chamber
 Where I shall join you in Nîmes
 While we drink tea together
 During those few hours of intimacy
 That your beauty will make beautiful for me

 We shall commit a hundred thousand follies
 In spite of the war and its miseries
 We shall be deliciously surprised
 By the trees in flower by Palm-Sunday
 By Easter by the first cherries

 We shall read in the same bed
 In the book of your body
 —It is a book to be read in bed—
 We shall read the charming poem
 Of all your dainty body's graces . . .

if I have not got brain-fever and at least I have anaemia of the brain. I understand your feelings and respect them, but for your part, try to realise all I have suffered. . . .'

Perhaps at this point he would have given up, have renounced a love that was so evidently one-sided. But early in April his regiment was ordered up to the Front. It was the event he had been waiting for, the real beginning of the great adventure of war. He needed a witness to this adventure, to his own joy and to the experiences that lay before him. So it was to Lou he wrote when he arrived at last with his battery at Mourmelon-le-Grand; and the letter, as ever in moments of excitement and exaltation, was in the form of a poem:

> Ma Lou je coucherai ce soir dans les tranchées
> Qui près de nos canons ont été piochées
> C'est à douze kilomètres d'ici que sont
> Ces trous où dans mon manteau couleur d'horizon
> Je descendrai tandis qu'éclatent les marmites
> Pour y vivre parmi les soldats troglodytes
> Le train s'arrêtait à Mourmelon-le-Petit
> Je suis arrivé gai comme j'étais parti
> Nous irons toute à l'heure à notre batterie
> En ce moment je suis parmi l'infanterie
> Il siffle des obus dans le ciel gris du Nord
> Personne cependant n'envisage la mort. . . .*

Lou herself has already slipped into the background; war has assumed the major role. Apollinaire was discovering in it the beauty he had imagined when the convalescents in the canteen had spoken of the fiery curve of shells in the night. A few days after

---

* My Lou I shall sleep to-night in the trenches
  That have been dug near our canons
  They are twelve kilometres from here
  These holes where I in my sky-blue coat
  Shall descend while the shells burst all around
  To live among the troglodite soldiers

  The train stopped at Mourmelon-le-Petit
  I arrived as gaily as I had set out
  We shall soon be off to join our battery
  For the moment I am among the Infantry
  Shells are whistling in the grey Northern sky
  Yet none of us imagines he might die. . . .

his arrival, he was promoted to the rank of corporal and appointed to maintain contact between the small groups of gunners scattered along this portion of the Argonne front. Lou, of course, was kept informed:

'As soon as I received the good news, I had my horse saddled and set off with the corporal who has replaced our sergeant, who was killed three days ago. He was to show me the way that I shall take each morning. My horse is splendid; I was mistaken, he is not dark chestnut but black, quite black, with a white star and a lecherous look in his eyes. My saddle is marvellous. The rain had stopped. It was five o'clock in the morning. I felt tremendously proud. Four months' service, and already I can make myself useful in a subordinate post (but a dangerous and confidential one). That's the sort of thing to make one pleased with oneself—even for a poet, whose job is rather like that of a whore, since we both prostitute our feelings to the public. Well, we set off, emerged from the wood, crossed the fields, arrived at the main road, going at a quick trot at that point, rounded a village by a muddy, overgrown path.

'There the firing started. I shall always remember it. The corporal said: "They can see us from here, we must pass quickly and if they fire, don't hesitate to jump off and hide behind a tree." When we came to the superb forest for which we were heading, and which is much finer than the one in which we live, there was a rending shriek. Poum! A shell exploded in the trees 25 metres away and 15 metres up. Leaves fluttered in the air. The horses are used to it. We broke into a gallop along the field at the edge of the forest, another shriek, Poum! at about the same height, but not in the trees, so we could see the reddish-yellow smoke that hung in the air. That was all, after that they were firing to the left, at one of the group batteries, but not at ours which is more to the right.

'Then we entered the lovely woods; there we left the horses in a hut and continued on foot, crossing extraordinary bridges made of rushes and water willow. We came back by the same way, but there was no firing. . . .'

But Apollinaire knew quite well that he was writing to a phantom. Louise had found other interests and hardly troubled to reply. The episode was over. It left behind it a store of poems that were to remain secret for many years and which he himself valued, at the time, above all the others. 'You will not be able to read my best poems, and I think some of them are really good,' he wrote that summer to Louise Faure-Favier, 'unless the person to whom they are addressed allows me to publish them after the war. And who knows what may become of such things!'* As for the moral effects, he may have been broken-hearted, as André Rouveyre, who knew Louise and had his own reasons for distrusting her, believed; but it left him none the wiser and no less ready to create illusions for himself and for others. This time the phoenix had hardly expired before it was flapping its wings again, in the form of a dark-eyed little school-teacher from Oran. Madeleine Pagès had been spending her holidays in Nice and was returning to Marseilles, where she was to take the boat for Algiers. It was January 1915; the liaison with 'Lou' was at its apotheosis and at the time, the meeting seemed to both of them merely a pleasant interlude.

Long afterwards, when Madeleine allowed the publication of over two hundred letters that Apollinaire had written her in the course of a single year, she recounted this first meeting in her own words:

'Settled comfortably in my corner, I was preparing to enjoy my solitude as far as Marseilles, when a soldier entered my compartment, excused himself vaguely as he passed in front of me and leaned out of the window to speak to a lady who had accompanied him. Was he an ordinary soldier or an officer? I could never recognise a rank. He was tall, yes, on the tall side, with rather short legs and a large chest; he wore a cap too small for him, pushed to the back of his head.

'My solitude was done for. I should have liked to change to the next compartment, but how could it be done without attracting attention? Meanwhile the soldier was talking in a low voice. 'You want to read some poetry? Well, read Baudelaire's *Fleurs du Mal*.'

* The poems to Louise Coligny-Châtillon first appeared in 1947 under the title *Ombre de mon amour*. The volume includes poems that justify Apollinaire's own opinion of them, but many are simply rhymed letters, hastily written under difficult conditions, which have spontaneous charm and documentary interest rather than literary value.

'The woman climbed up for a moment to bid the soldier goodbye. She was tall and slim and looked a little tired. I heard the soldier's voice again as he spoke to her: "Don't stay freezing on the platform. Go back to the hotel, the room is paid for till mid-day."

'The train started off, the day was even finer now. . . . There was the little pink, pine-bordered beach. . . . There was the sea. How lovely it was! I must have said so aloud, for the soldier came to stand beside me and we both gazed out, united in the pleasure of seeing it so beautiful and so blue.

'We talked about Nice, which he knew better than I did. I listened, fascinated, as he spoke of the Italianate houses where rags float like banners on cords thrown from one window to another. He spoke of the market place, of the *Paillon*, the *Collinettes*; I liked his slightly husky voice, his profile, the ringless hands with their indolent gestures. His eyes were dark brown, like his hair, his features magnificent; without his cap he looked really handsome. But it was ten o'clock already! Blushing hard, I offered him the sandwich of travel-friendship, which he accepted without difficulty. We both ate, feeling free and happy, while the train gathered speed, then, somehow we began talking about poetry. I think he asked me, as he swallowed a mouthful of ham, if I cared for poetry and I told him I loved it as much as life itself and that it seemed to me inseparable from life. This pleased him so much that I thought for a moment he was going to kiss me. I felt there was something he wanted to say to me, but he checked himself and we began to discuss various poets. He wanted to know which I knew and which I loved. We were laughing now as we snatched names and verses from each other:

Voici des fruits, des fleurs, des feuilles et des branches. . . .

Sois sage ô ma douleur et tiens-toi plus tranquille. . . .

'Do you know my beloved Villon, Mademoiselle?' I was enchanted and quoted at once:

Femme je suis povrette et ancienne
Qui rien ne scay; oncques lettre ne lus . . .

But these verses restored our gravity and I dreamed, with closed eyes, in my corner. I was listening to their echo as he had just recited them—never had they meant so much to me. It was as if he held them in his hand and enjoyed their contact as much as their sound. Yet he had recited, or rather, murmured them with a simplicity I could never have equalled. Astonished and vanquished, I yielded to him the poem I had begun. . . .'[2]

The young woman on the platform was, of course, Louise de Coligny-Chatillon. Three months later, when Apollinaire had admitted the truth to himself, in a couplet he could never bring himself to publish:

> La Comtesse s'en fut et revint un jour
> Poète adore moi, moi j'aime un autre amour*

he remembered 'the talkative little traveller with her long lashes and expressive face', on whom he had casually practised his talent for pleasing. He sent her a copy of *Alcools*, she responded with a parcel of good things. The correspondence begins, on his side, on a note of respectful flirtatiousness that quickly becomes tender, then passionate. The letters to Lou become letters to Madeleine, and the transition is almost unnoticeable. The style has changed a little; Lou had been a realisation; in Madeleine he could explore the infinite possibilities of the imagination. The two women were fundamentally different—Louise, sophisticated, unhappy and debauched; Madeleine a tender virgin, unawakened and safe in her small-bourgeois family—and their relationships with himself were apparently at opposite poles in the scale of love, yet they seem to have played exactly the same role in his life. They could almost, one suspects, have been interchangeable. Apollinaire needed to be in love almost as much as he needed to breathe. He needed a woman to idealise, a woman in whom he could confide constantly, to whom he could describe every detail of his daily life, every change of mood, and above all, who would act as the agency through which he could 'poetise' his existence. Without Lou, without Madeleine, war would never have yielded up for him its secret beauty. They, one after the other, were the necessary

---

* The Countess went away and came back one day—
Poet adore me, I have found another love

witnesses to all he experienced. In his poetry—which at this period is essentially war poetry rather than love poetry—they intervene, one after the other, and sometimes both together, as the element of dream, the indispensable illusion that touches off the mechanism by which life is transformed into poetry.

Lou had disappeared, leaving behind her a disappointment and bitterness which, as Apollinaire himself soon recognised, were amply counter-balanced by the poetic stimulus she had brought him. He had once accused her of rendering him 'as acutely sensitive as a prawn at the moment when it changes its shell', but the shell-less prawn had reacted to every emotion, to every sensation and had made full use of each. In June, while he was on the Argonne front, he printed fifteen copies of a small volume of poems entitled *Case d'Armons*, using gelatine, purple ink and pages torn from a squared copybook. 'Lou' is still present in these poems, and Madeleine makes her first appearance, although she has not yet become the tender and voluptuous dream of the later poems and letters.

The little volume contains too some of the first war poems—and Apollinaire was one of the very few poets who have written verse directly inspired by war. Most of the poets who have been caught up in war and have found the time and courage to write at all, have been inspired less by the event itself than by the emotions it has aroused in them, by patriotism at one end of the scale or revolt at the other, Apollinaire was as far from Péguy's solemn and splendid *Heureux ceux qui sont morts dans une juste guerre** as from Wilfred Owen's terrible indictment:

> What passing bells for these that die as cattle?
> Only the monstrous anger of the guns.

For him war, like the rest of life, was a series of moments to be captured at the exact point of impact on his own sensibility. The poems have a direct quality which he had abandoned since the days of *Rhénanes* and, though they are far from representing him at his greatest, they undoubtedly show him at his most human. 'At last I have the right to greet people I do not know', he had written in *Le Musicien de Saint-Merry*, meaning, perhaps, that he had

* Charles Péguy, like Ernest Psichari and Alain-Fournier, had been killed in 1914.

penetrated at last to the inner reality of others, just as Picasso and
the Cubists had been striving to penetrate to the inner reality of
inanimate objects by representing them simultaneously from a
number of different angles. Some of the poems of this epoch are
hasty, anecdotal, but there are moments of intuition when he
observes his subject, not from any one angle, nor even from a
multiplicity of angles, but from its secret core. 'I am alone on the
battlefield—I am the white trench, the green and russet wood', he
wrote at this time, then, watching the negro gunner who had been
brought without explanation from Dakar, he *became* the gunner
too:

> Je me souviens du si délicat si inquiétant
> Fétiche dans l'arbre
> Et du double fétiche de la fécondité
> Plus tard une tête coupée
> Au bord d'un marécage
> O pâleur de mon ennemi
> C'était une tête d'argent
> Et dans le marais
> C'était la lune qui luisait
> C'était donc une tête d'argent
> Là-haut c'était la lune qui dansait
> C'était donc une tête d'argent
> Et moi dans l'antre j'étais invisible
> C'était donc une tête de nègre dans la nuit profonde*

But this war which he was absorbing, which was becoming
part of himself while he became part of it, was no longer quite
the romantic adventure it had seemed from a distance. Life among

---

* I remember the very delicate very disquieting
  Fetish in the tree
  And the double fetish of fecundity
  Later a severed head
  At the edge of a swamp
  O my enemy's pallor
  It was a silver head
  And in the marsh
  It was the moon shining
  So it was a silver head
  Up there it was the moon dancing
  So it was a silver head
  And I was invisible in my lair
  So it was a negro's head in the deep night

the 'troglodyte soldiers' involved a sordid misery he had never imagined. René Berthier, the little corporal-poet who had adored and admired his 'Master in poetry' in Nîmes, had been evacuated with meningitis, brought on by the noise and terror of the guns; his own battery fought its way through oceans of mud, dug into more mud for brief repose. He himself, he assured Madeleine, was indifferent to danger, and indeed, found in this 'constant and admirable danger' a new stimulus. The hideous truth about war lay elsewhere. A letter dated July 1st reveals him in a moment of discouragement:

> 'I am writing to you among the awful horror of millions of great blue flies. We have arrived at a sinister spot where all the horrors of war, the horror of the site, the appalling abundance of cemeteries, is completed by the total absence of trees, of water, even of real earth. If we stay here long, I wonder what can be in store for us except death by the instruments of war. After a fine journey on horseback, lasting several days, sleeping quite comfortably on the ground, we find ourselves in holes so filthy that I feel sick even to think that I am here in one of them. Add to this our exhaustion, for everything here is so far distant that the work is a hundred times more tiring for men and horses. So much for me. Let us hope it will all be of some use. . . .'

In such conditions, and in the state of chastity which was so abnormal for a man of Apollinaire's temperament, *Tendre comme le Souvenir* becomes explicable. The volume contains over two hundred letters, written in a mounting crescendo of passion. In them, the writer reveals himself, consciously, almost painfully, as if he was tearing away, as a sort of burnt offering to love, the disguise of irony and reticence in which he had always shrouded himself. Perhaps there was an element of comedy, an intentional seduction, in the earliest letters. The facts he gives about himself, and specially about his relationships with other women, do not always correspond exactly to the truth. But however that may be, he was soon caught up in his own toils. Madeleine—the existence of Madeleine—became essential to him. She was the outlet for every emotion, every experience, every fleeting memory; the door of escape from the horrors of war into a paradise of mingled tenderness and eroticism. Out of her image he created a partner with

14

whom he was to fulfil that impossible conception of love that no real woman could ever have satisfied.

'How well I understand your exquisite reserve. I understand it and respect it too, and I shall always love and respect it. And you will see that though I shall always impose my will on you, yet you yourself will always take the first steps along the road of married happiness. You will make all the advances, I shall only obey, and you will obey me by keeping ahead of both our minds, and these minds will meet and mingle in such perfect intimacy that they will be one in two. And thus, my beloved, we shall form a veritable Trinity. Our perfect union will be the pledge of a diversity in which we shall never be alone, since there will be you, me and us. . . .'

And a few days later:

'I want you to be licentious with me, as the female is to the male, just as I want your mind to rise in company with mine to the highest conceptions of aesthetics, metaphysics, religion and moral philosophy. I want us to form a single being; although your brain already obeys me, and your body too, there are still a few obscure regions of your being where you are not yet entirely my Madeleine. Your girlish reserve must increase and become absolutely intransigent in regard to everything that is not me, but in my presence you must cast it off, ardently and completely. The only way in which we can express ourselves, apart from acts, is by words. Words give meaning and reality to acts. That is why they are so important. Few people have known real love and those who have done so have acted in a state of illegitimacy or vice. Two minds like ours must only act in a state of virtue, but as completely and passionately as those who have acted in a state of vice. . . .'

The 'state of virtue' which Apollinaire had in mind was marriage. Quite early in their relationship he had decided that their union must be regularised. He had written to Madeleine's mother, and obtained her consent to their engagement. The letters that passed between these two strangers form a correspondence between fiancés, and indeed, between lovers. Madeleine's letters have never been made public, but one can divine her replies and follow the rapid evolution of the young girl into the woman. In everything but the physical act of defloration, Apollinaire had made her his mistress. She had become his accomplice, following and encouraging aspirations in which intellectuality and sensuality mingled to create a tenebrous, ecstatic and impossible dream.

In August, Apollinaire was promoted to the rank of quartermaster, so presumably he did not allow love to interfere with military efficiency. Then, in November, he obtained a transfer to an Infantry regiment, this time as a sub-lieutenant.

The war was becoming increasingly fierce, conditions on the Front more and more horrible. The Infantry was more exposed than the Artillery and was sustaining even greater losses. Apollinaire was quite aware of this and he had probably applied for his transfer partly because he had always longed for the prestige of being an officer, and partly because it would ensure him a period of leave, during which he could join his fiancée in Oran. The marriage was being actively prepared. He was sending books, manuscripts, souvenirs, for Madeleine to keep until they could set up house together. Marie Laurencin had sent him a drawing from Spain and he sent it off immediately, as one of his most precious possessions ('It will be for *us*'), at the same time as two German cartridge bands that were to serve as napkin rings in the future ménage. In spite of all these preparations, he had never dared to mention his engagement to his mother.

'I am very fond of Mother and she of me', he had written, to explain his hesitations. 'But the Slav side of her character is so highly developed that she will always be jealous of anyone loved by her son. She will be delighted that I get married and will be jealous of you and tender towards you at the same time. It's too long to explain, but my mother's Slav nature will prevent her from having much to do with us, even though she will be very fond of you. . . .'

He was in the front line now, and by contrast the Artillery seemed comfortable. Two thousand eight hundred men and ninety officers of his regiment had been killed in less than three months. Conditions were appalling:

'. . . nine days without washing, sleeping on the ground, without straw, on earth full of vermin, not a drop of water except that used by the apparatus for spraying our masks with hyposulphate in case of gas. . . . The chalk trench is very bad and has to be constantly shored up with sacks of earth. The six-hourly round of inspection is a great bore but necessary, otherwise the men would go to sleep at the loopholes because of their exhaustion. I, who need very little sleep, only have to lie on the earth, like these poor children I command, and I go to sleep at once. . . .'

Under these conditions leave was delayed and it was not till Christmas day that Apollinaire arrived at Marseilles. The next boat brought him to Oran, where the Pagès family awaited him. No one ever knew exactly what happened, but it is not difficult to imagine the situation. The Pagès family were school-teachers, which in France, and specially at that period, usually meant Socialists of the doctrinaire type, with a philosophy of rather bigoted rationalism and, in general, a small bourgeois outlook on life. The mother, the numerous brothers and sisters, were charming to him. He was welcomed, received into the family, treated as a son-in-law. That much is clear from subsequent letters, and there, perhaps, lay the root of the trouble. It is hard to imagine an atmosphere more foreign to his nature, to his imperious instinct for independence and liberty of thought, joined to a certain nostalgia for aristocratic and religious traditions. Moreover, it must have been impossible, in this industrious and sensible atmosphere, to see in Madeleine his panther, his slave, and all the other aspects under which he had evoked her in her absence. It must even have been difficult to consider her as his mistress, and if she ever became so, it can only have been in conditions of sordid secrecy. It seems more likely that the amorous partner of his erotic dreams reappeared in the flesh as he had first seen her in the train between Nice and Marseilles—as a virginal and respectable young girl. Nothing could have intimidated Apollinaire more than this metamorphosis,* nothing could have seemed to him more

* Serge Jastrebzoff (Edouard Férat) told me, a few weeks before his death, the following story to illustrate Apollinaire's respect for young girls, which was slightly surprising in one of his unbridled erotic temperament. One day, he said, he had visited his friend in his apartment in the Boulevard Saint-Germain and was surprised to see that each of the innumerable negro statuettes that decorated walls and shelves had been adorned with a red frill to serve as a skirt. Apollinaire had explained, with a slight embarrassment: 'You see, I am expecting a visit from a young girl this afternoon.'

distasteful than to deceive these kindly people who saw in him only a fiancé like the fiancés the other sisters would bring one day to their home.

From the moment of his return, a fortnight later, the tone of the letters changed. They are the letters of an engaged man, conventionally in love, but they have singularly decreased in ardour. He had passed through Paris before rejoining his regiment, he told Madeleine, and had obtained Madame de Kostrowitsky's rather grudging consent to his marriage; Max Jacob had depressed him by predicting that the war would last for thirty years; he found Paris disagreeable, as he had on each of his short leaves in the capital, because of the profiteering spirit of so many civilians. The following day he rejoined his regiment, which was resting in the back lines. The letters contain details of his life, protestations of tenderness, exhortations to his fiancée to remain calm and patient and vague explanations as to the relative coldness of his style. In March his regiment moved up to the Front again. The fighting was furious, it was evident that an important attack was being prepared:

'My dear love, I have had two letters from you. We are just going up into the front line. I am writing to you in haste, with my helmet on. Don't know what we are going to do. In any case, I leave you everything I possess, and this is to be considered as my testament if need be.

'Well, I hope there will be nothing for the moment. I adore you. The weather is lovely.

'I want you to be strong now and always. . . .'

Next day, he sent a military postcard:

'My love, No sleep this night. No description possible. But the weather is fine. I think of you. We sleep under the sky. This morning saw a little squirrel, climbing and climbing up.

'I am tired and gay at the same time. My mouth is full of sand. I don't know if there will be a letter this evening. I hope so. . . .'

Two days later, on March 17, in a trench in the Bois des Buttes near Berry-au-Bac, Apollinaire was wounded by a piece of shrapnel that pierced the helmet and penetrated his skull just above the right temple. A summary operation was performed in the ambulance and he was evacuated to Château-Thierry, then to the military hospital of Val-de-Grâce in Paris. The doctor's report showed that he should have been trepanned immediately, but for some reason the operation was delayed and he was transferred to the Italian Hospital, where his friend Férat was a medical orderly. There he was cared for by several beautiful young women of the Italian nobility, which cheered him up considerably. He was correcting the proofs of a volume of stories that took its title from *Le Poète Assassiné*, the long story in which, back in the days following the break with Marie Laurencin, he had recounted the adventures of Croniamental, Tristouse Ballerinette and Horace Tograth; at the same time he was preparing a small volume of poems in collaboration with André Rouveyre. He had at least one solid reason for satisfaction. He had applied two years earlier for naturalisation, following Toussaint Luca's instructions, and had taken it for granted that, since he had volunteered and been accepted as a French soldier, he would be granted the rights of a French citizen. Unfortunately there was the affair of the statuettes and a thick (and often tendentious) file in the archives of the police. His association with the Cubist movement had not helped him either, and his application had been shelved for one objection after another. At last the long enquiry had come to an end and concluded: 'From the national point of view, nothing has been objected against him which could make him appear suspect.' The naturalisation had actually been granted at the moment when his regiment was moving into the front line and a few days before he was wounded. It was thus that he only learned much later that one of the things he had most ardently desired throughout his life had been realised at last.

But the wound, which appeared to be healing so well, had attacked some vital nerve centre. A creeping paralysis began to attack the left arm, accompanied by nervous depression.

To his Italian friend Sofini, he wrote:

'I have lost your military address. . . . I am terribly exhausted. I am unbelievably tired of everything, even of life if I dare say so. Morally, I am passing through a very difficult period. My left arm is still inert and I can only move it by making a great effort.

'Write to me, my friend.
'Hurray for France and Italy!'

And to Madeleine:

'My dear little Madeleine,
'I am tired and I find so little friendship in Paris at the moment that I am disheartened.
'There is egoism everywhere. I am much better but with fits of giddiness still and functional impotence of the left arm. I am not what I was from any point of view and if I followed my own inclinations I should become a priest or a monk. I am so far removed from my book that has just come out that I do not even know if I sent you a copy. If not, tell me so. I will send you one at once.
'A thousand kisses,
'Gui'

It had become evident at last that the patient could only be saved by trepanning. The operation was a terrible one in those days, but Apollinaire supported it with a courage and good humour that amazed doctors and nurses. The X-ray photographs of his wound interested him immensely: 'You say there is nothing new under the sun', he exclaimed to someone who refused to admit he had made any innovations in the art of poetry. 'And you say this to me, who have seen the inside of my own head!' The paralysis was checked and soon disappeared; presently he was convalescent. As soon as a little strength had returned, he began to work again—to work furiously, unreasonably, as if the word 'destiny' that had always held such intense and mysterious meaning for him, had acquired a new and more precise menace.

But after this operation, Apollinaire was never again the man he had been. He had grown stouter than ever in hospital; under the bandaged forehead the eyes held an expression of haggard anxiety that was never to leave them. He had fits of irritability; the childish vanity that had always marked his character increased, and as it increased he grew more and more susceptible.

As for poor Madeleine, consumed with anxiety far away in Oran, she received a telegram reassuring her after the operation, then, months after, two more short notes, then there was silence.

The illusion had been shattered long before in Oran and Apollinaire no longer had the strength or courage to continue a correspondence that had become an affair of routine and duty. Another dream had been shattered.

> O ma jeunesse abandonnée
> Comme une guirlande fanée
> Voici que s'en vient la saison
> Des regrets et de la raison. . . .*

---

* O my youth abandoned
  Like a faded wreath
  Now comes the season
  Of regrets and of reason

                    (*Vitam Impendere Amori*)

Tristan Tzara and friends of *Le Cabaret Voltaire*
(T. Tzara, second from right, back row, with Philippe Soupault beside him
Front row, extreme right, Paul Eluard)

Guillaume Apollinaire at the Italian Hospital in Paris

XIV

'Many of these Gods have perished'

Beaucoup de ces dieux ont péri
C'est sur eux que pleurent les saules
Le grand Pan l'amour Jésus-Christ
Sont bien morts et les chats miaulent
*Dans la cour je pleure à Paris**

When Apollinaire emerged from hospital, with his bandaged
head and the almost-new officer's uniform that had grown a little
too tight for him, he found himself in a changed city. It was the
month of August 1916. The horrible, long-drawn-out battle of
Verdun was still in progress and the end was still in doubt. The
slaughter all along the Western Front showed no signs of abating
and most of his fellow officers had been killed or wounded. Yet
he sometimes regretted leaving the Army. After the close comradeship of his regiment, it seemed to the convalescent that the
civilians at home knew and cared little about the war and lived
wrapped in their own egoism. The profiteering spirit was rife
everywhere and every imaginable kind of goods was being
treated as material for speculation. Certain astute souls had even
foreseen the possibilities in painting and the few artists who had
escaped mobilisation were surprised to receive visits from unknown dealers, who offered high prices for canvases at which
they hardly troubled to glance—except to ensure that they had
been duly signed.

It was one of the first symptoms of the new, commercial attitude
that was to consider art less on its own merits than as a promising
or unpromising investment. These enterprising merchants even
scented a profit from Cubism, and began acquiring as many
Cubist paintings as possible against the day when they would

* Apollinaire: *Vitam Impendere Amori.*

come into favour again. Picasso was already considered sound business and was making a great deal of money, while most of the original band from the *Bateau Lavoir* could command higher prices than they had ever dreamed of.*

Apollinaire's own situation was uncertain. France was desperately short of men, and specially of trained officers. The wounded were evacuated, patched up and returned as soon as possible to the trenches. Dalize, Mac Orlan, Vildrac, had all been wounded in the early days of the war and were back on active service, so was Georges Braque, who had received a terrible head wound and, like Apollinaire, had been trepanned. Apollinaire had not yet obtained his discharge and his two months' convalescent leave was almost at an end. Finally André Billy, who had influential friends in many quarters, obtained for him a post in the periodicals department of the Censorship. There he began a new career as a civil servant—though he still depended upon the army and was still in uniform—constrained to daily and punctual attendance in an office. There it was his mission to delete from the pages of all the weekly and monthly reviews anything that might be considered as useful to the enemy or defeatist in spirit. As he himself contributed to a good many of the publications that passed through his hands, he often had the pleasure of stamping one of his own articles, 'passed by the Censor', and adding his initials.

During the first years of war, any artistic activity that was not directly patriotic in character, had seemed a little suspect. Now the war had begun to seem almost normal and Paris was resuming her intellectual life in a rather timid, sporadic way. Louise Faure-Favier's apartment on the Quai Bourbon was one of the focal points where writers and artists home on leave could meet, almost astonished to find each other still alive, and try to revive for a few short hours the joyful spirit of 1914. It was one of the few places in this alien world in which he now found himself, where Apollinaire could still feel at home. Rachilde, wife of Alfred

---

* The boom in Cubist painting reached its height by about 1920 and remained there for three or four years. The American invasion of Montparnasse had a good deal to do with this inflation of a form of art that was already losing its vital impetus. Anyone who painted in a sufficiently angular style could be sure of getting a good price for his canvases at that time, but the true Cubists were already beginning to look beyond Cubism.

Vallette, had become a regular visitor. The *Mercure de France* was appearing regularly again—and was the only literary magazine of any note to do so—and she counted on Madame Faure-Favier to keep her in touch with her husband's contributors. René Dalize and Louis de Gonzague Frick appeared each time they came home on leave; Fernand Léger explained there one afternoon how he had composed a picture at the Front in Champagne, using a piece of wood sawn from a felled tree trunk and scraps of coloured paper in place of paint; Blaise Cendrars had lost an arm and would limp up the stairs, mutilated, but as sure of himself as ever, to read extraordinary scenarios for films which, if they had been realisable, would have opened up a new era for the cinema. And there was Fernand Fleuret, and André Derain, and Picasso with his Russian wife, Olga, with whom, since they had no other language in common, he conversed in appalling French, while she replied with an accent as incomprehensible as his own.

One of the first public manifestations of the revival of the capital's artistic life was an exhibition of paintings by André Derain. It was attended by the artist himself, wearing the uniform of an officer of the Artillery. Derain had withdrawn from the Cubist movement as soon as it broke definitively with Fauvism, but he had never declared himself its enemy as his friend Vlaminck had done. Apollinaire himself, though he had long been considered as the mouthpiece of Cubism, had always refused to confine himself to appreciating only Cubist paintings, and was as ready as ever to preface the catalogue:

'After the truculency of his youth,' he wrote, 'André Derain now inclines towards sobriety and prudence. The effort this has cost him has produced works of a grandeur that seems almost religious at times. This expressive grandeur can indeed be described as antique. He has borrowed it from the great masters and also from some of the early French schools, especially that of Avignon, but there is nothing artificially archaic about it.

'The works exhibited here by André Derain thus reveal a temperament that is both audacious and disciplined. In a great part of his later works we are moved by the signs of the effort he has forced himself to make in order to conciliate these two tendencies. He had almost fulfilled his aim of achieving a harmony full of realistic and sublime beatitude.

'It is by encouraging audacity and moderating temerity that Order is achieved. But to do this needs great sincerity. André Derain is an absolutely sincere artist.'

Certain friends—André Billy and Fernand Fleuret, for instance —who had been alarmed by what they considered a tendency to excessive modernism, were relieved. The preface sounded almost like a condemnation of Delaunay, perhaps even of Picasso. In the literary field it might even presage a return to punctuation in his own work! And indeed, the words Order, Harmony, Discipline, were to be heard more and more frequently on his tongue. Sometimes, indeed, he seemed almost aggressively determined to show himself in the light of a model French officer. Certainly he wanted to forget and to make others forget that he had been intimately connected, barely three years earlier, with Walden, with *Der Sturm*, with Klee, Kandinsky, Macke and Marc.*

His friends were gradually beginning to realise, in fact, that they were in the presence of a new Apollinaire, rendered cautious by experience, inclined to regret old audacities and showing an unexpected reverence for some of the fetishes he had attacked most violently a few years earlier. Some of them felt he had become sensible at last; others were dismayed. All realised that his wound, the long illness that followed, and perhaps the succession of sentimental disappointments had changed him profoundly. He still had fits of melancholy and occasionally of uncontrollable rage and seemed to become more and more vain and susceptible. On the other hand, he seemed to have gained an extraordinary gift of insight, a profound charity, a power of sympathy that brought profound comfort to his friends when—as so many of them were at this terrible period—they were in distress. He was working immensely hard, but dissipating his strength and talents in journalism rather than in anything creative. He suffered from and resented the spite of certain colleagues jealous of his literary position or the *Croix de Guerre* he wore on his uniform, far more

---

* Macke and Marc were killed on the German Front; Walden fled to Russia to escape conscription and disappeared in the turmoil of the Revolution.

than he would have done in the days when he was ready to provoke any detractor to a duel and then to forget the offence among
a host of other interests.

It was at this point that Apollinaire came into contact with a
new generation, with men who had been almost boys before the
war and were just returning to Paris, exempt from military service
or invalided out of the Army. He must have been aware to some
extent of their existence just before the war, since he had written
to Toussaint-Luca in May 1914:

> 'The term *alone* by which I described myself and that I lamented
> in my letter only applied to my love life and I was not alluding
> to my literary life. Yet there too, if I must tell the truth, I feel
> myself somewhat isolated, since the spirit of artistic and poetic
> initiative is seldom to be found in the generation that im-
> mediately follows our own, and you know how the liberal
> spirit is losing ground among it. I regret this, but I am told
> things are different among the youngest generation of all. I hope
> this is true. . . .'

Now this 'youngest generation of all' was suddenly beginning
to manifest itself and to reveal its fervent admiration for Apollinaire and its determination to adopt him as master and leader. He
had still been in hospital when he had received a visit from Pierre
Albert-Birot, a very small, very thin young man with diabolic
black eyebrows, who had been hesitating, like so many intellectuals at that time, between poetry and painting. For him, as for so
many others of his age, the mere phrase, *Perdre mais perdre vraiment
pour laisser place à la trouvaille* had left an echo that would never
quite be stilled. 'We must destroy all the old laws so as to discover
the new law that will correspond to our epoch', he wrote, and,
early in 1916, in a still unpropitious atmosphere, he had founded a
review in order to group together the remnants of the avant-garde
in the search for this new law. It was necessary, at that moment, to
provide some sort of patriotic justification for this enterprise, so
Sic opened with a manifesto that reads a little like an excuse:

> 'It is in the French tradition: to destroy shackles.
> 'It is in the French tradition: to see everything and understand
> everything
> 'It is in the French tradition: to seek, to discover, to create

'It is in the French tradition: to be in the advance guard
'It is in the French tradition: to desire to live
Let us follow tradition!'

Sic was to become one of those culture-media in which the
future begins to move and take shape.

'There was a time', wrote Birot in his first editorial, 'when
you could not understand such and such a thing that you
understand to-day; remember how inexistent that thing was for
you BEFORE and with what force it has come to exist for you
SINCE. Remember, remember, and never say, "I do not understand such and such a thing, therefore it does not exist. Come
with us, let us watch, see, listen and seek together . . ." '

Apollinaire contributed to nearly every number of *Sic* and
realised, with mingled pleasure and apprehension, that a whole
group of ardent and talented young men was looking to him to
show them the way, to reveal to them the secrets of the art of
the future.

The following year, Pierre Reverdy—whom Max Jacob used to
call the Man-Poet, in opposition to certain Grocer-Poets, or
Professor-Poets who were then in vogue—was invalided out of
the Army and returned to Paris. He had been almost a boy when
he had assisted at the foundation of Montparnasse, so he could
truly claim to have been reared in the Cubist incubator. He had
been publishing poems that corresponded strangely to certain
paintings by Braque or Picasso, and insisting that a poem can
also be an *object*. The idea had been in the air for some time:
Mallarmé had likened the effort of the poet to that of an alchemist
'isolating from some cluster of elaborate images a certain idea
which a few rare words will protect for ever from death'. Claudel,
too, had considered each of his poems essentially as 'an idea,
isolated by a blank space'; and in the train between Nice and
Marseilles, an observant girl had noticed how Apollinaire himself
had recited the poems of Villon 'as if he held them in his hand
and enjoyed their contact as much as their sound'. Now, in 1917,
Reverdy founded the review *Nord-Sud* that was to play such an
important role in revealing a new generation and a new intellectual
attitude.

Nord-Sud was founded as a literary counterpart to pictorial Cubism. It was sober, simple and rather solemn in tone. *Les Soirées de Paris* had been ostensibly the organ of pre-war Cubism, but Apollinaire had been too ironic, too imaginative, too many-sided to keep any single purpose exclusively in view. Reverdy was more coherent and less liable to be side-tracked by such fascinating irrelevancies as Fantomas. The first number summed up, simply and methodically, the position of Cubist painting at this point in its history. It shows how far the young generation had moved in the direction of Abstraction since the *Demoiselles d'Avignon*, or even Metzinger's portrait.

'We must not confuse serious works with the more or less justifiable and more or less honest (artistically speaking) fantasies of painters who have nothing to contribute to the movement and are attracted only by an excessive modernism or by less avowable motives.

'Cubism is an eminently plastic art, but a creative art rather than one of reproduction or interpretation.

'As the subject now counts only as one of the elements of the picture, it is understandable that the painter will not attempt to reproduce its aspect, but to make use of that which is eternal and constant in it (for instance, the roundness of a glass) while excluding the rest.

'There lies the explanation of the deformation of objects, which has never been given to the public. It is a consequence and must not be considered as an arbitrary whim of the painter. Otherwise we shall never free ourselves from the caricatural deformations which find their excuse in the expression that we consider now as old-fashioned: 'a way of seeing things'.

'In view of all this, it will be easy to understand why we refuse to admit that a Cubist painter can paint a portrait. There must be no confusion possible. We are concerned with creating a work, not some human head or object constructed according to new laws which could not sufficiently justify the appearance it would take on as a result of those laws.

'It is this form of creativeness . . . which will mark our epoch.'

And in the same number, Paul Dermée analysed with the same

precision the position of poets who had followed the same artistic evolution:

> 'A day came when *fine poetry* died: from that time on a poem meant a lyric unity. Yet neither the total freedom in which lyricism disperses like smoke, nor the external constraint of some conventional form, is suited to the creation of a work of art. The constraint must come from within; the work of art must be conceived in the same way that an artisan conceives the fabrication of a pipe or a hat; each part must have its proper place, exactly determined according to its function and its importance. It is the object that counts here and not one or other of its elements.'

Apollinaire had been the first to attempt this exact transposition of Cubist theory, so it was natural that this group of young writers should adopt him as their patron:

> 'The war goes on,' wrote Reverdy in his first editorial, 'but we know in advance how it will end. Victory is a certitude now. For this reason, we feel it is time to save literature from the neglect into which it has fallen, to reorganise it among ourselves.
>
> 'There was a time when the young poets sought out Verlaine, dragging him from the obscurity into which he had fallen. It is only natural that we should judge the time ripe to group ourselves round Guillaume Apollinaire. More than any man of our day, he has traced new paths, opened up new horizons. He has earned our fervour, our admiration.'

This was the sort of recognition Apollinaire had always longed for. He was to be the new Verlaine, the man who had created an epoch in his own youth and to whom the new generation looked for guidance along the paths he himself had revealed to them. He was to be the 'rocket-signal' flaring into the night (it is significant that he gave this title—*Fusée-Signal*—to one of his first contributions to *Nord-Sud*). He was to be the bearer of a new message, that he alone was capable of revealing to those who awaited it with such avidity:

> O bouches l'homme est à la recherche d'un nouveau langage
> Auquel le grammarien d'aucune langue n'aura rien à dire
> Et ces vieilles langues sont tellement près de mourir

Que c'est vraiment par habitude et manque d'audace
Qu'on les fait encore servir à la poésie. . . .*

This was indeed the sort of language to appeal to the new poets
introduced by Birot and Reverdy. Most of their names were still
quite unknown. They were André Breton, Philippe Soupault,
Louis Aragon—that elegant and inseparable trio of romantically
uneasy spirits—and Tristan Tzara, with his enormous, destructive
laughter that spared nothing and no one. War had destroyed the
natural order of their world just as they were emerging from
adolescence, their early adult years had been moulded by destruction and violence. They associated themselves with Cubism because it represented in their eyes the spirit of revolt, a break with
the past, but it soon became evident that they were preparing to go
far beyond Cubism as it existed at that time, or even indeed, as
Reverdy or Dermée had defined it.

'There was a great impatience to live,' recalls Tzara, 'disgust with
all the forms of so-called modern civilisation, with its very foundations, with logic, with language. The revolt took forms in which
the grotesque and absurd far outweighed aesthetic values. It
must be remembered that literature was invaded at that period by a
sentimentality that disguised any element of humanity, that a
pretentious bad taste sprawled over every form of art and sym-
bolised the force of the Bourgeoisie in its most odious aspect.'[1]
Few writers of the past seemed to have any relevance for this
'lost' generation for whom there could be no more pejorative
term than 'Literature'. There was Rimbaud who had proclaimed
his love for 'idiotic paintings, decorated doors, stage scenery,
backcloths for acrobats, signboards'; there was Jarry, since whose
time, said André Breton, literature had been 'moving among mine-
fields'. And among their elders there was Apollinaire, who had
handed down to them from his own experience certain messages
to which circumstances had rendered them specially receptive:
*Perdre mais perdre vraiment pour laisser place à la trouvaille. . . . Allons
plus vite nom de Dieu allons plus vite. . . . A la fin tu es las de ce monde
ancien. . . .* The destruction that had been an intellectual exercise

* O mouths, mankind is seeking a new language—In which no grammarian
of any known language will have any part. And those old languages are so near
their death—That it is truly only by habit and lack of courage—That they are
still made to serve poetry. . . . (*La Victoire*).

15

in 1913 had become an artistic necessity by 1917. Louis Aragon has recalled how:

> Lorsque j'avais vingt ans pour moi la grande affaire,
> Etait de désapprendre et non d'avoir appris
> Il me semblait rouvrir les portes de l'enfer
> Par le simple refus du cœur et de l'esprit. . . .*

But neither he nor any of these young poets could yet have explained just where they were going, or on what mighty runaway horse they had mounted.

*   *   *

So it was to Apollinaire they looked, with truly touching confidence, to reveal to them the new law that was to emerge from the destruction of the old. How, they were constantly asking him, would he define 'the modern spirit?' What would be the art of the future, the 'new language' he had announced?

André Breton, who was to become the inventor and leader of Surrealism, was one of the most assiduous of these young disciples. The two men met almost every day and took long walks together in the late afternoon, when Apollinaire had escaped at last from his office and Breton from the psychiatric department of the military hospital to which, as a medical student, he was attached at this time.

'At the period when I saw him so often,' he has recounted, 'Apollinaire had unlimited prestige in my eyes. It lent immense importance to the least of his gestures, to the least object he owned. If, for instance, I happened to find him shaving when I called on him, any idea that I might be in the way was immediately driven out by two verses which seemed to murmur in my ear:

> Hiver toi qui te fais la barbe
> Il neige et je suis malheureux . . .

---

* When I was twenty my one concern
  Was not to have learned but to unlearn
  I thought I could reopen the gates of hell
  By a mere refusal of heart and mind. . . .

(Louis Aragon, *Les Yeux et la Mémoire.*)

Between us two there thus came into being an antidote to this usually banal business of shaving, which, transferred on to the plane of poetry, became the very atmosphere of a snowy Christmas day. It seemed to me that I was not exactly talking to a man, even to a man I admired beyond all others, but to an intermediary power, capable of reconciling the world of natural necessities with the world of men.'

Breton was already absorbed at this period in the new theories arising from the discoveries of Freud and Jung concerning the role of the subconscious in man's mental life. Already he had an obscure presentiment of the importance which this suppressed and submerged force in human nature would assume in post-war literature. For him, at least, the 'new language' was already taking form. It was to be 'that psychic automatism by which we propose to express, either verbally, or in writing, or by any other means, the true functioning of the mind. The mind will dictate to us directly, in the absence of all control by reason, without any kind of aesthetic or moral preoccupation.'[2]

Naturally, he expected to find his idol in agreement with him. Many of the ideas which he, Soupault and Aragon were soon to work out together in the 'Surrealist Manifesto' had already been expressed, either directly or indirectly, by Apollinaire. Had he not prophesied already:

> Profondeurs de la conscience
> On vous explorera demain

Was he not the author of *L'Enchanteur Pourrissant*, of *Onirocritique*, those strange, almost delirious works which seemed to spring directly from the unplumbed depths where lurk myths long rejected by the conscience of civilised man? Had he not described himself, in the *Soirées de Paris*, as a 'sur-naturalist'? Breton had good reason to hope that he would seize hold of this new form of expression and this new truth, that had not yet received a name;* that he would become its theorician as he had been the theorician

---

* In a letter to Paul Dermée, dated March 1917, Apollinaire wrote: 'After thinking over the question carefully, I prefer to adopt the word *Surréalisme*, rather than the "Surnaturalism" I used at first. *Surréalisme* does not yet exist in the dictionary and will be easier to manipulate that *Surnaturalisme*, which has already been used by philosophers.'

of Cubism. It was not long, however, before he discovered that they were talking at cross-purposes. Apollinaire's interest in prophesy seemed to Breton too systematic, the light he sought to throw on the things of the subconscious too crude, so that it blinded rather than revealed. He was ready to skim over the surface of the subject but not to accord it the long meditations which Breton asked of him. His mind was preoccupied with too many things; he seemed to be trying to grasp them all at once, feverishly, as if he felt it vitally necessary to discover and possess all the knowledge of the world without delay. As they tramped through the streets of Paris on their long daily walks, Breton was often struck by the expression of haggard anxiety on his face. It would be dissipated for a moment by some sight or scene which caught his eye and interested or amused him. For a moment the old, gay laugh would break out, then he would grow tense again, talking as brilliantly and wittily as ever, but always with this new, desperate avidity. He remained the same enchanter as of old, but something had changed. For the first time, something new and exciting in the world of art was taking shape, at his very side, and he let it pass by, almost with indifference.

'Guillaume Apollinaire', wrote Breton later in the first 'Surrealist Manifesto' which he dedicated in homage to his old friend, 'often seemed to us to have allowed himself to be carried away by an impulsion of this kind [psychic automatism], but without sacrificing to it the banal procedure of literature. . . . Nerval possessed admirably the *spirit* of Surrealism; Apollinaire, on the contrary, possessed only the *letter*, and still imperfectly, so that he was incapable of giving a valid explanation of it.'

But before Surrealism, there was to be Dada. In Zürich, the young Rumanian, Tristan Tzara, who was about twenty years old at this time, was the centre of a turbulent band of extremists—French, Germans, Italians, Futurists, political refugees, intellectuals and people who felt themselves to be victims of social injustice. Out of this mass of uncoordinated elements, which had little in common except a furious desire to change everything, he was welding together the movement that soon became known as *Dada* and founding his Dadaist review, *Le Cabaret Voltaire.*

The name itself was an indication of the spirit of the movement. It meant, Tzara would explain, a cow's tail in the dialect of the Krou negroes; a cube or a mother in one of the Italian dialects; a wooden horse or a nurse in Russian and Rumanian. *Le Cabaret Voltaire* took as its motto the arrogant phrase of Descartes: 'I do not even wish to know if there have been other men before me', and printed it like an insolent challenge across its cover.

Picabia had arrived in Switzerland, coming from Spain and bringing with him the review '391' he had founded in Barcelona. In spite of the difference in age, the two men were kindred spirits. The destruction and profanation of idols had long been Picabia's favourite distraction and he entered at once into the spirit of Dada. He and Tzara were soon preparing a Manifesto:

'Those who join us retain all their freedom. We recognise no theory. We have had enough of Cubist or Futurist academies, those laboratories of formalist ideas. Is the aim of art to earn money and caress the nice Bourgeois? Rhymes ring out with the same sound as coins and inflections slide along the profiled belly. Every group of artists has finally arrived, astride various comets, at the same bank. A door opening on the possibility of lounging among cushions and food.

' . . . We have the right to issue proclamations, for we know what it is to thrill and to awake. Returning, drunk with energy, we plunge the trident into the uncaring flesh. We stream with curses in a tropical abundance of vertiginous vegetation, our sweat is gum and rain, we bleed and burn with thirst, our blood is vigour. . . .

'All pictorial or plastic art is useless; let it become a monster to terrorise servile spirits instead of a sugary decoration for the refectories of animals in human dress. . . .

'Dada is the signpost of abstraction; advertisements and business affairs are also elements of poetry. . . .

'Let each one of us cry forth the great work of destruction and negation to be accomplished. Let us sweep out, clean up. . . . Everything that proceeds out of our disgust is Dada. . . .'

It was through the advice and recommendations of Picabia that Tzara obtained contributions to the *Cabaret Voltaire* from men of different nationalities who seemed likely to share his own ideas, on whom he counted to prepare the spiritual revolution that would destroy in the name of destruction itself. There were Picasso, Cendrars, Marinetti, Kandinsky—and, of course, Apollinaire.

Apollinaire had been pleased by the invitation and sent off a poem—*Arbre*, in the 1913, Simultanist style—without troubling to read the review or discover its tendencies. Very soon, though, disquieting facts began to leak through to him. A number of Germans were connected with *Le Cabaret Voltaire* and this just at the time when he himself was doing all he could to efface the awkward memory of his own connections with Walden and *Der Sturm*. Moreover, Dada was going further than he had gone even in his most iconoclastic days, and infinitely further than he was prepared to go now. He had always insisted, and would continue to insist, that the element of surprise, the taste for the unexpected word or juxtaposition of words, was one of the main characteristics of the modern spirit. It had distinguished his poetry, as well as Salmon's, from that of the Symbolists, even before they had turned their backs on Symbolism and gone their own way; and it had always been the very essence of Max Jacob. But things had been moving very fast in the last few years. The movements to the birth of which he himself had contributed were gathering a frightening momentum. With Dada, 'surprise' had developed into the desire to scandalise at all costs. Tzara, Arp, Picabia, Marcel Duchamp, like Marinetti before them, had dedicated themselves to the creation of scandal. 'It was necessary to arouse hostility, at the risk of passing for sinister imbeciles', recalls Georges Ribemont-Dessaignes, who was an active organiser of these 'necessary' scandals when the movement came to Paris. And they consisted of those typically 'Dada' weapons; 'shameless publicity, provocation, lies, insults—'.

It was all too evident that Tzara and his friends had had in mind the Apollinaire of the *Antitradition Futuriste,* the Apollinaire who had demanded 'words at liberty' and the destructions of traditions. Apollinaire, the functionary, the future candidate for the *Académie française* found himself in an embarrassing position. Dada was even more alien to him than the first gropings of Surrealism, yet, as in Surrealism, he was forced to recognise himself uncomfortably in its origins. The great myth-maker was losing control of his myths.

Anyway, it was too late to draw back. Tzara himself was contributing to both *Sic* and *Nord-Sud*. Breton, Soupault and Aragon held aloof for the moment, but were soon seduced into contributing to the Dada review. The Dada spirit was gaining ground among the young writers in Paris. *Sic*, after its quick bow to 'French tradition' soon took a more iconoclastic turn, published a 'sound poem' imitating the noise of an aeroplane and declared:

'A scientist has proclaimed in the Assize Courts: "There is arsenic everywhere, I could find it in the arm of a chair." Like arsenic, beauty is to be found everywhere, except in works of art.'

The general mood was anti-art, or at least against all classified (and thus stultified) forms of art. *Nord-Sud* was already publishing poems that were connected only in the remotest way with Cubism. Even Reverdy was beginning to realise that his position was untenable. Cubism supposed a certain self-imposed poverty of experience which had held an understandable attraction by contrast to the easy and frivolous pre-war days, but which repelled a generation for whom renunciation had proved a matter of destiny rather than choice. Cubism confined itself, as Jean Cocteau complained, 'to such objects as can be found on a table in a café, or to a Spanish guitar . . . nor would the Cubists admit that one might travel, except along the North-South omnibus route that led from the Place des Abbesses to the Boulevard Raspail'. He might have added that no Cubist painter ever dreamed of painting outside his own studio and that they had all abandoned, from the first, the landscapes of Montmartre to Utrillo, Modigliani and such drunken and eccentric sharp-shooters of art. In any case, the war had brought about a rupture with the past so decisive that neither men nor the forms through which men expressed themselves could ever be quite the same again. Cubism was dying just as it was becoming fashionable. From this time on, the truly creative works of painters and poets would stem from the victory of Cubism, but would no longer be Cubist.

XV

The New Spirit

At the end of 1915 Diaghilev had made a brief appearance in Paris. Social gaieties during those grim days had to be disguised as charity, so the great performance of the *Ballets Russes* on December 29, with Igor Stravinsky in person conducting his *Firebird* was presented as a gala in aid of the British Red Cross. All the available artists of the avant-garde—Cubists, Futurists and anyone who could claim to have made some original contribution to poetry, painting or music—had been invited. Diaghilev badly needed new blood. He had quarrelled with his star dancer, Nijinsky; some members of his troop had been swept into the armies of their respective countries; others were not prepared to face the perils and discomfort of travel in wartime. So he had been busy during his short stay in Paris contacting likely recruits, and before leaving he had appealed individually and collectively to this little nucleus that still represented Montparnasse to collaborate in the ballet.

There had been an immediate response. Perhaps the sudden enthusiasm for a form of art that had left the Cubists indifferent for nearly seven years was due to a certain exasperation resulting from a long diet of simplicity and austerity. In the ballet, in the deafening, hallucinating music of Stravinsky, in the brilliant décors of Bakst, in the wild leaps of Massine, the younger generation had discovered an echo of its own exuberance. Only the most orthodox die-hards of Cubism were scandalised to hear that Picasso had left with Jean Cocteau for Rome, where they were working with Léonide Massine on a new ballet, while Erik Satie composed the music in Paris.

The first performance of *Parade* was held in February 1917, and part of the audience, which had come to the first night in the

simple expectation of seeing something resembling the classical
Russian ballet, was understandably outraged. The characters
looked indeed more like the mobile constructions of some crazy
architect than conventional dancers. An angular pantomime-
horse clodhopped about among the revellers—some more or less
human, some apparently belonging to a strange race of robots—in
a garishly-coloured fair-ground. Strident music accompanied
grotesque gestures. There was no attempt at the grace and harmony which people had come to associate with ballet. Naturally
most of the critics were furious, but a few discerning spirits
realised that here, whether they liked it or not, was a manifestation
of the new approach to art.

'Here for the first time', wrote Apollinaire in his preface to
the programme, 'we find painting allied to dancing, plastic art
to mime. . . . This new alliance—for until now the connection
between scenery and costumes on the one hand and chore-
ography on the other was entirely artificial—has given birth, in
Parade, to a sort of sur-realism which will, I imagine, be the
first of a series of manifestations of the New Spirit. . . .'

'The New Spirit'—the words were constantly on his lips now.
They occurred again and again in his conversation and in his
writings and his friends soon realised they were almost the symp-
tom of an obsession. The copyright of Baudelaire's works had
just expired and it was Apollinaire who prepared and prefaced a
complete edition of the poems for *La Bibliothèque des Curieux*.*
Naturally, they became a pretext for a discussion of what really
constituted the 'modern spirit', which, according to him, had
been first incarnated in Baudelaire. The essay reflects Apollinaire's
own hesitations. Baudelaire is reproached for his morbidity, for
having considered life 'with a passion of disgust which had the
effect of transforming trees, flowers, women, the whole universe
and even art itself into something pernicious'. Finally, he con-

* The publication of *Les Fleurs du Mal* in the series *La Bibliothèque des
Curieux* sheds a revealing light on the attitude to Baudelaire less than half a
century ago. This series specialised in pornographic works and the fact that
he had prefaced a number of the volumes told badly against Apollinaire at the
time of 'the affair of the statuettes'. *Les Fleurs du Mal* thus appeared in what
seems to-day an incongruous company: Aretino, Cleland's *Fanny Hill,* Sade
and the *Erotika Biblion* of the Comte de Mirabeau.

cluded that Baudelaire had not been capable of penetrating this 'modern spirit' with which he himself was impregnated, and the question of exactly what that spirit was remained without any precise answer.

Apollinaire was still dwelling on the problem of the cinema. Here, he was convinced, lay secrets which, once discovered, could be applied to all the other arts, and would perhaps provide the key to this elusive 'modern spirit'. For several years he had been experimenting with scenarios, librettos, scraps of plays, all inspired by cinema technique, which he had never had time to finish. Pierre Albert-Birot, visiting him in hospital, had seen the first act, or at least the sketch for the first act, of a fantastic play-opera which he had started to compose shortly before the war. Now that Picasso, Cocteau and Satie had produced their ballet and that the ballet-form was rousing so much interest and discussion in Paris, Birot proposed that he should produce some kind of an opera in his turn, using this fragment as a starting-point. Apollinaire was delighted with the idea; Serge Férat started at once to design costumes and décors; Germaine Albert-Birot to compose the music; Max Jacob to rehearse the choir. After a number of technical hitches, *Les Mamelles de Tirésias* was produced at the *Théatre Maubel*, on June 21, 1917.

The curtain rose on a scene representing the market-place of Zanzibar. In the background an actor representing the people of Zanzibar was enthroned among a number of curious musical instruments designed to punctuate and accompany by their rhythm the speeches declaimed by the actors.

In the foreground, Theresa, strung about with saucepans, brooms and such symbols of housewifery, was engaged in a lively quarrel with her husband. She was tired of docile obedience, of having children, of the boring life of a woman, and felt an overwhelming ambition to become a soldier, a member of Parliament, a Cabinet Minister, or to exercise some other such virile function.

At this moment, to the amazement of an audience still unaccustomed to such shocks, a massive beard appeared on Theresa's chin, her vast bosom opened and revealed a number of balloons which she tossed joyfully to the spectators, while declaring that she was now a man and had changed her name to Tirésias. To complete the transformation, she took her husband's clothes and forced him to change into her own, while to his wife's cries of 'No more children! No more children!', he opposed a forceful speech on the necessity for procreation and concluded that, since the woman refused to do so, the man must take her place.

At this point the choir intervened, with Max Jacob and Paul Morisse singing among them, to the noisy encouragement of their friends. By the time they had finished, the actors were ready for the second scene, which showed the husband nursing his children in the same market-place. He had given birth, he explained, to 40,051 of them in eight days and the country was now threatened with famine. Thereupon arrived a wicked and sterile policeman, come to arrest him and put an end to this dangerous situation. A lively argument, in which the policeman refused to listen to his assurance that the problem could easily be solved by a little order and organisation, was interrupted by the appearance of a fortune-teller, whose head, blazing with lights, illuminated the whole theatre. The newcomer broke out in her turn in praise of the virtues of fecundity, and was revealed in the ensuing struggle as Theresa, returned home and repentant. The policeman, immediately converted, promised the happy couple to have numerous children in his turn, and the curtain fell in a tumult of booing and applause.

The play-opera-ballet (for it is difficult to give it an exact designation) got a mixed reception. Some of the critics had enjoyed themselves, but others were moved by the same righteous rage into which experiments of all kinds had been throwing them for the last twenty years.

'The inharmonious clown Erik Satie', wrote *La Grimace,* 'has composed his music on typewriters and rattlers. . . . His accomplice, the dabbler Picasso, speculating on the eternal stupidity of mankind . . . Guillaume Apollinaire, poet and naive visionary, managed to get all the critics, all the habitués of Parisian first-nights, the scoundrels of the *Butte* and the drunkards of Montparnasse, to witness the most extravagant, the most senseless of all the lucubrations of Cubism. . . .'

It was exactly the sort of attack to upset Apollinaire, who could not bear to be taken for a *farceur* or to have doubts thrown on his sincerity. The prospect was even darker next day, when an important group of Cubist painters, many of whom owed their fame and prosperity largely to him, issued a statement to the Press, disavowing him and accusing him of rendering them ridiculous by his extravagances. Perhaps it was these attacks that moved him to write a rather solemn preface to the published edition of Tirésias and claim, to the amazement or amusement of his friends:

> 'My Surrealist play was written above all for the French, just as Aristophanes composed his comedies for the Athenians. In it, I pointed out to them the grave and universally recognised danger to a nation that desires to be prosperous and powerful when it allows its birth-rate to decrease, and showed that the remedy is simple and lies in procreating children.'

It was generally taken for granted that Apollinaire was joking, in his own ironic way, but one of his friends was amazed to receive a letter deploring the attacks of the Press against a play destined 'to change the spirit of the nation and persuade it to raise its birth-rate'. Arguments over this epic—and unique, since there was only one performance—evening's entertainment have been breaking out sporadically for over forty years without coming to a conclusion. Was *Les Mamelles de Tirésias*, as Jean Cocteau claims, 'the first deliberately anarchic play, the first act of liberation by a poet who could no longer support an aridity that excluded all element of surprise', or was it a piece of patriotic propaganda addressed to a nation more preoccupied with the delights of love than with their proper consequences? Perhaps the truth about the play is that it can be taken in either way and that Apollinaire was playing, not for the first time, a double game. The word 'Surrealist', coupled with the declaration of noble and moral intentions, suggests that he was addressing himself simultaneously to two very different audiences. A sociological play concerned with the problems of depopulation, pauperism and feminism might be a step in the direction of the Academy and that ribbon of the Legion of Honour for which he fruitlessly longed. On the other hand, a 'Surrealist' play, fantastic in plot, scenery and music, would consolidate his position as the leader of a new generation seeking for a new kind of art. It was the kind of ambiguity he most enjoyed; and if he was to some extent the dupe of this ambiguity created by himself, the charm of the process can only have been increased thereby.

The New Spirit

His young friends of *Sic* and *Nord-Sud* naturally interpreted
Tirésias as an immense act of anarchy and applauded without
reserve. It was a step towards the destruction of Art and of
Literature (with capital letters) which would leave room at last for
the expression of the new spirit, the new truth. They were beginning more and more to distrust all conventional art forms, the
whole heritage they had received from their elders. Even men like
Max Jacob, or Cendrars, were regarded with slight suspicion as
'literary'. As for Apollinaire, who was in fact more of a Man of
Letters than any of them, he apparently managed to disarm them
by an extraordinary charm and persuasiveness. His very presence
was such a vital stimulant that it hardly mattered whether they
agreed with him or not.

Their presence was as necessary to Apollinaire as his to them.
The sadness and disquietude he hid beneath the enchanting mask
of gaiety made him dread solitude more than anything else. The
loss of loves and friends had marked him pitilessly and now, in
September 1917, the oldest and dearest of his friends disappeared
in his turn. René Dupuy—the charming, irresponsible Dalize,
with his opium, his gambling debts, his delicious erudition and
the literary talents he had been too nonchalant to develop—was
killed in action. He had led his men in a desperate charge, running,
holding a stone in front of his face because of his fear of dis-
figurement, and dropped as he ran, his body riddled with bullets.

Barely a month later, a different kind of blow fell. Apollinaire
had been looking forward to the time when he could revive *Les
Soirées de Paris*, and offer a platform to the new vanguard of art
and letters and pursue his mission of reconciling the 'long quarrel
of order and adventure'.[1] Serge Férat, who had been such a liberal
patron to *Les Soirées*, was prepared to finance the review once
more. Then, in October, came the revolution in Russia and the
Jastrebzoffs, cut off from the source of supplies, found themselves
as impecunious as the rest of their friends. Férat took his reverses
with good humour, went into journalism and enjoyed himself
inventing, in collaboration with Apollinaire, fictitious messages
from 'our correspondent on the Russian front'. It was a pleasant
occupation but a poor consolation for the loss of the review from
which they had expected so much.

Les Soirées de Paris was to have been a platform for the 'new spirit' of which Apollinaire—and indeed all the younger writers and painters—were talking so much. Now, after swallowing the disappointment as best he could, Apollinaire decided to explain his point of view in a public lecture in the *Théâtre du Vieux Colombier*. The lecture on *L'Esprit Nouveau,* followed by readings from selected poets, was held on November 26. It was given a great deal of publicity and attended by a fervent crowd, many of whom had come to the theatre rather in the spirit of disciples awaiting a definitive revelation. Everyone was there—Breton, Soupault and Aragon; Reverdy, Dermée, Birot; old friends like Cendrars, Léger, Picasso, Jacob, Salmon, Férat and Hélène d'Oettingen; old antagonists like those members of *L'Abbaye* who were not involved with their regiments. The young men of *Sic* and *Nord-Sud* were hoping for a scandal, or at least an explosive declaration of principle in the Dada style.

There was to be nothing of the sort. Apollinaire spoke with the old charm, the old authority and with the new and pathetic prestige of the scar that circled his head—*l'étoile de sang qui me couronne à jamais.** Perhaps it was only when he had finished speaking that his audience realised how far he was from the Apollinaire of *Les Soirées de Paris.* The keynote had been struck from the very beginning:

'The new spirit which we can already distinguish claims above all to have inherited from the classics solid good sense, a confident spirit of criticism, a wide view of the world and the human mind, and that sense of duty which limits or rather controls manifestations of sentimentality.

'It claims moreover to have inherited from the Romantics a curiosity that impels it to explore all those domains in which may be discovered material for a literature by means of which we can exalt life in any form whatsoever.

'The exploration of truth, the search for truth in, for instance, the domain of ethnology, just as much as in that of the imagination . . . such are the main characteristics of the new spirit.'

It was a call to order, a solemn denunciation of those very wildernesses of the spirit which he had opened up to a new generation. It was a retraction that could not be disguised by a

* This star of blood that crowns me for ever more (*Tristesse d'une Etoile*).

passing bow to the happy effects of 'surprise', to 'typographical
artifices' and to free verse 'through which lyricism takes its free
flight'. It was an enunciation of nationalistic principles—the
very principles which had served his critics for so long as a weapon
against him:

> 'Whatever happens, art will become more and more national.
> The poet will always be the expression of a class, of a nation.
> ... A cosmopolitan form of lyric expression can produce only
> hazy works without accent or construction, which would have
> the same value as the banalities of international parliamentary
> rhetoric. . . .'

This Guillaume Apollinaire, wounded in battle and terribly
scarred by life, who stood on the platform of the *Vieux Colombier* and destroyed much of what he had built up with such joyous
vigour . . . how should he be judged? Was he trying to efface a
compromising past and create an image of himself that would
flatter public opinion and smooth the path to the Academy and
official honours? Was he playing a double game, such as he had
played with Tirésias? Had his trepannation fundamentally altered
his character? Surely he, who longed above everything to be the
acknowledged leader of new generations, must have realised how
ill a lecture which was in fact a barely disguised declaration of
conformity, served his cause with them? 'I regret that I cannot
give our readers an account of Monsieur Guillaume Apollinaire's
lecture on the New Spirit', wrote an anonymous reporter in the
next number of *Nord-Sud*, 'since on that particular Saturday I was
occupied with a game of marbles in another quarter.' There could
hardly have been a more cruel disavowal of their visionary Verlaine.

Perhaps the truth lies quite simply in this—that he had lost
confidence in himself, in his capacity for loving and being loved,
in his infallible instinct for picking out writers and painters who
could make some valid contribution to the myth of the twentieth
century; in the gift of prophesy that he believed had enabled him,
like 'a hill rising above other men', to view that still unformed
myth as a coherent whole. Perhaps, faced with all the logical consequences of the Cubist break with tradition, he had found himself in the small hours of some feverish night faced with the question: had he been always and consistently mistaken?

If Apollinaire at this point had lost the power of believing in himself, it would explain the state of indecision that shows in all his work at this period and the impression of mortal disquietude to which his friends, and especially André Breton, have borne witness. If he could no longer believe fully in his own prophesies, he remained none the less a prophet; if his visions of the future suddenly appeared to be illusions, he was none the less a visionary and could never be anything else. He was still the same sorcerer as of old, but like his own Merlin, found himself faced with a world inexplicably changed even though it had its source in his own spells.

Everything seems to show that it was in this frame of mind that Apollinaire composed his lecture and prepared his second volume of collected poems, written between 1913 and 1917. The same hesitations explain, too, *La Jolie Rousse,* that final poem which plays the same explanatory role as *Zone* played in *Alcools.* In 1913 Apollinaire could no longer feel himself to be the poet of *Rhénanes* or even of *La Chanson du Mal-Aimé.* In January 1918 he was no longer the man who had composed *Les Fenêtres* or *Lundi rue Christine.* He needed to take stock of himself. Just as *Alcools* had opened with a summing up of his position at the moment of publication—*A la fin tu es las de ce monde ancien*—*Calligrammes* concluded with a summing-up of experience:

> Me voici devant tous un homme plein de sens
> Connaissant la vie et de la mort ce qu'un vivant peut connaître
> Ayant éprouvé les douleurs et les joies de l'amour
> Ayant su quelquefois imposer ses idées
> Connaissant plusieurs langages
> Ayant pas mal voyagé
> Ayant vu la guerre dans l'Artillerie et l'Infanterie
> Blessé à la tête trépané sous le chloroforme
> Ayant perdu ses meilleurs amis dans l'effroyable lutte
> Je sais d'ancien et de nouveau autant qu'un homme seul
>   pourrait des deux savoir
> Et sans m'inquiéter aujourd'hui de cette guerre
> Entre nous et pour nous mes amis
> Je juge cette longue querelle de la tradition et de l'invention
> De l'Ordre de l'Aventure
> Vous dont la bouche est faite à l'image de celle de Dieu
> Bouche qui est l'ordre même

Soyez indulgents quand vous nous comparez
A ceux qui furent la perfection de l'ordre
Nous qui quêtons partout l'aventure

Nous ne sommes pas vos ennemis
Nous voulons nous donner de vastes et d'étranges domaines
Où le mystère en fleurs s'offre à qui veut le cueillir
Il y a là des feux nouveaux des couleurs jamais vues
Mille phantasmes impondérables
Auxquels il faut donner de la réalité
Nous voulons explorer la bonté contrée énorme où tout se tait. . . .*

And the long poem finishes in a pathetic appeal to these unknown judges, his readers of the future—and perhaps in a final avowal of impotence:

* Here I stand before you all a man of good sense
    Knowing life and as much of death as a living man may know
    Having felt the pains and joys of love
    Having been able at times to impose his ideas
    Knowing several languages
    Having travelled a good deal
    Having seen the war in the Artillery and the Infantry
    Wounded in the head trepanned under chloroform
    Having lost his dearest friends in the appalling struggle
    I know as much of the old and the new as one man may know of both
    And not thinking at present about this war
    Between ourselves and for ourselves my friends
    I judge this long quarrel between tradition and invention
    Between Order and Adventure
    You whose mouths are made in the image of that mouth of God
    Which is Order its very self
    Be indulgent when you compare us
    With those who were the perfection of order
    We who are everywhere in quest of adventure.

    We are not your enemies
    We wish to take for ourselves vast and strange domains
    Where mystery flowers offering itself to whomsoever would gather it
    There are new fires colours never yet seen
    A thousand imponderable phantasms
    To which we must to give reality
    We wish to explore goodness that vast country where everything is
        silent . . .

16

Mais riez riez de moi
Hommes de partout surtout gens d'ici
Car il y a tant de choses que je n'ose vous dire
Tant de choses que vous ne me laisseriez pas dire
Ayez pitié de moi*.

* But laugh, laugh at me
  Men from everywhere especially you people here
  For there are so many things I dare not say to you
  So many things you would not allow me to say
  Have pity on me.

XVI

'The Slandered Stream'

*Un peu profond ruisseau calomnié la Mort.**

The nostalgia for order had never, in fact, been entirely absent from this often disorderly existence. The Flugi blood, after all, had run in the veins of prudent Dom Romarino, with his devotion to duty, as well as in those of frivolous and volatile Francesco. The Flugis had been poets or soldiers, sometimes one, sometimes the other, and had acquitted themselves efficiently in both roles. Even Angelica de Kostrowitsky had a feeling for tradition and a strong sense of what was fitting. So it is hardly surprising that Guillaume Apollinaire, with middle age looming in sight, should have turned his back on the wilder aspects of youth. Villon who, like himself, had been ready to turn his hand to anything, who could 'laugh in tears', who had been an impossible lover and loved dangerous friends, had shown signs of taking the same turning. Perhaps, if he had not disappeared into legend, somewhere on the road between Paris and Saint-Maxence, he would have settled down, with a lawful wife and the King's Pardon in his pocket, to enjoy the fruits of his reputation.

No French poet, surely, has ever been as near to Villon as was Guillaume Apollinaire in his youth. Fernand Fleuret, who had often led him and others of their band into temptation, has listed the common themes that form the greater part of the inspiration of *Alcools*: 'Chance loves, a difficult destiny, regrets for lost youth, the flight of time, sterile idleness, death'; and common characteristics: 'realistic and subtle, sceptical and credulous, virile and weak, he is the people of Paris, he is the very People. . . .' Like Villon, Apollinaire was the poet of Reality. But Villon had

* Stéphane Mallarmé: *Tombeau.*

lived in the comparatively simple times of the fifteenth century, while Reality four hundred years later has become infinitely complex—dangerous as radium for those who examine it too closely and with results just as unpredictable.

But Apollinaire at thirty-seven was very unlike the man he had been ten years earlier. Perhaps he had seen, heard and guessed too much. His ears seemed to be tuned now to echoes of Goethe, with his dreams of universal harmony, rather than to Villon. To some of his friends it seemed as if he was attempting in his turn to realise in himself the synthesis of all wisdom. Only in place of the Goethean serenity there was the feverish disquietude, the air of haggard apprehension, that had so painfully impressed the young André Breton, and the word 'destiny' was more and more often on his lips.

La Jolie Rousse had been a gesture of farewell to the old life and had revealed an unaccustomed shrinking and hesitation on the brink of the future. It had marked the choice for Order, but that choice seems to have been made with reserve and an uneasy conscience. As for the title, it is less irrelevant than it appears at first. Apollinaire had sustained many disillusions, had been deprived through the whole of his life of the tenderness he had always longed for. Now he had made at last the acquaintance of a young girl with flaming red-gold hair, who represented for him exactly that 'ardent reason' which he had come to identify with Truth. Jacqueline Kolb knew how to soothe his anxiety, watch over his health, drive away the fears and depression that so often beset him. With her beside him he sometimes re-discovered the old capacity for joy, which he recognised as the most precious of all gifts and feared so much to lose:

> Nous n'aimons pas assez la joie
> De voir les belles choses neuves
> O mon amie hâte-toi
> Crains qu'un jour un train ne t'émeuve
>   Plus
> Regarde-le vite pour toi.*

* We do not sufficiently love the joy
  Of seeing fine new things
  O hasten, my dear
  Fear the day when a train will move you
  No longer—Quick, see it and make it your own.

Apollinaire and Jacqueline Kolb were married at the Church of Saint-Thomas d'Aquin on May 2, 1918, with Picasso, Ambroise Vollard, Lucien Descaves and Gabrielle Picabia as their witnesses. They set up their home in the apartment in the Boulevard Saint-Germain and life continued in the same hectic rhythm. Apollinaire would rise early, make coffee while he hummed the five or six notes to which he invariably composed his poems. Then there was the day's work at the Ministry, interspersed with the harassing labour of journalism on which he depended for the greater part of his income. He was forcing himself to produce a novel, at the urgent request of his publishers, and to compose the libretto for an opera he had imagined during a conversation with Diaghilev. The publication of *Calligrammes* had increased his celebrity, brought new obligations and forced him to face new attacks.

'My dear André,' he wrote to André Billy, who had published an important review of the volume, 'I have delayed a long time in writing to thank you for your sensitive and subtle article on *Calligrammes*. It was the work of a lover of poetry and of a true friend. May I do as much for you one day! Note that I find you too severe on the subject of the typographical clichés. They are a modern contrivance of which it would be a mistake not to make use. It is the first book of this sort and there is no reason why others should not perfect this poetry I have inaugurated and one day we may have calligrammatic books of great beauty. However that may be, this book is the fruit of the war; it is full of life and I believe it will touch people more than *Alcools,* if fortune smiles at my poetic reputation. As for the reproach that I am destructive, I deny it formally. . . . The *merde* set to music in my Manifest-Synthesis published by the Futurists did not apply to the work of the Ancients, but to their names opposed as a barrier to future generations. . . . If I cease this kind of research one day, it will be because I am tired of being treated as a lunatic simply because this research seems absurd to those who content themselves with following in the old tracks. But God is my witness that I only have tried to add new domains to art and literature, without in any way refusing to recognise the masterpieces of the past and the present. . . .'

He was deep in the difficult situation of trying to please

everyone at once. Overwork had taken toll of his strength. Shortly
before his marriage he had been transported to the Italian Hospital
with pneumonia. Jacqueline, disguised as a nurse, had remained
beside him with the complicity of the doctors and the comfort of
her presence and his own robust constitution triumphed over the
illness. Now, in the autumn of 1918, as the world waited in tense
expectancy for the end of the war, the deadly epidemic of Spanish
influenza broke out and was soon sweeping through France.
Apollinaire caught the disease, struggled against it for a few days,
then, when everyone believed him to be out of danger, had a
relapse. He, who had never feared death during the war, fought to
live with desperate energy, but by November 9 it was obvious
that nothing more could be done for him. The armistice was being
prepared just at that time and the announcement was expected at
any minute. All through the day he had listened to the crowds
chanting in the street below his window: 'Down with Guillaume!
Down with Guillaume!' and in his delirium it had seemed to him
that all Paris had risen in a hostile demonstration against himself.
... *Mais riez riez de moi* ... *Ayez pitié de moi*.... He died at
6 p.m., clutching at the doctor's hand and begging, 'Save me,
Doctor, I still have so much to say!' He was thirty-eight years old.

The end had come so unexpectedly that his wife remained alone
all through the night and it was not till early next morning that
Louise Faure-Favier could be fetched. Soon after, André Salmon
arrived, then other friends. The news had spread quickly and
soon the little apartment was full of silent, grieving men and
women and the flowers they had brought in tribute. Max Jacob had
been one of the first, so grief-stricken that for once he forgot to
transform emotion into burlesque. For the next three nights he
was to watch by his friend's body. 'We have spent so many hours
laughing together, that I can well spend a few more crying beside
him', he noted during this period of vigil. 'Neither the successes
of my friends, nor that of France in her hour of victory can
revive what this death has withered in me for ever. I never realised
he was 'my life' to this extent.'

Madame de Kostrowitsky arrived in the middle of the morning.
A telegram had reached her just as she was preparing to attend a
wedding, and those present were astounded by the sight of this
woman dressed in all the finery of jewels, furs, plumed hat, with

tears running down her painted cheeks. A sob broke from her throat, 'one of those sobs that seem to rise up from a mother's very entrails', recounts Louise Faure-Favier, as she threw herself down by the body of her son, crying: 'My little boy!'

Yet ten minutes later the mother was making exactly one of those scenes her son had dreaded all his life, reproaching the young widow simultaneously for having failed to send for her in time and for having cut in half a certain rug that had been a gift from herself. Three days later she attended the funeral service in the same church in which Apollinaire had been married a few months earlier. She led the procession to the cemetery, escorted by Max Jacob and Serge Férat and recounted to them in detail all the faults in his character from childhood on. When the ceremony was over she strode away, taking leave of no one, speaking to no one and clutching to her bosom his uniform cap. No one could tell what she was really feeling. As Apollinaire had explained to Madeleine Pagès, her Slav nature was incomprehensible to ordinary mortals.

A last glimpse of Angelica de Kostrowitsky is provided by that indefatigable diarist Paul Léautaud. After the death of her son she had learned from the obituary notices a fact that had entirely escaped her during his lifetime—that he was a famous man and a celebrated poet. One day she appeared in the office of the *Mercure de France,* asked for Monsieur Léautaud and demanded an explanation. Léautaud presented her with Apollinaire's books and tried to give her some idea of what he had come to represent for the world of art and letters. When he had finished, she thanked him and informed him proudly, 'My other son is a writer too. He writes financial articles for an important paper in New York.'

A few months later she died in her turn of the same terrible epidemic, followed within a few days by the faithful Jules Weil. Albert de Kostrowitsky, the only remaining member of the family, died during the same year in Mexico.

*   *   *

So the story of Guillaume Apollinaire ends on a question mark, as every story of a life interrupted in its prime must do. His friends are old or ageing men to-day. Some of them are Academicians, with all the decorations of which France is so prodigal to her distinguished sons—official figures who already have their seats reserved in the Pantheon of French literature. They take it for granted that he would be among them to-day if he had lived, that he would attend the same solemn functions as themselves, and like themselves retain a taste for laughter and the good things of life. Others have kept to the revolutionary paths into which he did so much to guide them, refusing official honours and dynamiting accepted ideas. They agree too that Apollinaire would have been an Academician by now, and deplore it. Some of his friends are famous all over the world; others have exercised a long and secret influence over the élite of several generations. All, without exception, recognise something of Apollinaire that lives on in themselves and know that without him they would not have lived, worked and created exactly as they have done.

Yet the question he raised all through his life remains as unanswerable as ever. 'Who is he?' they used to ask on the terrace of the *Closerie des Lilas,* and even those who were closest to him admit that they still do not really know. The mere facts, of course, have come to light, but the real problem remains intact. We owe to him some of the loveliest lyric poems of modern times, but not even *La Chanson du Mal-Aimé,* not even *Vendémiaire,* not even *Le Musicien de Saint-Merry* could justify Max Jacob's prophesy that, 'the twentieth century will prove to be the century of Apollinaire', which is proving its truth as time moves on.

Was this extraordinary influence on his time and ours, then, a question of personality? All his friends have borne witness to the radiant charm that enabled him to convince anyone of anything—sometimes (as in the case of the Douanier Rousseau) before he was fully convinced himself.

'No man of our time', wrote André Billy in his obituary article in *Sic,* 'has aroused so much fury, or provoked so many sneers. All the forces of stupidity, ignorance and routine were leagued against him. Of what has he not been accused? But it was sufficient for him to appear, to smile, and his opponents, like the beasts of Orpheus, would immediately crouch and purr. I have seen that happen a hundred times. . . .'

But no amount of charm, even supported by an undeniable sense of publicity, could have so triumphantly survived death.

Apollinaire's judgements, moreover, were often unsure, and few of his pronouncements on aesthetics were entirely original. It is surprising how many of them can be traced back to men like Marcel Schwob and René de Gourmont, who are now almost forgotten. He had taken at least as much as he had given in his association with Picasso, with Max Jacob, with Delaunay, with Cendrars, and none of his own formulae can be taken as definitive. He lives on, surely, by his prolongations, and they lead back to the same question: Who was he?

Perhaps he himself has provided an answer, better than anyone else has been able to do. *Je suis ivre d'avoir bu tout l'univers....* Perhaps we should see Apollinaire as a vast sponge, assimilating, soaking up his times; responding to every trend, to every personality; and by some alchemical process transforming everything into living Myth, restoring to all what he had taken from each one. He was as multiple as Cubism, a personification of the Cubist age. And just as in the Cubist vision of life no one angle is more 'real' or more 'true' than another, so every aspect of Apollinaire was at once true because it was part of the whole and false because it was not the Whole. The essence of his genius lies, perhaps, in the fact that he was never wholly himself. Perhaps the true answer to the question that was so often whispered as he passed should have been: Everyone and No one.

Notes

CHAPTER ONE

1. Maurice Barrès in an obituary article published in 1910.

CHAPTER TWO

1. Article in the special number of *La Table Ronde* consecrated to Apollinaire.

CHAPTER THREE

1. *Les Sapins (Alcools)*.
2. *Schinderhannes (Alcools)*.
3. *La Loreley (Alcools)*
4. Republished in *L'Hérésiarque et Cie.*
5. *L'Hérésiarque et Cie.*
6. *Le Poète assassiné.*
7. *La Rose de Hildesheim* in *L'Hérésiarque et Cie.*
8. *Le Poète assassiné.*

CHAPTER FOUR

1. G. Apollinaire's Preface to the *Collected Works* of Baudelaire.
2. From a translation by A. J. Bull.
3. Madame J-M. Durry has spoken with great perspicacity of this characteristic of Apollinaire's poetry during her lectures on *Alcools* at the Sorbonne.

CHAPTER FIVE

1. A. Valentin, *Pablo Picasso*. Albin Michel, 1957.
2. Article in *La Plume*, April 1905.
3. *La Plume.*
4. *Les Peintres Cubistes.*

CHAPTER SIX

1. A. Valentin, *Picasso.*

CHAPTER EIGHT

1. From the series of radio-interviews which brought sudden celebrity to Léautaud in 1950, just before his death.
2. *La Femme assise*, published posthumously.
3. Max Jacob published *Saint-Matorel* in 1911, following it up with *Les œuvres burlesques et mystiques de Frère Matorel* a year later. It was his first published prose work and gained him sudden celebrity, although in a restricted circle.

CHAPTER NINE

1. From an unpublished fragment of Paul Léautaud's diary.

CHAPTER TEN

1. A. Gleizes, *Le Cubisme*.
2. Letter from Delaunay to Macke in Berlin (1912).
3. In *Calligrammes*.

CHAPTER TWELVE

1. From *La Femme assise*, the least successful of Apollinaire's works and conclusive proof that he was never meant to be a novelist.

CHAPTER THIRTEEN

1. *Trois Histoires de Châtiments divins* in *L'Hérésiarque*.
2. *Tendre comme le Souvenir*, letters from Guillaume Apollinaire to Madeleine Pagès.

CHAPTER FOURTEEN

1. Tristan Tzara, in a series of radio-interviews of the type that brought fame to Paul Léautaud.
2. *Manifeste surréaliste*.

CHAPTER FIFTEEN

1. *La Jolie Rousse* (*Calligrammes*).

Index